PREACHING ON WAX

RELIGION, RACE, AND ETHNICITY
General Editor: Peter J. Paris

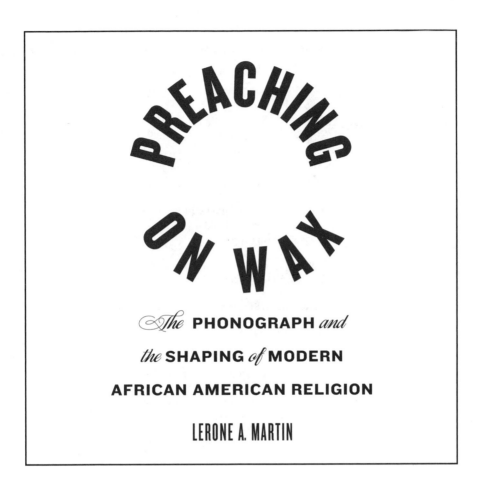

PREACHING ON WAX

The **PHONOGRAPH** *and*
the **SHAPING** *of* **MODERN**
AFRICAN AMERICAN RELIGION

LERONE A. MARTIN

NEW YORK UNIVERSITY PRESS
New York and London

NEW YORK UNIVERSITY PRESS
New York and London
www.nyupress.org

LIBRARY OF CONGRESS CATALOGING-IN-PUBLICATION DATA
Martin, Lerone A.
Preaching on wax : the phonograph and the shaping of modern African American religion
/ Lerone A. Martin.
pages cm
Includes bibliographical references and index.
ISBN 978-0-8147-0832-3 (hardback) — ISBN 978-1-4798-9095-8 (pb)
1. African Americans—Religion. 2. Phonograph. 3. Radio broadcasting—Religious
aspects. I. Title.
BR563.N4M37 2014
261.5'208996073—dc23
2014024572

For my grandparents—

John A. and Agnes S. Martin

and

James and Katherine Cosper

Urban migrants who helped to shape modern America . . .

CONTENTS

FIGURES

ACKNOWLEDGMENTS

Writing this book required me to spend a lot of time alone. It was, at times, a very lonesome labor. Yet all the labor was not mine, it was shared by many. I am truly grateful and indebted to a large community for their selfless support, assistance, and contributions to my life and this project. I must begin with my foundation: my parents Larry Alfred and Rose Marie Martin. Dad and mom, I am because you are. Without your countless sacrifices, years of toil in Ohio's industrial factories, support, and love, none of my accomplishments would even be in the realm of possibility. Dad, you have been and continue to be the dean of the university of hard work. Your example set the bar in our family. From the Usher board to the overtime board, I have literally watched you work your fingers down to the bone to support our family. I can only hope you find in these pages a glimmer of that same work ethic. Mom, you will always be my "rose." Your being epitomizes the flower for which you were named: beauty and grace adorned with thorns. Your graceful pursuit of beauty, truth, integrity, equality, and religious piety grounded our family in the joy and awesome responsibility of being human. And your thorns, frankly, kept us in line! While I was completing this project and neck deep in archival materials, your sincere telephone inquiries of "Son, how is your paper coming along?" were a source of joy. The genuineness of your voice helped me to keep a healthy perspective on this project. Mom and Dad, I love you both dearly. As children of urban migrants, I hope the following pages provide you both with a usable past that can, perhaps, help illuminate our family's present.

To my four older siblings, thank you for your prayers and unwavering support. To my only brother Tony, please know that to me you will always be the coolest person to ever walk the earth. No matter how old we get, you will always be my Big Brother; able to leap tall buildings in a single bound. To my sisters Nicole, Danielle, and Libra, thank you for your love, questions about my work, and the sincerity of your interests. Your curiosity was a pure joy even as it forced me to better articulate my ideas. To my large but close-knit extended family of Martins and Cospers—stretching from metro Atlanta to Afghanistan, to Southern California all the way to northwest Ohio—I offer to you all my heartfelt love and gratitude for your support and love.

To Reverends Derrick and Tonee Morant and Higher Ground Christian Ministries Center in Fostoria, Ohio: thank you for helping me to discover purpose and passion. To Pastor Robert A. Culp and my family at First Church of God, Toledo, Ohio, Pastor Kevin Early of Metropolitan Church of God in Detroit, and Reverend Rodney Francis and Washington Tabernacle in Saint Louis, Missouri: thank you all for your trust, love, and prayers.

I continue to benefit from the scholarship, mentoring, and community I experienced at the hands of Emory University's Graduate Division of Religion, Laney Graduate School, and the Office of University and Community Partnerships. The same must be said for the Center (formerly Program) of African American Studies at Princeton University, Princeton Theological Seminary, Anderson University department of religion, the Fund for Theological Education, and the Louisville Institute. Wallace Best, Liz Bounds, DeMario Cash, Nathan Connolly, Joseph Crespino, Wayne Croft, Dianne Diakite, Sharon Flucker, Nichelle Fry, Kharen Fulton, Brett Gadsden, Eddie S. Glaude, Jr., Jerry Grubbs, Geddes Hanson, Leslie Harris, Derek Hicks, E. Brooks Holifield, Dorcas Ford Jones, Paul Kelly, Nafees Khan, Gary Laderman (dissertation advisor), Earl Lewis (mentor, fellow basketball warrior, and friend), Celeste Lee, James W. Lewis (Anderson), James W. Lewis (Louisville), James Logan, Steve Luke, Brian Mack, Amber May, Purvi Mehta, James Morehead, Brendan Moriarty, Michael Leo Owens, Peter Paris, Bobbi Patterson, Mika Pettigrew, Miriam Petty, Leroy Quashie, Michael Rich, Noliwe Rooks, David Sebastian, Nathaniel Smith, Val Smith, Merle Strege, Lisa Tedesco, Michael Thigpen, Rhonda Thompson, Judith Weisenfeld, Cornel West, Susan Whitlock, and Matthew Williams all deserve special mention for the scholarly guidance and encouragement they provided along the way.

The faculty, staff, and students of Eden Theological Seminary in Saint Louis, Missouri, continue to be a source of grace. Eden provided me with the space, resources, and trust to hone my ideas and teaching. My Eden colleagues—Travis Ables, John Bracke, Allen Callahan, Leah Gunning Francis, David Greenhaw, Christopher Grundy, Deb Krause, Kristen Leslie, Clint McCann, Damayanthi Niles, Martha Robertson, Laurel Koepf Taylor, and Mai-Anh Le Tran—all taught me not only how and why my scholarship and teaching mattered, but also how to communicate it. Renee Taylor and the dynamic duo of Aaron Rogers and Minenhle Khumalo provided much needed research assistance. And Donita Bauer, Milton Brown, Chris Davis, Stephanie DeLong, Pat Garnett, Dorothy Gilliam, Velma Gonzales, Jackie Hamilton, Byrce Krug, Theon Miller, Randy Ott, Bev Rowlinson, Bev Scanlon, Carol Shanks, Carl Schenck, Stella Schoen, Al Schon, Denise Stauffer, Caron Strother, Kathleen Thomas, EJ Williams, Michelle Wobbe, and Mariyln Woods made it all possible. A heartfelt thank you to all.

As this project entered the final writing stages, my postdoctoral fellowship in the John C. Danforth Center on Religion and Politics at Washington University in Saint Louis proved to be a godsend. In addition to the resources and time to complete the project, the input of the Center's outstanding community of scholars was invaluable. R. Marie Griffith read and suffered through the dissertation, muddled chapter drafts, and numerous incarnations of the manuscript. She offered pivotal advice every step of the way. Since the days I stumbled into her office as a (clueless) first-year seminary student, she has been a model of kindness and scholarly rigor. Words will eternally fall short in my attempt to express my gratitude to her. The faculty at the Center also offered timely suggestions on the manuscript as well as mentoring. I am forever indebted to Darren Dochuk, Mark Jordan, Rachel Lindsay, Laurie Maffly-Kipp, and Leigh Schmidt for their scholarly contributions to this project. My fellow postdoc at the center, Anne Blankenship, and dissertation fellows Rachel Gross and Emily Johnson, and visiting graduate students Sherrema Bower and Hannah Hofheinz all provided much needed community, while Debra Kennard, Laura Delmez, Sheri Pena, and a cadre of student workers (including Erica Beach, who after reading a chapter draft provided much needed perspective and laughter when she asked the simple yet profound question: "What's a phonograph?") were remarkable in their organization, help, and resourcefulness. Truly this project benefited greatly from the Center, a community whose commitment to scholarly excellence and rigor is only surpassed by its collegiality.

A very special thank you is also in order to the broader and thriving intellectual community at Washington University in Saint Louis: Jean Allman, Kurt Beals, Monique Bedasse, Irver Berstein, Daniel Bornstein, John Baugh, Philip Byers, Adrienne Davis, El Hadji Samba Amadou Diallo, Valerie Dixon, Garrett Duncan, Gerald Early, Jonathan Fenderson, Diana Hill, Ron Himes, Korina Jocson, Dale Kretz, Suzanna Krivulskaya, Mary Laurita, Sonia Lee, Jeffrey McCune, Steven Miller, Vernon Mitchell, Amber Musser, Sowande Mustakeem, Mungai Mutonya, Shanti Parikh, Michelle Purdy, Trevor Sangrey, Barbara Schaal, Jennifer Smith, Sharon Stahl, Bill Tate, Holden Thorp Wilmetta Toliver-Diallo, Virginia Toliver, Anika Walke, Rebecca Wanzo, Chancellor Mark S. Wrighton, Rafia Zafar, and a host of others all made me feel welcome during my time at Washington University.

I would have been lost without the assistance of a group of archivists, librarians, and researchers from across the country and pond. I thank Matthew Barton, Kevin LaVine, and the Recorded Sound Division at the Library of Congress; Charles Reynolds, Kristen Castellana, and the entire Music Library staff at the University of Michigan; Aaron Smithers and everyone at the Louis Round Wilson Special Collections Library at the University of North Carolina Chapel Hill; Kerrie Williams of the Atlanta Fulton Public Library System Auburn Avenue Research Library; Lucinda Cockrell at the Center for Popular Music of Middle Tennessee State University; Theresa Koenigsknecht at the Indiana Historical Society; James Harlan of the Wayne County Indiana History Museum; Leonard DeGraaf at the Thomas Edison National Historic Park; The David Sarnoff Library in Princeton, New Jersey; Lance and April Ledbetter of Dust-to-Digital; Simon Barker, Shelly Saguaro, Lorna Scott, and Neil Wynn at the University of Gloucestershire in Cheltenham, U.K.; Charles Haddix of the Audio Division of the LaBudde Special Collections at University of Missouri-Kansas City; Sara Fitzgerald, Matthew Wier, and the Emerson Library Staff at Webster University; Michael Boddy at Eden Theological Seminary; Leigh Greenhaw, Charles McManis, David Deal, Justin Fong and the Intellectual Property Legal Clinic at the Washington University School of Law; and Rudolph Clay, Makiba Foster, Gail Wright, Marty Cavanaugh, Ted Chaffin, and Steven Vance of Olin Library at Washington University in Saint Louis. Thank you all for your invaluable assistance during my research.

Several friends deserve special mention for both their scholarly input and priceless friendship. Josef Sorett has been a sharp interlocutor and even better friend. He has been a constant voice of scholarly clarity as well as wit and humor throughout this project. Jonathan Walton continually provided friendship and razor sharp analysis. I am thankful for his pastoral way of challenging me and telling me when I needed to go back to the drawing board. Roshni Patel always offered questions that cut to the heart of the matter. Thank you for always pushing me toward clarity and to the "so what" of every paragraph! Greg Ellison II always made sure that I did not neglect self-care during the writing process. Jamil Drake always managed to find time between his family and his own scholarly commitments to lend a listening ear and encouragement. Lee and John provided much needed chatter and distraction at Bread Co. Paul Oliver invited me into his home while I was conducting research in the U.K. and provided invaluable direction and guidance and Michael Roach of the European Blues Association was my unofficial tour guide, research director, and friend. And finally, Mons provided support, laughter, patience, and an enduring scholarly ear.

Last but certainly not least, I wish to express my gratitude to NYU Press and my editor Jennifer Hammer. Jennifer, thank you for not only believing in me but also for constantly reminding me of the importance of this project. To be my editor, clearly you have the "patience of Job." You handled these pages with an unsurpassable level of care, concern, and gracious scrutiny, while Constance Grady and Dorothea Halliday kindly ushered me through the production process. Thank you all!

These pages, then, are a glimpse of all that the aforementioned family, loved ones, friends, and colleagues have invested in me. Any and all shortcomings are surely my own.

There are two primary economic calculations that are used throughout this book: Income value and Economic Status. Income value is used to determine the relative "cost" of a particular commodity. Rather than using the consumer price index to measure price according to inflation, income value uses a wage index or the GDP per capita to measure the relative income that would be used to buy a particular commodity. This is the best means of understanding how affordable a specified item was to the average person in the past.

Economic status is used to determine how a person or income ranked compared to other income earners in a particular historical period. It measures income or wealth relative to a wage or more general earnings, such as the wages of manufacturing workers or per capita GDP. It is the best way of revealing the relative standing of a person and/or income during a specified period. All data, definitions, and calculations are based on 2012 figures, retrieved using the U.S. Department of Labor, Bureau of Labor Statistics' *National Occupational Employment and Wage Estimates*, http://www.bls.gov/oes/current/oes_nat.htm#00-0000 and Lawrence H. Officer and Samuel H. Williamson, "Measures of Worth," MeasuringWorth, 2010, www.measuringworth.com/worth-measures.php.

Introduction

Phonograph Religion

The preacher sat in the sweltering sun, anxiously waiting for the train. The Atlanta summer of 1926 had proven to be one of the warmest in the city's history.[1] However, nothing, not even record-breaking temperatures, could stifle the spirit of Reverend James M. Gates. The rural native turned urban migrant preacher was headed to New York City for a month-long preaching tour. Few would have guessed that Gates, an unschooled sharecropper born in rustic Hogansville, Georgia, a generation after slavery would become a highly sought-after clergyman. He had been preaching in Atlanta for more than a decade with little to no local fanfare, but by September 1926 he had become a nationally known preacher.[2] When the train finally arrived, the country preacher headed to the "colored" section of the Jim Crow train, en route to preach to the masses.[3]

This, however, was no ordinary preaching revival. Reverend Gates was headed to the city to record his rhythmic sermons for leading record labels. The recording capital of the world came clamoring to him after the resounding sales of his first phonograph sermon with Columbia records in Atlanta. The sermon was priced at almost twice the national average hourly wage, comparable to over thirty dollars today. The cost, however, did not dissuade consumers. The first release sold out so quickly, the label hurriedly pressed over thirty thousand copies of his second sermon to meet the demand. When retailers swiftly sold out, Columbia placed a supplemental order of another 20,000 copies the very next month. Americans got phonograph religion.[4]

When Gates arrived in New York City, more than ten labels vied to get him in the studio, including industry stalwarts Paramount and Victor (later RCA-Victor). The entrepreneurial preacher obliged them all. The studio jaunt provided a striking juxtaposition. The rural folk preacher was the featured attraction in some of the most technologically advanced studios in the business. When Gates visited Okeh Records's sophisticated studio in Manhattan's Columbus Circle he recorded sermons in rural black expression, namely, in the form of the chanted folk sermon accompanied by his studio congregation. There, overlooking Broadway, one of the city's most famed and modern commercial thoroughfares, Reverend Gates recorded, "Ain't Gonna Lay My Religion Down," a warning of the dangers of urban living upon traditional "down home" religion. He adjusted such vernacular sermons to fit the limited time parameters of a double-sided 78 rpm wax record and delivered them to the tune and pace of the jazz and blues era.[5] Gates employed a new method to preach an old gospel message.

During his career, Gates recorded over two hundred such sermons, making him a leading spokesperson of old-fashioned revivalism. A white southerner attested to Gates's plain-folk appeal. "[I have] heard [D. L.] Moody, Billie [sic] Sunday, and Dr. [Charles] Fuller," the mayor of Cedartown, Georgia, reportedly admitted. But when he heard Reverend Gates preaching, he was convinced that "there is not a man, living or dead, who could make it so plain."[6] Mainstream (white) publications of the day, such as the *New York Times*, *Variety,* or *Time Magazine*, did not feature or comment on Gates's revivalism as they did Moody, Sunday, and Fuller. However, in the eyes of many plain folk, Gates's gospel labors were just as significant.

The popularity of Reverend Gates's old-time media ministry made him a commercial icon. Labels advertised his sacred wares according to the latest commercial trends, giving him a seemingly ubiquitous presence in the black consumer market. Ads featuring Gates's face and sermons graced all the nationally circulated black newspapers as well as posters in local stores, handbills, record brochures and journals, and mail order catalogs. The pervasive commercials often pitched Reverend Gates alongside ads for top-billed artists such as Louis Armstrong, Bessie Smith, and Duke Ellington. In addition to celebrity exposure, Gates also enjoyed celebrity living. During his New York City recording sessions, he often stayed at Harlem's luxurious and chic Hotel Olga: a precious ritual for a man who had lived in dirt floor shacks with no running water for the first forty years of his life. While residing at the "black Waldorf-Astoria" Gates lounged, dined, and rubbed shoulders with hotel regulars such as Harvard-trained philosopher and first black Rhodes scholar Alain Locke, baseball great Satchel Paige, and Armstrong. Preaching on wax transformed the folk preacher into a celebrity preacher.[7]

The outcome of this phonograph religion was pervasive. The record industry eagerly sought other black preachers who could inject folk religion into the studio pulpit, and black clerics lined up to do so. Labels jostled with one another to market their black media preachers, advertising and retailing their pricey sacred wares in a variety of local shops and chain stores. Consumers, in turn, zealously bought them. There was a harvest of souls who thoroughly enjoyed hearing the gospel preached in the old-time style on the phonograph and plenty of money for preachers and record labels to reap in the process.

• • •

This book explains why a critical mass of African American ministers, like Reverend Gates, teamed up with major phonograph labels to record and sell their sermons and why black consumers eagerly purchased them. More specifically, it chronicles and evaluates how this "phonograph religion" significantly contributed to the shaping of modern African American Christianity.

There has been much work in the study of American religion that chronicles the significance of mass mediums such as print, radio, film, television, and the Internet in the practice(s) of Protestant Christianity. The field, however, has been slow to recognize the phonograph as an equally vital tool within these religious traditions. This book takes up this neglected task by tracing the phenomenon of African American Protestant clergy who utilized the phonograph to sell and broadcast their sermons during the interwar period.

Many white mass media religious celebrities came to the fore during the early part of the twentieth century. Noted evangelists Aimee Semple McPherson and Charles Fuller, for example, became iconic names through their trailblazing use of radio. Black clergy have not traditionally been seen as attaining the same kind of "big name" status in their communities through religious broadcasting. Indeed, African Americans did not have the same kind of access to radio as their white counterparts. However, black clergy utilized other means to get their message out and join the chorus of modern religious broadcasting. Scores of African American preachers teamed up with leading phonograph record labels to record sermons and transmit their spiritual messages to a broad—and, it turned out, eager—African American consuming public. As a result, these black phonograph preachers played an active role in the shaping and continued vibrancy of black Protestantism during the interwar period.

The revitalization of black religion during this era has largely concentrated on the experiences of the black literati. However, chronicling the rise of professionally trained ministers and scholars, black institutional churches and schools, and the artistic musings of the black literati on "the folk" does not tell the whole story. While the black literati of the Harlem Renaissance were examining and debating the "primitive" nature of black Christianity in Broadway plays such as *The Green Pastures* and acclaimed writings such as *God's Trombones: Seven Negro Sermons in Verse*; black "folk" were busy crafting their own ideas and practices of religious revitalization. This renaissance of black religion was not written down in intellectual tomes. Rather, it was recorded on wax.[8]

The phenomenon began, in many ways, with the Great Migration. From 1900 to 1930, more than 3 million African Americans left their rural homes in search of better lives in urban America. More than half of this black rural diaspora moved to the urban south, while there were about 1.4 million southern-born African Americans living in the urban north and west.[9] This widespread urbanization severely changed patterns of consumption, community, and domesticity, as well as canons of civil and religious authority. This fundamental shift in worldview altered the way Americans understood and practiced religion. Formally held beliefs and authorities were brought into question. In a word, religion and the role it played in black life changed dramatically during the Great Migration.

Protestant clergy perceived the colossal population and cultural transformations as a clarion call for revival. Their efforts were not necessarily aimed at launching a collection of large religious gatherings of emotional fervor. Such efforts largely fell out of favor during the interwar period. As one clergyman of the time noted, the increasingly urban nation demanded "a different type of revival." Rather, clergy labored to remake or "revive" the faith and its social mission according to the new social and cultural mores. Some clergy, mostly liberal Protestants, augmented creeds, dogmas, and practices as a means to grapple with the modern era. Evangelical clergy, however, attempted to hold fast to traditional beliefs. Eager white Protestant clergy such as McPherson and Fuller responded by taking old-time revivalism to radio: a new medium for an old message. Evangelical black clergy in turn harnessed the phonograph as an instrument for the urban revitalization of black Protestantism. Phonograph religion was a revival on wax.[10]

Phonograph religion, then, retooled African American Protestantism for the modern era in four primary ways. First, preaching on wax made black Christianity a mass-produced commodity. To be sure, African Americans, born a generation or so after slavery, grew up seeing the conspicuous presence of black clergy in the national marketplace. Following the Civil War, African American clerics began to endorse and sell novel branded products such as home wares and medicines as a display of bourgeois respectability and as a means to raise funds to support black faith communities and institutions.[11] However, phonograph religion went a step further; it packaged the central ritual and tenet of Protestant Christianity for the marketplace: the preached word.

The aim of phonograph religion, in part, was to address the materialization of modern consumer culture. An unprecedented rise in recreational spending during the interwar period marked the emergence of modern-day consumer rites. Urban life offered the rural diaspora regulated working shifts as well as higher wages and salaries with daily and weekly cash payrolls as opposed to the inconsistent income of farm life. Urban migrants were endowed with more cash *in hand* than many had ever had before and the leisure time and freedom to spend it. This was evident in the rise in recreational spending. In the first twenty years of the twentieth century, the average household expenditure for non-necessities—such as cars, cosmetic products, home wares, and records—grew by only 1 percent. However, from 1920 until the end of World War II, the average family expenditure for these items grew by almost 10 percent. The period witnessed the largest incremental increase in leisure spending in American history. Americans were buying phonographs, blues and jazz records, cars, clothes, and a host of other mass-produced goods with unparalleled alacrity. However, religious institutions by and large did not benefit from the economic boom. The hike in recreational spending coincided with a decline in the percentage of income Americans devoted to religious work. Urban residents, native and migrant alike, were increasingly devoting their dollars to the nonessentials of the consumer market and less to religious life. "The uncertainties of 1919 were over," wrote F. Scott Fitzgerald in 1937. It was the Jazz Age, "an age of excess" when America went "on the greatest, gaudiest spree in history."[12]

Phonograph preachers packaging their sermons as desirable commodities as a means to address and redress such trends, while the phonograph industry welcomed the chance to broaden its market share. These complementary desires resulted in the mass-production of black Protestant sermons by leading record labels. From 1925 to 1941 approximately one hundred black preachers teamed up with the phonograph industry. Their spiritual wares were advertised and sold in numerous places including black newspapers, posters, handbills, department stores, mail-order catalogs, record label shops, and furniture stores. The preached word, along with black popular music, art, film, and beauty products became a mechanized product in the burgeoning consumer marketplace of the twentieth century.

The rural diaspora welcomed the recorded folk sermons. They were purchased across the country in large numbers. The chanted sermon was a ritual that many believed was a core tenet of Christian worship. The sermons many heard in black urban churches lacked such cadence. A sermon without the rhythmic chanted pace was, to many black migrants, not a sermon at all. Phonograph religion helped the transplanted faithful to hold fast to their faith in a strange new land.

Second, phonograph religion shifted black Protestantism by laying the foundations of modern religious broadcasting in black Christianity. Religious broadcasting, as religion scholar Jonathan L. Walton notes, is not just the widespread utilization of sound mediums for proselytization, but also the industries that aid clergy in producing, merchandizing, and marketing their spiritual products.[13] The phonograph trade electrically recorded, packaged, and aurally transmitted black preachers and their sermons across the nation prior to widespread black radio preaching.[14]

The collapsing of temporal and spatial boundaries was a definitive characteristic of modern culture. Scientists (Einstein), inventors (Alexander Bell and Thomas A. Edison), and thinkers and artists (James Joyce) of the period "were united by their desire to challenge the traditional bounds of space and time."[15] Jazz music trumped the parameters of musical time, and automobiles altered notions of distance and time. It was the ethos of the era. Likewise, phonograph religion released black clergy and the essential ritual of preaching from the temporal and corporeal confines of the pulpit and preaching moment into the sonic arena of modern life and consumer culture. Seen in this way, the transmitters of phonograph religion were apostles of modern black church work and the architects of popular black religious broadcasting.[16]

In addition to commodification and broadcasting, recorded sermons created commercial celebrity preachers in black Christian practice. The era has largely been known for the emergence of modern black celebrities in sports, art, and entertainment. However, the nationwide packaging, marketing, and selling of the revival on wax made phonograph preachers commercial celebrities as well. This iconic status aided clergy claims of authority and influence during the rise of black cultures of urban professionalism. Some black clergy pursued education, elected office, and associations with elite organizations to bolster their standing. Popular phonograph preachers, however, eschewed such channels, basing their status on broad commercial appeal.

The study of American religion has traditionally positioned such celebrity as an anomaly and a departure from black Christianity. Such practices have long been considered the arena of white Protestants and the black urban "sects" and "cults" of the 1930s. The contemporary presence of wealthy black celebrity preachers and their branded products, some argue, is actually evidence of a "new black church" or in the case of a black Pentecostalism, an expression of neo-Pentecostalism.[17]

However, commercial celebrity became a significant aspect of traditional black Christian practices when phonograph religion transfig-
ured Baptist and Pentecostal clergy into mainstays of black celebrity
culture. Popular preachers on wax pursued and basked in the same
commercial publicity, public adulation, and compensation of leading
black entertainers of the day. The phenomenon is not new; it simply has
not received the same scholarly attention as racial uplift and community mobilizing in black religious experience. Designations, then, such
as "new" or "neo" are misleading. The difference between black commercial celebrity preachers of then and now is one of technological and
financial scale, not religious ideology.[18]

Finally, and closely related to this, the iconic clergy of phonograph
religion altered not only the sources and channels of black clerical
authority, but also its tone. As black religious broadcasters wedded their
cultural and social clout to the market and celebrity—rather than profession, custom, and education—their ability to authoritatively address
and protest societal ills was attenuated according to the dictates of the
market.

In all, this book argues that the placement of black Protestant preachers and their phonograph sermons on the market shelf significantly
changed the face of African American religion and culture during the
interwar period by establishing the black religious practices of sermon
commodification, broadcasting, commercial celebrity, and the modern
nature of religious authority.

•   •   •

The phonograph puts this story in play. Chapter 1 then offers a broad
look at the prominent role of the phonograph in American life and culture during the early twentieth century. The phonograph was not limited to music; it was also the primary home entertainment medium for
speeches, letters, news, books, family records, children's stories, and
even advertising. Thomas Edison, the inventor of the phonograph,
anticipated the day when he would "see a phonograph in every American home." His dream became a reality.[19] The chapter relies on the
voices of consumers to highlight the ways in which the talking machine
altered American life.

Chapter 2 examines how black faith communities responded to the emergence of race records—black popular music recorded by and for African Americans. Many established black churches demonized this manifestation of the black entertainment industry in one way or another. Despite such efforts, a host of evangelical black clergy responded to the rise of race records by joining the phonograph industry. Their response to race records was steeped in the time-honored practice of American evangelicalism: duplicating and utilizing forms of popular entertainment and communication as a means of proselytization and religious revitalization. The phonograph, in their eyes, was a utensil of church work. Chapter 3, then, centers on the rise of phonograph sermons, tracing the production, marketing, advertising, and selling of these mass-produced spiritual commodities.

Chapter 4 focuses on the popularizing of phonograph religion. The revival on wax went into full swing when phonograph preachers began to channel the linguistic folk style of race records into the studio pulpit. The record-breaking sales of these phonograph preachers carved out a lasting blueprint for popular black religious broadcasting. The final two chapters explore the life and career of Reverend James M. Gates. As the most popular and prolific sermon recorder of the era, Gates set the tone and standard for successful black media ministry. As a case study, his life grounds the celebrity and authority of phonograph religion. Chapter 5 traces how the popularity of recorded sermons made Reverend Gates a commercial star, established and molded in the black celebrity culture of the era. This new preacher derived his authority not from the world of letters and elite black institutions and organizations, but from the commercial marketplace and the social mobility associated with celebrity. Chapter 6 examines the relationship between recorded sermons and dominant notions of race, class, and gender. The spotlight is placed on Reverend Gates's experience of corporate retail and his 1930 sermon "Say Goodbye to Chain Stores" to reveal how the market simultaneously amplified and attenuated black religious broadcasters' ability to address inequality.

In the end, the story of phonograph religion has implications for the past and present. It broadens our narrative of African American and American religion by injecting a new cast of historical actors, media, and corporations into our understanding of how religion in America was shaped and formed during the twentieth century. In doing so, it invites scholars and casual observers of black religion and churchgoers alike to a more sober assessment of contemporary times. Black religious commodities, broadcasting, celebrity, and popular social authority are not in fact new phenomena in black life. Rather, these practices largely stem from preaching on wax.

"The Machine Which Talks!"

The Phonograph in American Life and Culture

Thomas Edison was awestruck. Following the first successful test of the talking machine in November 1877, the inventor recalled, "I was never so taken aback in my life!" He was not alone in his astonishment. The *Scientific American*, a popular science magazine (published continuously since 1845), was also flabbergasted. In December 1877, Edison presented his novelty to more than a dozen scientists and admirers gathered in the journal's New York offices. Edison turned the crank of the phonograph and the prerecorded tinfoil cylinder squeaked out, "How do you like the phonograph?" The small assembly looked on in disbelief. "No matter how familiar a person may be with modern machinery and its wonderful performances," the publication proclaimed, "it is impossible to listen to the mechanical speech without his experiencing the idea that his senses are deceiving him." It was not a deception. The phonograph recorded and reproduced sound across the chasms of mortality, time, and distance.[1]

The experience was so jolting, Edison questioned if the world was ready. In past times, he told a reporter, the public would have probably "destroy[ed] the machine as an invention of the devil and mob[bed] the agents as his regular imps." Perhaps now, Edison hoped, the modern world was ready to accept a talking apparatus. The 1878 gathering of the National Academy of Sciences in Washington D.C., revealed that society was initially divided on the issue. Several observers fainted when he presented "the Talking Machine." One observer was overcome with an eerie feeling of evil as the phonograph repeated Edison's words, shouts, and whistles. The unnerved eyewitness remarked that the phonograph "sounds more like the devil every time." The academy's council, however, praised Edison above all others, declaring, "These other men are only inventors—You, sir, are a discoverer!" Following the astonishing presentation, Edison went to the White House and gave President Hayes and his wife a private demonstration. The showing turned into a celebration, lasting until the wee hours of the morning.[2]

Unlike the enthusiastic witnesses at the White House, some cultured observers, such as noted scholar Georges Duhamel, were stunned into skepticism. The accomplished intellectual, born in 1884, witnessed the rise of the phonograph with great distrust. Duhamel, in his *In Defense of Letters,* warned that the communicative abilities of the phonograph (as well as radio) would destroy the foundation of Western culture, particularly reading and book publishing.[3] Similarly, a Yale professor expressed distrusts of the phonograph, telling one journalist that the very existence of a "talking machine is ridiculous!"[4] Detractors believed that a device that preserved and relayed sound was ghostly and culturally detrimental at worst, absurd and useless at best.

The trepidation was understandable. The talking machine revolutionized the aural world. The "sound writer" allowed listeners the unprecedented opportunity to hear almost any variety of sound they wanted time and again. In the first press release for the phonograph, Edison stated that the machine was the first "apparatus for recording automatically the human voice and reproducing the same at any future period . . . immediately or years afterward."[5] Furthermore, he explained to an awestruck *Washington Post* reporter, "This tongue-less, toothless instrument without a larynx or pharynx, dumb, voiceless matter, nevertheless mimics your tones, speaks with your voice, utters your words, and centuries after you have crumbled into dust will repeat again and again, to a generation that could never know you." Edison's explanation led the reporter to ponder if the device came from heaven. "If every idle thought and every vain word which man thinks or utters are recorded in the judgment book," the reporter wondered, "does the recording angel sit beside a celestial phonograph, against whose spiritual diaphragm some mysterious ether presses the record of a human life?"[6] For many, only transcendence could explain the incomparable machine.

Religiously inclined or not, the public was fixated by the phonograph. The *Chicago Daily Tribune* noted that no other invention had "created

Figure 1.1: Listeners enjoying the talking machine through the customary small rubber tubes at a public venue. Source: U.S. Department of the Interior, National Park Service, Thomas Edison National Historical Park.

such an interest and attracted such widespread attention as the Phonograph."[7] In 1902, the U.S. Census Bureau concluded, "Of the many wonderful inventions during the past quarter century perhaps none has aroused more general and widespread interest among all classes of people than the machine which talks; and for this reason, together with the fact that it has been widely exhibited, nearly everyone is more or less familiar with the so-called talking machine."[8] Americans were taken by the sound writer.

The phonograph became the primary entertainment medium in American life and a cornerstone of modern domestic life. Beginning in the early twentieth century, wealthy residences and impoverished domiciles alike possessed at least one talking machine. In our contemporary moment, the primary entertainment mediums are televisions, computers, and smart phones. In the first few decades of the twentieth century it was the phonograph. Before radio was broadly adopted in American homes, the talking machine brought all aspects of American life into the home. Emile Berliner, the inventor of flat disc records—easier to use and store than Edison's cumbersome tinfoil cylinders—foresaw the centrality of the phonograph. Shortly after unveiling his wax disc in 1888, the German immigrant told a gathering of Philadelphia's Franklin Institute for Science Education that the uniform ease with which his new discovery could record, reproduce, and copy sound would give way to a new form of popular entertainment. "Whole evenings," he predicted, "will be spent at home going through a long list of interesting performances . . . of prominent singers, speakers, and performers."[9] Berliner was clairvoyant. Americans would indeed gather at home and various other spaces to enjoy music, current events, landmark speeches, political debates, and religion—all through their phonographs.

The Phonograph in American Consumer Culture

The phonograph began as a commercial amusement device in train stations, taverns, hotels, small businesses, and various exhibitions. By 1890, the city of Atlanta, for example, had a total of nine commercial machines. For a nickel, consumers could behold the marvel of hearing the round wax cylinders squeak out a musical rendition through a pair of small rubber tubes (Figure 1.1). Despite the fee, such commercial use proved popular and lucrative. Edison representatives traveled to Atlanta and were pleased to learn that their "Nickel in the Slot" phonographs were receiving a "great deal" of use in the city. One Atlanta newspaper observed that the device had "won a place in the affections of our people from which it can never be dislodged." One city saloon phonograph reaped over $1,000 in just four months. The phonograph was the emerging avenue of commercial entertainment.[10]

The phonograph industry grew at an exceedingly fast pace. In 1897, the nation purchased about half a million records. Two years later, about 2.8 million records were consumed annually, and the number kept rising. Before World War I, there were eighteen established phonograph companies. Collectively, they sold 500,000 phonographs. Near the end of World War I, the number of phonograph manufactures had risen from eighteen to two hundred and their combined phonograph production climbed from a half million to 2.2 million.[11]

Three companies—Edison, Columbia, and Victor (RCA-Victor beginning in 1929)—dominated the widespread growth of the phonograph. Within a decade of the invention, Edison's phonograph division employed 600 men. By the turn of the century, sales of Edison's phonograph products exceeded $1 million, a percentage of gross domestic product (GDP) that amounts to a contemporary equivalent of $734 million. At the company's peak, worldwide phonograph sales topped 140,000 and record sales were just short of 8 million. Columbia, founded in 1888, brought innovation to the industry and eventually surpassed Edison. The company, which introduced the nation to double-sided records in 1908, amassed assets of $19 million ($4.8 billion today) near the end of World War I. The Victor Talking Machine Company, however, was the most lucrative. Founded in 1901, the company grew at a shocking pace. In its initial year, the company sold 7,570 phonographs. For its tenth anniversary in 1911, annual sales had increased 1,600 percent to 124,000 phonographs. Toward the end of World War I, the company was housed in a 1.2 million square foot facility and endowed with assets of $33 million, a contemporary equivalent of $6.57 billion. By 1921, the wealthy company was selling approximately 55 million records a year and enjoying a higher advertising expenditure than prominent companies such as Colgate, Goodyear, and Kodak. In all, Victor's advertising costs ranked second among all U.S. businesses, trailing only its celebrated Camden, New Jersey neighbor: Campbell's Soup.[12] The Victor advertising logo, entitled "His Master's Voice" (an image of a white dog listening intently and curiously to a phonograph), was seemingly ubiquitous in American life. Today, the image and slogan remain a cultural icon.[13]

The three titans of the phonograph industry were the bastions of big business. During the industry's height, Americans were annually spending $250 million ($51.4 billion today) on products bearing the names of Edison, Columbia, and Victor. At their pinnacle, the companies collectively had annual profits in the range of $125 million ($25.7 billion today).[14] The phonograph industry was a staple in American consumer culture—a sphere that helped to shape the experiences, tastes, habits, and cultural practices of the early twentieth century and beyond.

Figure 1.2: 1918 phonograph advertisement showing prices ranging from $22.50 to $900. Source: *Atlanta Constitution*, December 24, 1918, 7.

The Ubiquity of the Phonograph in American Daily Life

The Victrola solidified the phonograph's place in American homes. The Victor Talking Machine Company introduced the device in 1906. The home entertainment center was comprised of enclosed parts and hidden speakers (a sound horn) in an oak or mahogany casing. In addition, the cabinet provided shelf space for storing a music library, making it simultaneously a sound medium and an exclusive piece of home décor. The *Talking Machine World*, the premiere journal for the phonograph industry, declared at the close of World War I, "The phonograph is about to enter a period of unparalleled popularity as a national household article."[15]

The innovation was extremely popular. President Woodrow Wilson took his enclosed phonograph with him for his journey to the Paris Peace Conference following the close of World War I. The president boarded the George Washington ocean liner for his trip across the Atlantic Ocean equipped with his stylish phonograph and library of one hundred records. Few things could make the long journey feel more like home than the domestic entertainment medium.[16] The nation followed suit. A 1925 study of thirty-six small U.S. cities concluded that more than half (59 percent) of homes had a phonograph. The device was equally popular in large cities. A 1927 study of home equipment in cities of 100,000 or more found that 60 percent of homes owned a phonograph, compared to 23 percent who owned a radio.[17] The phonograph, once a novelty, had become a centerpiece of the American home.

In 1921, Mrs. Mary Kelly, a mother of five, wrote to the Edison phonograph company saying as much. "I have had my life made worth living since it [the phonograph] came into my home." The Providence, Rhode Island, resident praised her inexpensive phonograph for improving her quality of life. Mrs. Kelly was attached to her phonograph. She disclosed that she planned to save money not for a radio but for an expensive mahogany cabinet phonograph, declaring, "There is no case too grand for such a glorious machine!"[18]

The industry attempted to meet all aesthetic and economic tastes. Phonographs were soon available in an assortment of models, including designs in the likeness of small grand pianos, overnight bags, suitcases, leather purses, handbags, and eventually small players that could be concealed behind walls and ceiling tiles. Such designs varied in price. In 1918, one leading company advertised its arsenal of phonographs in the price range of $22 to $900 (Figure 1.2). The price range is significant compared to the average annual family income, which was approximately $1,500 at the time.[19] Nevertheless, some consumers thoroughly enjoyed the elite priced phonographs. In 1921, George Rhulen of Tacoma, Washington, wrote to the Edison Company to express the joy he derived from his $285 Edison phonograph (the equivalent of approximately $3,700 today).[20]

The phonograph became a seminal commodity of conspicuous consumption in the modern home. Garvin Bushell, a member of the first band to record a race record, recalled that the kind of phonograph one purchased was a symbol of one's social and economic significance. His family purchased their first Victrola for Christmas in 1917. Bushell marveled at the "handsome" cabinet and was spellbound by the musical quality of the machine. In addition to its acoustic value, the family recognized the cultural significance of the device. "Back in those days," the Springfield, Ohio, resident recalled, "The larger the horn, the more convinced the neighbors were that the 'Joneses' were quite successful." To put such status on display, families would place their phonographs in front of a window or an open door so everyone who passed the house would be put on notice.[21] Having a phonograph was one thing. Possessing an elaborate record player, however, was a pronounced social and cultural statement.

In addition to home entertainment, portable phonograph models provided amusement for the country's increasingly mobile society. Traveling models were available in brown, mahogany, or oak. The Outing Talking Machine Company promised customers that their eight by fifteen inch portable phonograph, priced at $37.50 (approximately $494 in 2012), was "the Master of Movable Music." The company slogan proclaimed, "One handle, handles it." For those looking for even smaller players, "Kompact" [sic], maker of "the camera-size phonograph," maintained that their 5 by 7-inch portable players, priced just below $15, produced the "full tone quality and volume equal to that of any of the large size portables on the market." One national mail order catalog advised that their mobile sound medium was "suitable for the home, but so light and compact that it will furnish music anywhere." The Artophone Talking Machine Company, based in Saint Louis, found that their suitcase-styled phonograph was particularly popular with African Americans. The portable player, priced at $13.85, provided the increasingly migrant population of blacks with musical accompaniment for the journey. A New York City phonograph dealer attested that such small players were especially popular with customers living in the city's small apartments. Moreover, the dealer noted, the portable players were ideal for summer driving excursions as well as traveling to resorts and cottages.[22] Americans wanted their phonographs wherever they went.

H. L. Mencken begrudgingly witnessed the phenomenon. In his 1920 portrait of American culture, *The American Credo*, the famed cultural critic quipped about those growing up around the turn of the twentieth century and their relationship with the phonograph. Those reared in the twentieth century, unlike their more "reasonable" nineteenth-century forbearers, "put their inheritance into phonographs and Fords."[23] To Mencken's chagrin, many Americans viewed the two items as a perfect match. Robert and Helen Lynd recognized the popularity of the pairing in their landmark 1920s study of modern culture. "Phonographs have become so much a part of living," they noted, that one family strapped their luggage to the running boards of their Ford so they could "put the Victrola in the back seat" during their summer travels. The family excitedly proclaimed, "Wherever we lived all summer, we had our music with us."[24] Not surprisingly, in 1923 a Detroit furniture store reportedly sold two hundred and fifty small portable players in one week in the motor city. The presence of car radios, let alone secure reception, was rare in the 1920s.[25] However, portable phonographs could be trusted to provide a consistent assortment of audio accompaniment during driving excursions.

The plethora of such exquisite phonograph designs attracted consumers seeking the latest incarnation of the machine, sometimes to their own detriment. One Michigan phonograph aficionado complained that when people purchased phonographs, too often they "depend more on the eye than the ear!" He wrote to the Edison Company, "they look at the case and forget to listen to the music until it is too late."[26] Although the host of designs may have sacrificed sound quality, Americans wanted their phonographs to suit their tastes, pocketbooks, lifestyles, and travels.

The Utility of the Phonograph

Phonographs were popular because they seemingly had something for everyone. The device enabled customers to audibly bring entertainment into their private homes and spaces ostensibly on demand. Frank Burns of Pennsylvania declared that his phonograph records "bring the artist-singer or player to your home." Similarly, Lawrence Dreger of Pittsburgh enjoyed his phonograph because of the medium's ability to bring "the artists to your very home and a little imagination makes you think that they are standing in your very midst. You think you see them in person."[27] Customers were overtaken with such imagination. Adolph Lonk of Chicago testified, "When I sit next to the Edison and listen to some song it wakes up my imagination just as it does to all other people. If it is winter and a person listens to a spring time song the person can almost believe it is springtime. . . . I would not sell my Edison for any amount of money." The phonograph made events timeless and spaceless by enabling listeners to experience a remote event and/or performance, all from the comfort of their own homes.[28]

Moreover, phonograph recordings enabled consumers to enjoy a variety of cultural expressions that they otherwise would not have heard due to social, economic, or geographical limitations. Couples like Mr. and Mrs. Ira K. Harris of Pittsburgh, Pennsylvania, were able to hear a variety of concerts regardless of their distance from the concert venue, thanks to their player. "When there is a concert we wish to hear, we pool the price of our admittance, leaf through our catalogues—Victor, Columbia, and Edison—and purchase the program and we listen to that same concert many times." Small-town couples like Mr. and Mrs. Frank Eaton of Lima, Ohio, enjoyed their phonograph "because we have no other way of hearing the Opera."[29] Likewise, Mary Piest, an employee at Chicago's infamous Cook County Hospital, admitted that she was "not a woman of leisure and means." However, she was so thankful she could spend the evening listening to "the music of our great composers after a day of working and seeing all kinds of tragedies." The phonograph's ability to bring "good" music into her home despite her limited social and economic status, compelled Mrs. Piest to state, "I would not part with my Edison machine even for a good deal."[30]

Likewise, the phonograph enabled Phillip Gibbons to enjoy the entertainment of his choice. The Oregon resident and his wife preferred popular amusements such as "jazz music and foxtrots" to classical music. "What few we have of these so-called higher class records have been played extensively," the jazz enthusiasts admitted, "and we have done our darndest to learn to like them." In fact, he continued, "Sometimes some of our more highly educated relatives drop in and go into spasms of joy on hearing them and discourse learnedly about them." However, the dance lover concluded, "We are afraid we will never properly appreciate them."[31] Whether one desired classical or popular expressions, the phonograph could meet all consumer tastes.

The phonograph was also cherished because it helped Americans stay connected to their pasts through ethnic music expressions. This was particularly true for the countless immigrants who poured into America's cities. Phonograph companies competed vigorously for the patronage of America's immigrant populations. Collectively, phonograph companies produced records in at least thirty-two foreign languages. The competition for this market was fierce. Nathaniel Shilkret, an executive of Victor's Foreign Department, recalled, "With other recording companies competing, it was necessary to attend Polish weddings and affairs, Jewish theaters, Italian vaudeville, German cafes, etc.—sometimes meeting immigrants arriving in America for concert tours." Foreign recording, he concluded, "was a hectic department, and I found little time for sleep."[32]

Immigrant communities could find records in their own native languages in record stores across the country and in chain store catalogs. Sears stereotypically advertised Columbia's Foreign Language records, including "some splendid old German songs, weirdly sweet Hungarian music, Swedish and Norwegian airs that remind one of the far away Northland, vivacious French selections, comical Hebrew songs that make you laugh, patriotic Polish airs, harmonious Russian selections, beautiful Italian songs that carry one's thoughts to the sunny Mediterranean, and Spanish love songs."[33] The phonograph enabled America's growing immigrant populations to enjoy the familiar sounds of their respective homelands in their new and unfamiliar urban surroundings.

These ethnic recordings provided immigrants with vivid memories of family.[34] The Utz family, who were of German origin, adored their phonograph because the German recordings "[r]emind us of friends and places."[35] Such records were widely popular. Following World War I, the Edison record service department received such a high demand for these ethnic recordings that their facilities were "taxed to the utmost to produce sufficient quantities . . . to meet the requirements of the public."[36] The talking machine's ability to aid in such linguistic and expressive continuities made the device a favorite of immigrant groups.

Sacred music also contributed to the popularity of the phonograph. The Fisk Jubilee singers of the historically black Fisk University were one of the most successful sacred music recorders. The group began recording for Victor and its rival Columbia Records in 1909. Their 1916 Columbia release, "Sweet Low"/"Shout All Over" was one of their most popular records, shipping 108,144 copies, compared to the industry average of ten thousand copies during the heyday of race records.[37]

Churchgoers praised such sacred recordings. Mrs. Harry Mangan heard a phonograph record for the first time while attending church. Her New Jersey Presbyterian Church hosted an exhibition to demonstrate to the faithful how the talking machine could aid worship. The sound writer bellowed out sacred hymns. The parishioners were amazed. Mrs. Mangnan was so moved by the experience that she pledged to purchase a talking machine for the spiritual nourishment of her own home. Mr. and Mrs. Frank A. Eaton were a step ahead of the Mangans. The pious couple owned their own phonograph as well as an assortment of religious records. The Eatons often centered their familial devotional life on the talking machine. A rendering of the Twenty-Third Psalm was a family favorite. The experience of listening to sacred music on the phonograph was so fulfilling, Mrs. Eaton admitted, that sometimes it "takes the place of church."[38]

Listeners such as J. T. Trigg of Missouri would only purchase "sacred music" and "good church songs." Trigg viewed the phonograph as a moral teacher. Christian recordings, he wrote, "Give our boys better training. It imprints a good song on the mind in place of a bad one, in other words it teaches them to sing a Christian song in place of a non Christian song." He continued, "the few Christ-like songs that I have, my children will play one of them on the machine and sing these songs well at church."[39] Similarly, A. J. Pleasants, Sr., stationed at Camp Eustis in Virginia, loved the hymn "Nearer My God to Thee." The Army serviceman saw the device as a tool of evangelism. Pleasants's neighbors were not religious; nonetheless, "[d]uring the months that our windows are open, our neighbors lend their ears, without protest." This, according to Pleasants, was quite a feat given the character of his military neighbors. The lay evangelist believed his phonograph was bringing souls closer to God.[40]

Sacred music was so popular that customers complained when their personal religious preferences were not available. Mrs. A. D. Colegrove of Corry, Pennsylvania, thoroughly enjoyed "Hymns for Sunday Use." However, she complained that the Edison catalog did not have "many sacred ones that have pleased me."[41] G. G. Sanchez of Oregon inquired why Edison had not recorded any songs of Christian Science founder Mary Baker Eddy.[42] Morton Sherdahl, a Norwegian Lutheran residing in Evanston, IL complained that "The three most beloved church hymns of the Norwegian Lutheran Church of America" were not found in Edison's catalog.[43] The phonograph had become a popular and common aid for religious practices.

Figure 1.3: William Jennings Bryan recording his "Cross of Gold" speech with musical accompaniment for Gennett Records, 1921. In the days of acoustic recording, phonograph performers centered their performance on the recording horn, which captured the sound and transferred it into the etched grooves of the phonograph disc. Source: *Palladium-Item*, Richmond, Indiana, courtesy of Wayne County Historical Museum, Richmond, Indiana.

The popularity of the phonograph, as both Edison and Berliner had predicted, was not solely related to music. The primary sound medium in American life also provided a plethora of aural experiences to satisfy a seemingly infinite number of consumer desires. The phonograph enabled history lovers to enjoy several historic addresses on the phonograph. The famed presidential debates between William Jennings Bryan and William Howard Taft were re-created for the phonograph. Bryan, a leading evangelical and fundamentalist known for his defense of Fundamentalist Christianity, was credited with being the most popular orator of his day. He recorded several of his famous political addresses. "The Labor Question" expounded on his populist views for the electorate. "The wage earners," the famed orator bellowed out, "comprise so large a proportion of our population that every public question concerns them."[44] Bryan's "The Cross of Gold" was perhaps his most famous political speech. It was originally delivered at the Democratic National Convention in 1896 to resounding applause, assuring Bryan the party's nomination. The presidential hopeful closed the speech by declaring that business interests "shall not press down upon the brow of labor this crown of thorns. You shall not crucify mankind upon a cross of gold!" Gennett Records, a small label in Richmond, Indiana, recorded the heralded address in 1921 (Figure 1.3). The label sought to profit from the rhetoric and oratory of the populist politician and minister with the "golden tongue." The *Chicago Defender*, a leading African American weekly newspaper, advertised the recordings as "marshal[ing] all the force of his eloquence, enthusiasm, and convincing argument!"[45]

Several recordings were made of the famous fireside chats of President Franklin D. Roosevelt. The Sears mail order catalog advertised such presidential recordings as well as "Address by the late President McKinley at the Pan-American Expedition." The relaying of important speeches was not limited to presidents or presidential hopefuls. Booker T. Washington, for example, recorded a version of his 1895 "Atlanta Compromise" speech in 1908 for Columbia Records. The record was even advertised in the NAACP organ *Crisis*. Marcus Garvey, an avid admirer of Washington and founder of the Universal Negro Improvement Association (UNIA), recorded a standard address, "Explanation of the Objects of the Universal Negro Improvement Association," for See Bee Records, a small independent black label. The "stump" speech enabled the mass movement leader to address his worldwide following.[46] The phonograph enabled such storied addresses not only to be preserved, but also to be transmitted to homes across the expanding country and globe.

Comedy records also aided the popularity of the phonograph. Minstrelsy (some even in the form of sermons) and "Coon Songs" enjoyed wide popularity. Few were more lucrative or controversial than "Amos 'n' Andy." Victor recorded the minstrelsy-based serial comedy. The records were sold to customers as well as leased to radio stations across the country. The phonograph recordings enabled the show to become the first syndicated radio program in American history.[47]

The phonograph was also a heralded educational tool. Okeh Records, for example, produced Typewriter Lesson Records. Such records provided educational instruction for those who could not afford—or, as was the case for many African Americans, were prohibited from obtaining—formal professional training. Several labels also produced children's records for educational purposes. Columbia inked a deal in 1917 with Harper & Co. publishers to record children's songs to accompany Harper's children's books.[48] The Talking Book Corporation specialized in children's educational records, featuring games, children's songs, stories, and plays including Shakespeare, Jack and Jill, Old King Cole, London Bridge Is Falling Down, and Simple Simon.[49] Emerson Records produced the "Child's Speaking Book." One speaking book on the animal kingdom featured pages of colorful cardboard animals with phonograph records affixed to their center. The recordings offered detailed information on the featured animal. The books canvassed the entire known animal kingdom. The company lauded the books as providing "a most novel and instructive toy for children."[50]

Victor and Columbia made concerted efforts to have their phonographs and records in schools across the country to help with pedagogy and the dispersal of information and new knowledge. The city of Atlanta praised the installation of phonographs in the city's public schools as marking "the beginning of an important epoch in the progress of education in the South." Moreover, according to school officials, the technological development and the host of special educational records were poised to "mean more in advancing the cultural side of public school education, both in cities and smaller towns, than any other system or invention of the present generation."[51] One schoolteacher wrote to

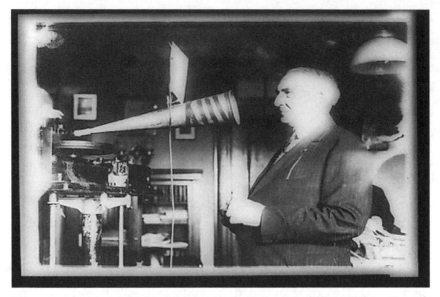

Figure 1.4: President Warren Harding continued to make phonograph addresses following their utility in his victorious bid for president in 1920. In this 1922 picture, probably dated April or May of that year, he is recording an address. The president's "teleprompter" is perched slightly above the recording apparatus. The location of this recording is unknown. It was probably made in the presidential study at the White House. Source: Library of Congress, Prints and Photographs Division, Washington, D.C. LC-USZ62-64386 (b&w film copy neg.) LOT 12282, v. 1.

Victor's Educational Department about the significance of her school acquiring its first phonograph. Annie Pike Greenwood praised the company's "Victrolas for the Kiddies" for aiding the reading, writing, and singing ability of her students as well as their religious instruction. She explained to the company, "You would appreciate all it means, if . . . you could see the light in my pupils eyes as they gather around the Victor to hear the records."[52]

Similarly, Professor Jacob Henry Landman of the College of the City of New York commended the use of the phonograph in teaching, particularly history. The historian reminded his colleagues that record labels "gladly provide the teacher with an assortment of phonograph records for use in exchange for free advertising in the school or college paper." Such use proved popular. Customers complained to Edison, Inc., about the company's lack of educational records.[53] Indeed, the medium became a cutting edge pedagogical tool.

The phonograph also proved to be an effective means of advertising. Emerson Records produced marketing records in which "[o]n One side . . . is placed an advertisement," according to an advertising agent, "and on the other an actual phonograph record which tells of some phase of the commodity or person to be advertised." John Wanamaker, founder of the "Grand Depot," one of the earliest department stores, reportedly ordered $1.2 million in advertising records. The records were given away for free so that advertisers such as Wanamaker could "speak directly to his customers." Using records as a marketing tool was a state-of-the-art advertising technique that engaged more senses than the typical mediums of newspaper advertisements, posters, and flyers.[54]

Presidential candidates also enjoyed this utility. Political hopefuls used the device to record and transmit campaign messages. Like their commercial counterparts, these recordings featured a candidate's picture on one side of the record and his voice on the other. Political competitors William Taft and William Jennings Bryan made records for Edison and Columbia to help them in their respective bids for president in 1908. According to the *Talking Machine World*, Victor also recorded the presidential candidates "on the heels of the remarkable success" of Edison's presidential recordings. Woodrow Wilson and Theodore Roosevelt also utilized the mass media device for their 1912 presidential contest, recording with both Victor and Edison. Wilson, aiming at Roosevelt's Progressive Party, recorded "Governor Wilson on the Third Party." Roosevelt, in turn, recorded "The Liberty of the People." Victor asked Roosevelt to also record a recreational record, one stripped of political speech, so "future generations," regardless of partisan commitments, could simply admire his voice. According to one Victor employee, Roosevelt retorted, "No! I don't care a damn about the preservation of my voice." The campaigning "Rough Rider" saw the phonograph primarily as a mass medium for politics, not recreation.[55]

Emerson records backed the production of presidential campaign records for both presidential candidates in the 1920 election. A. H. Carlyle, head of the Southern States Phonograph Company, displayed the presidential campaign records of Republican running mates Warren Harding and Calvin Coolidge at a meeting of the Atlanta Ad Men's Club. Carlyle assured the predominantly Democratic audience that "several thousand" records were also being produced for Democrat running mates Harvey Cox and Franklin Roosevelt. Such campaign records were distributed and given away at will. In a world without established commercial radio, let alone television, phonograph records offered candidates and presidents the opportunity to address the broadest public possible (Figure 1.4).[56]

The phonograph was employed as a medium for relaying current events as well. As a mass medium, the phonograph transmitted information to listeners across the country. This was particularly true for illiterate populations as well as in rural areas that lacked access to daily newspapers, suffered from irregular radio broadcasts, or were without transportation to urban centers of knowledge and information. Subsequently, record labels produced a host of event records to relay and preserve important events.

Jack Johnson, the first black heavyweight boxing champion, made several recordings toward this end, including a three-disc series retelling his historic "Great White Hope" bout with Jim Jefferies in 1910. Johnson recorded the disc series for the American Cinephone Company in Columba's studio. In a placatory manner, Johnson eloquently described the fight round by round. A silent film company filmed the heavy weight champion in street clothes to accompany the recordings. This combination of silent film and the retelling of the fight via the phonograph was a feasible means to circumvent the ban on the popular silent film footage of the actual bout. Moreover, recordings like Johnson's were the best means to a mass aural play-by-play in the years prior to the first live broadcast of a professional sporting event in 1921.[57]

Columbia Records produced a record series covering the *Scopes v. the State of Tennessee* trial (more commonly referred to as "The Scopes Monkey Trial"), one of the biggest national events of the early twentieth century. The trial typified the Fundamentalist-Modernist cultural war that was waging in America's Protestant faith communities and institutions of higher learning. The 1925 trial convicted John Scopes of teaching evolution in the classroom. Chicago's WGN radio station broadcasted the trial, but only 10 percent of American households possessed a radio in 1925. Columbia in turn produced and recorded event-based songs retelling the events of the trial. Columbia employee Frank Walker recalled that over 60,000 of the records were sold on the Dayton, Tennessee, courthouse steps. "There were thousands of buyers of phonograph records that had no other means of communication," Walker reported. The phonograph was therefore a viable medium to disseminate the latest in current affairs. For some, it was the primary news medium, for others it complemented other media.[58]

In addition to music, current events, education, and speeches, recorded sermons solidified the phonograph's place as the country's primary medium of sound in the early twentieth century. In 1888, Emile Berliner predicted that religious leaders would avidly employ his flat disc for religious broadcasting. He foresaw "his Holiness, the Pope" utilizing the phonograph "to broadcast a pontifical blessing to his millions of believers." The sacred pronouncement, Berliner continued, would be "copied ad infinitum," shipped, and sold across the globe.[59]

The pontiff did utilize the device. Pope Leo XIII made a private recording for President Cleveland in 1893. Columbia issued the first pontifical recording to the public in 1903.[60] American Protestants, however, most readily fulfilled Berliner's prognostication. In 1921 William Jennings Bryan recorded "The Virgin Birth," "The Lord's Prayer," and "Psalm 23," as well as "Nearer My God to the Thee" to the accompaniment of a string quartet for Gennett Records. The *Chicago Defender* emphasized the fundamentalist nature of the religious addresses, proclaiming that the "Virgin Birth" sermon "completely outlines the doctrines he advocated at the Dayton, Tennessee" Scopes Monkey Trial. Moreover, if customers wanted to hear more of Bryan's fundamentalist Christianity, the advertisement promised, "his other records set forth completely the fundamental features of his teachings." To "hear these records," *The Defender* declared, was to "[h]ave them in your home!"[61]

Several white preachers followed suit. Reverend Gust F. Johnson of Minnesota's Swedish Tabernacle had success with a 1924 Christmas sermon on Victor Records. The label advertised the sermon in Scandinavian newspapers and through direct mail. They projected to sell about five thousand copies to their Minnesota customers.[62] Victor also recorded two sermons by Reverend Clarence M. Grayson in 1928. The Mississippi Baptist clergyman recorded "Judas Sold Christ" and "God's Indictment." In 1927, Paramount recorded several sermons by Birmingham pastor Reverend James Oscar Hanes in its Chicago studio. An all-male choir accompanied the eight sermons by the Methodist clergyman.[63]

In addition to becoming the first woman to preach on radio, Aimee Semple McPherson, founder of the International Church of the Four Square Gospel, recorded sermons on her Foursquare Religious Recordings label. Charles Fuller, founder of Fuller Theological Seminary, used the phonograph to syndicate his "Old Fashion Revival Hour" radio broadcast. In the early 1930s, prior to broadcasting nationwide, the preacher recorded his sermons on the phonograph and mailed the recordings to independent stations throughout the country. Fuller wanted syndication. During one Easter vacation, he recalled having the "thrilling experience" of hearing one of his phonograph sermons over the radio.[64] For evangelical clergy, every medium was an opportunity to spread the gospel

•   •   •

The phonograph provided the sound track for American life in the early twentieth century. The device brought music, speeches, news, remote events, and sermons to American homes and public spaces in an unprecedented manner. However, beginning in the early 1920s these leisure transmissions were increasingly provided by radio. By 1930 more than half of all white homes owned at least one radio. That number rose to close to 90 percent the following decade. Edison, the father of the phonograph, saw the writing on the wall. He left the phonograph business altogether. The phonograph industry was in dire need of new markets to stave off the encroachment of radio.[65]

African Americans were an ideal niche market. A growing number of African Americans left the seasonal pay- and credit-based economy of rural America for the daily and weekly wages of urban labor. City life offered African Americans the tangibility of a regular cash income and the leisure to spend it. Radio, however, was still out of reach for many. The average cost of a radio did not dip below $50 until the late 1930s, the contemporary equivalent of over $800. Herb Schiele of the Artophone Phonograph Corporation, a major industry wholesaler based in Saint Louis, attested that even though radio was increasingly popular in the early 1920s, his company continued to prosper because of black patrons by and large, "didn't have money to buy radios in those days." Indeed, by 1930 only 7 percent of African American households owned a radio. To be sure, African Americans encountered radio in a myriad of ways outside the home. However, due to high cost (let alone low rates of home electricity), radio was not as commonplace as phonographs in black homes. Radio did not eclipse phonographs in black homes until World War II, when radio ownership in black homes reached over 50 percent.[66]

This advent of radio primarily in white America made the phonograph industry's policy of racial exclusion no longer cost effective. Thus, beginning in 1920 labels finally expanded their attention and production activities toward black audiences. African Americans, like immigrant populations, rushed to purchase records and spend their leisure time enjoying aural recordings that mirrored their own cultural expressions and practices. The industry named these recordings "race records." The popularity of these records secured the phonograph's place as a key purveyor of entertainment and leisure in black life, a role that had previously been the undisputed arena of the church.

"Ragtime Music, Ragtime Morals"

Race Records and the Problem of Amusement

Zora Neale Hurston was astonished by the way the phonograph altered black leisure. During her undergraduate fieldwork, the noted anthropologist and folklorist observed that the majority of African Americans in the 1920s no longer spent their leisure time in church or church-related events as in times past. Rather, in addition to movie theaters, she reported to her Columbia University professor Franz Boaz, "the bulk of the population now spends its leisure with . . . the phonograph and its blues [records]."[1] African Americans had long enjoyed the phonograph before the interwar explosion of black phonograph artists. The *Crisis,* the official magazine of the National Association for the Advancement of Colored People (NAACP), noted that "sixty-five percent of the phonograph records" made by one phonograph company were bought by African Americans, despite the fact that the "company employs only one colored artist regularly."[2] Race records, however, made the phonograph even more prominent in black life. Beginning in 1920, record labels, about fifteen in all, flooded the market with African American blues and jazz artists, helping national record sales to top one hundred million for the first time in history. By the end of the decade, an average of ten new race records hit the market every week and black consumers cheerfully bought them. The popularity of these "race records" contributed to an interwar economy that witnessed the largest incremental increase in recreational spending in American history as well as the decline in the percentage Americans gave to religious work.[3] The phonograph sat at the center of an emerging black recreation and entertainment industry that rivaled the church for the time, authority, and patronage of black communities.

Race records disrupted and challenged not only the church's entertainment monopoly, but also its cultural hegemony. The nascent black leisure market became a space where ideals of race progress, politics, citizenship, and propriety were contested. Black ministers, professors, teachers, and literati established the acceptable discourses, cultural labors, and recreational activities of racial progress. The working class and folk expressions of race records, however, did not subscribe to such wisdom. In fact, the articulations of the black entertainment industry publicly challenged the social and cultural authority and legitimacy of this ruling class, particularly regarding traditional notions of gender, racial advancement, and Christian morality.[4] Black recreational life, as Hurston noted, had a new locus outside the church and a host of new spokespersons and peddlers.

Black mainline churches responded to the phenomenon of race records in two primary ways. Some thought the best way to combat the influence of black popular music on wax was to reprioritize church work by making faith communities alternative venues of entertainment and amusement that could compete for the allegiance and patronage of black consumers. Others, while agreeing that race records were a hindrance to racial uplift and Christian faith, insisted that under no circumstances should the church be engaged in the amusement market. The entertainment industry, they argued, was best left in the hands of professional and educated race men. The responses of black faith communities and race leaders were somewhat divided. However, they were unified in one matter: the popularity of "the phonograph and its blues" was a central black cultural phenomenon that had to be addressed for the sake of racial progress and Christendom.

The Phonograph and the Black Entertainment Industry

By the end of World War I, the music industry had produced more than $335 million worth of goods.[5] However, this success was achieved without a significant concern for black consumers. Music suppliers marketed records to various American immigrant groups and recorded hundreds of titles in at least thirty-two foreign languages.[6] However, the gatekeepers of the entertainment medium refused to make recordings exclusively for African American consumers. One record executive confessed, "We had records by all foreign groups—German records, Swedish records, Polish records; but we were afraid to advertise Negro records."[7] J. A. Sieber, an advertising manager for a leading record company, asserted that economic concerns were the real reason for refusing to record black popular music and artists for black audiences. He argued that the phonograph industry was convinced that "colored people were . . . mighty poor record buyers, and cash visits by colored customers were rare and far between."[8] The Victor Talking Machine Company held similar views. The firm maintained, "Our experience has taught us that our customers judge records entirely by the way they sound to them, and care nothing at all about the race of the singer." Victor defended its recording policies, stating, "We do not believe that records by Negro singers would appeal to our Negro customers. . . . We have quite a number of records by negro singers—Tuskegee, Fisk Jubilee . . . but we do not believe that a very large proportion of these records are to be found in negro homes."[9] According to the industry, recording African American artists for black consumers was not cost effective.

Subsequently, there were largely two categories of black phonograph performances: minstrelsy records that cohered to the degrading stereotypes of the Sambo, Coon, and Pickaninny; and classical renderings of the spirituals by black college groups. The recording of George W. Johnson set the pattern. Billed the "Whistling Coon," he became the first African American to record on the phonograph in 1890. Artists such as Bert Williams and Louis "Bebe" Vasnier followed suit. The Fisk Jubilee Singers began recording their sacred songs in 1909. Both categories were geared toward and advertised for white consumers as "darkey" songs and "negro dialect."[10]

However, the emergence of a predominately white radio market coupled with the growth of the black salary and wage-earning classes situated African Americans as a new target market. From 1910 to 1930 the number of black professionals more than doubled and the number of black automotive workers increased by almost 2,800 percent.[11] The increase in daily and weekly pay and the regulated workday of urban America provided the means and time for African Americans to enjoy the variety of urban commercial amusements that cropped up in the twentieth century. The phonograph was among the first items consumers looked to buy with their newfound expendable income. As one phonograph industry insider observed, the working classes "made money at a rate that they never dreamed of and the first thing that they turned to for the enjoyment of their new surplus was the phonograph."[12]

The Okeh record label pioneered the untapped niche of black popular music for the expanding market of black cash and salaried workers. Perry Bradford, a well-known vaudeville performer and composer, proposed the idea of recorded black popular music to several record companies. Bradford, who had migrated to Atlanta from rural Alabama in 1901, thought the success of his vaudeville and minstrel shows and compositions was evidence of the commercial profitability of black popular music on the phonograph. He continually lobbied the phonograph industry, "There's fourteen million Negroes in our great country and they will buy records if recorded by one of their own."[13] Columbia dismissed Bradford's business venture, stating they "wouldn't think of recording a colored" popular artist. Victor, however, gave Bradford a chance. They recorded Mamie Smith, one of Bradford's popular black vaudeville singers. In keeping with the industry's prevailing practice of limiting black artists to minstrelsy, the company classified the singer's studio visit in their recording ledger as a "comic" performance. But Victor elected not to release the recording. They feared that recording a black artist would risk the company's prestige among white consumers.[14]

Okeh Records, however, took Perry Bradford up on his offer. The upstart label was so generic that it rarely even listed the identity of its performers in its advertisements. Fred Hager, Okeh's recording manager, decided to record Mamie Smith in New York City singing Perry Bradford's "That Thing Called Love" and "You Can't keep a Good Man Down," on February 14, 1920, even though he received countless racist letters and threats of impending boycotts. Smith became the first black vocal artist to record black popular music, pioneering the race record genre. Okeh did its best to hide the race and name of its new artist. It inconspicuously advertised the record's July release along with other titles. Nevertheless, news of the novelty spread. The *Chicago Defender* publicized the recording in March, almost four months before the record was placed on the shelf. In an article that featured a picture of Mamie Smith, the newspaper proudly announced:

> Well, you've heard the famous stars of the white race chirping their
> own stuff on the different makes of phonograph records . . . but we have
> never—up to now—been able to hear one of our own ladies deliver the
> canned goods. Now we have the pleasure of being able to say that at last
> they [phonograph companies] have recognized the fact that we [African
> Americans] are here for their service; the Okeh Phonograph Company
> has initiated the idea by engaging . . . Mamie Gardner Smith . . . and
> apparently [she is] destined to be one of that company's biggest hits.[15]

Mamie was indeed a hit. The record reportedly sold 75,000 copies
during its first month. One Atlanta record retailer remarked that the
record was so popular that it sold out before he even had the chance
to properly package the record. "We get 'em [records] in there . . . we
didn't even put 'em in a bag. Just hand them to 'em and take a dollar.
Hand them out just like we was selling tickets at a theatre window."[16]
For many consumers, buying Mamie's record was truly akin to
purchasing a ticket for a blues performance, one that could be enjoyed
countless times at one's convenience.

The hefty price tag of the record indicates just how much consumers were willing to pay for the pleasure of listening to black folk music.
A dollar was a significant price for anything in 1920, let alone a nonessential commodity. After World War I, the average hourly wage for
manufacturing labor was 53 cents. The purchase of the $1 record, then,
was about two hours' wages for the average laborer. This corresponds to
spending about $40 today based on average manufacturing wages. The
cost of the race record was significant, but it did not deter listeners from
lining up to buy it.[17]

The risk Okeh took by recording black popular music yielded great
returns. Leading scholar and activist W. E. B. Du Bois had initially
shrugged off the label's foray into black popular music, deeming it
nothing more than an "experiment." He was stunned by the ground-
swell of support for the trial run. He observed with astonishment
that Mamie Smith's record "was so successful that the demand for her
records among colored folk was so great that the company was not
able to fill its orders." Indeed, Okeh was having difficulty keeping pace
with demand for the record. The label had found a niche market. As
one dealer surmised, Mamie Smith's record was "a Negro style that they

wanted and never had had [*sic*]." Once the record was released, he glee-fully reflected, "They just lapped it up like nobody's business."[18]

Mamie's follow-up record, "Crazy Blues," was recorded on August 10, 1920 and released in November. The record, accompanied by a large window display featuring Mamie Smith, was sent to record dealers just in time for the Thanksgiving holiday. It purportedly went on to sell one million copies. With this unprecedented success, Bradford bragged that he had received $53,000 in royalties. Touring also proved lucrative for Bradford and Mamie Smith. In January 1921, Mamie Smith, accom-panied by her "Jazz Hounds," played to an estimated crowd of 18,000 in Norfolk, Virginia. The concert admission price was $1 per ticket. Mamie was paid $2,000 dollars for her performance, comparable to approximately $150,000 today. After the concert, 10,000 records were sold, also at $1 each. By May of the following year, Mamie's minimum appearance fee still stood at an astounding $1,000 per performance, at a time when the average family income was only about $1,500.[19] Smith, a former cleaning woman, became a rich black celebrity.

Smith's success contributed to the rise of race records. Within months of Mamie Smith's profitable release, leading phonograph com-panies released their own black artists. By June 1921, Cardinal Records recorded international celebrity Josephine Baker, as well as blues leg-end Ethel Waters. Pathe Records introduced Lavinia Turner, while Richmond, Indiana, label Gennett recorded Daisy Martin. Georgia Tom (Thomas Dorsey) made blues records with Paramount and sev-eral other labels. Okeh's Victoria Spivey burst on the scene, selling an astounding 150,000 copies of her "Black Snake Blues."[20] The industry exploded with race record artists.

Bessie Smith was one of the most successful and lucrative race record artists. She began recording for Columbia in 1923. The label joined the race record frenzy, attempting to flood the market with popular black artists. Bessie's recording of "Downhearted Blues" that year reportedly sold 800,000 copies in six months and 2 million for the year. African Americans as well as whites snatched up the records of the woman who became known as "The Empress of the Blues." Smith's segregated "whites only" concerts sold out across the south. Columbia had a star on their hands. The label quickly signed her to an exclusive contract. Her 1924 contract obligated her to record a minimum of twelve songs per year at a salary of $200 per song, assuring her of a minimum of $2,400 every year. Moreover, her jam-packed weekly performance fee stood at $1,500. In current terms, Bessie's recording contract amounted to the equivalent of someone earning approximately $160,000 a year, while her performance fee was equivalent to roughly $100,000 per show/week. Bessie often kept her bundles of cash with her, usually in overalls she wore under her dresses. During a 1925 Columbia recording session, a twenty-three-year-old Louis Armstrong remembered seeing the stash: "She had so much money, it killed me!" Even without royalties—Columbia slyly retained those—Bessie was a wealthy celebrity. Given her handsome salary, one can only imagine how much money Columbia made from her.[21]

One thing, however, was clear: the race records industry was a lucrative business. As the *Music Trades Magazine* observed in 1924, "The sale of Negro records is becoming more and more of a volume proposition for phonograph dealers all over the country." Moreover, the monthly industry magazine promised executives that "[d]ealers who can offer the latest blues by the most important of all colored singers of blues selections, are in a strategic position to dominate in the sale of records."[22] Labels adhered to this forecast, showering the market with race records. Roughly fifty race records were released within a year of Mamie Smith's groundbreaking song. By 1927, the three leading race record producers (Okeh, Paramount, and Columbia) released a staggering collection of 1,305 race records. In all, from 1920 to 1942 approximately 1,200 African American artists were issued on some 5,500 blues recordings.[23]

The popularity of race records accentuated the role of the phonograph in black life. Legendary gospel singer Mahalia Jackson, born in 1911, recalled how the release of race records permeated her native New Orleans. "Everybody was buying phonographs . . . just the way people have television sets today and everybody had records of all the Negro blues singers—Bessie Smith . . . Ma Rainey . . . Mamie Smith . . . all the rest." Many white households in the Big Easy listened to classical music on their phonographs, Jackson remembered, "but in a colored house you heard blues. You couldn't help but hear blues—all through the thin partitions of the house—through the open windows—up and down the street in the colored neighborhoods—everybody played it real loud."[24]

An east coast race record fan recalled in 1923 that he and his friends constantly listened to artists like Louis Armstrong and King Oliver

"until our arms were worn out from working the phonograph handle." The group listened until "the record was worn out."[25] The child
of a West Virginia wage earner had fond memories of "every pay-
day . . . Mama would send us kids down to the store to get the latest
blues records. . . . Everybody else we knew would be there too and we'd
carry those records home, stacked in our arms." As a result, throughout
the small town neighborhood, "you could go from street to street and
hear those blues records blasting out from the open doors."[26]

Rushing to the store to pick up the latest race record was also a common scene in urban black communities. A Los Angeles record dealer
claimed that his shipments of the latest race records usually sold out
within an hour.[27] H. C. Speir, a Jackson, Mississippi, music store proprietor and talent scout, calculated that his African American clientele
outspent whites "fifty to one." The white Mississippi native, born in 1895,
regarded the influx of black customers as an offense to whites. He instituted segregated entrances and listening booths to accommodate his
newfound race record business. But the store's Jim Crow practices did
not deter black consumers. The store, which opened in February 1925,
averaged about $500 in race record sales, or over six hundred records,
every Saturday. Although Speir considered his black patrons undesir-
able and ignorant, he welcomed their money.[28]

Art Satherly, a Paramount employee, recalled that long lines of
black consumers at record stores was a common Friday night scene in
Atlanta and Birmingham. Similiarly, while working in "the Carolinas,"
the British-born executive marveled that neither Jim Crow nor insuf-
ficient funds deterred race record buyers. Prohibited from entering the
store, black consumers would form "a queue all around the stores, bor-
rowing from each other to get the latest Blind Lemon or Ma Rainey or
what have you!" Likewise, a Chicago storeowner testified that whenever
popular artists such as Mamie Smith, Bessie Smith, or Rainey released
a new race record, "Colored people would form a line twice around the
block." Their desire for it was so intense, he remembered, that sometimes bootlegged records "sold in the alley for four or five dollars
apiece." For some, purchasing the newest race record was worth taking
a small loan or even spending an entire day's wage.[29]

Earl Montgomery had a similar experience in Greenwood, Mississippi. Montgomery, an executive for Paramount distributor Artophone,

recalled that the black patron of a drug store offered him $5 for an advance copy of Leroy Carr's wildly popular "How Long Blues." The anxious buyer told Montgomery that possessing the record—a blues tune that employs the metaphor of a departing train for an estranged lover—before it was actually released to the public, would surely aid him in bringing his sexual plans for the evening to fruition.[30] No doubt, consumers were willing to go to great lengths to get their hands on the latest race records.

Perhaps the periodic race record style shows and cabarets most vividly reveal the encompassing impact of race records on black life. The 1926 Okeh Summer Cabaret and Style Show in Chicago, the city's second show of the year, was held on June 12 in the main auditorium of the Coliseum. The label rented the spacious arena for an astounding $1,000 per night, comparable to an expenditure of more than $60,000 today.[31]

The gala was advertised in four of the city's black periodicals for over a month, including an extra "Music Edition" of the *Chicago Defender*. The *Talking Machine World* deemed the newspaper ads "as play[ing] a most important role" in advertising the revue. In addition to the newspapers, 65,000 posters, handbills, and theatrical one-sheets were used to herald the show. Moreover, prior to the feature presentation all Chicago's movie houses ran slides announcing what one black periodical called "the monster cabaret and style show." A week before the extravaganza, "a street team" of bandwagons, floats, and a "unique Crystal Wagon" traversed the streets of Chicago's black neighborhoods "in the proverbial circus style" to promote the concert and style show. Furthermore, one hundred black taxi drivers were paid to affix stickers on their cars announcing the show and their vehicles as the official transportation to and from the festivities.[32] The thirty-three record stores on the south and west sides of the city served as ticket agents. Large canvas banners on each store announced the special ticket prices: 75 cents for an Okeh record, and $1.10 for a ticket, comparable to about $68 today. Customers received a 25 cent discount (about $15) if they purchased both. Collectively, the licensed Okeh dealers reportedly sold over 20,000 tickets.[33] The event was the cultural centerpiece of the summer.

On the day of the event, the Colored Musicians Union paraded the streets together with automobiles and bandwagons in a show of support. Twenty truckloads of food and confections were brought in while local businesses donated several carloads of gifts and prizes. The *Chicago Defender* declared that the Coliseum's VIP reservation list "show[s] that every man and woman on Chicago's south side who is important socially, politically, or otherwise will be there."[34]

The doors opened at 8 p.m. to an estimated crowd of eighteen thousand. Eighteen Okeh race record artists performed from 9 p.m. until 1 a.m., including Louis Armstrong, Sara Martin, and the singing and comedy duo of Butter Beans and Susie. A state-of-the art "Western Electric Public Address System" was rented for $600 (over $30,000 in average wages today) for the evening, ensuring that the crowd would be able to enjoy every bellow, croon, moan, and note of their favorite artist or group. Likewise, a team of electricians installed "the most artistic and costly lighting system" ever used in the Coliseum to make certain all eyes could see the performers and their every move. The constellation of phonograph stars, trendy audio and visual technology, and the large crowd led one observer to describe the scene as a "carnival city of brilliant lights and festive booths and riotous banners."[35]

A number of contests followed the exuberant performances. The women's fashion show began at 1 a.m. Five women's clothing stores on the city's south side sponsored and judged the competition. Forty contestants were assessed in "sport, street, party, and evening wear." The winner was awarded an assortment of gifts from the leading boutiques. The dance contest commenced at 3 a.m. The singles' and couples' competitions pitted "the leading colored dance schools and classes" against one another. As the summer sun dawned in the sky, male and female contestants displayed their prowess in the latest jazz dance crazes, vying for a portion of the $250 prize money (comparable to about $16,000 today). The *Chicago Defender* summarized the event as a "monster never-to-be-forgotten show."[36]

The popularity and scale of such events put on display how race records were not only central to black entertainment, but also highly influential in the black public sphere. Black nightlife, dance culture, fashion, and commerce were all taking their cultural cues from race records. One only had to stroll through virtually any black neighborhood, attend a black leisure event, beauty salon, or barbershop, or peruse a black periodical to witness the comprehensive nature of the race record phenomenon.

Writer and poet Langston Hughes praised such commercialization of black popular expression. Hughes, dubbed the "Bard of Harlem," believed that jazz and blues were "inherent expressions of Negro life in America." At the very least, he argued, the packaging of such black cultural forms and practices would "forcibly" bring the artistic expressions of common black folk "to the attention of his own people among whom for so long, unless the other race had noticed him beforehand, he was a prophet with little honor. . . . Let the blare of Negro jazz bands and the bellowing voice of Bessie Smith singing the blues penetrate the closed ears" of black intellectuals, middle class communities, and their churches. This, argued Hughes, would help the "smug" black middle classes and their faith communities discover racial pride. As historian Erin Chapman points out, Hughes's sentiments spoke for all those who believed that, as Hughes termed it, "the present vogue in things Negro" in the leisure marketplace would actually aid the advancement of the race. The participation of the black working class in cultural production, consumption, and as commodities themselves on the phonograph (as well as in art and literature), could bolster black claims of humanity, full citizenship, racial progress, and spiritual flourishing.[37] However, African American faith communities deeply opposed these claims even as they debated the relationship of the church to the black entertainment market.

The Problem with Race Records

The *New York Times Sunday Magazine* spoke for many black churchgoers when it succinctly surmised that jazz and blues music were nothing but a contagious "exhibition of how-not-to-be."[38] Established black faith communities believed that race records promoted immoral forms of amusement and recreation that hindered black morality and racial advancement. Guided by racial uplift ideologies, these churches framed their concerns for race records in terms of cultural politics. Racial uplift aimed to rehabilitate the image and cultural practices of African Americans through an embodiment of Western bourgeois assimilation and associated notions of social purity, respectability, thrift, and chastity.[39] Racial uplift posited that there was a direct relationship between recreational activities and morality. Leisure activities had the potential to impede or stimulate the assimilation and social equality of African Americans. This was especially the case with black popular music. In a heralded sermon that was later published in several white and black newspapers, a Yale-educated black minister plainly explained this relationship between black popular music and morals. "There is a close relationship between music and morals. . . . Ragtime music makes ragtime character, just as noble music makes noble character." In short, amusement and leisure activities, particularly music, signified moral and racial commitments or the lack thereof.[40]

The Woman's Convention, Auxiliary of the National Baptist Convention (WC) and the National Association of Colored Women (NACW) are emblematic of this view. The women of the National Baptist Convention, the largest black religious body in America, worked closely with the NACW. The interrelated organizations not only shared members and leadership—such as Nannie Helen Burroughs—but also an avid disdain for race records. Historian Evelyn Higginbotham notes that the WC "adhered to a politics of respectability that equated public behavior with individual self-respect and with the advancement of African Americans as a group." Black Baptist women "felt certain that 'respectable' behavior in public would earn their people a measure of esteem from white America." All forms of "folk" cultural practices—popular dancing, expressive worship, and of course jazz and blues music—were disavowed and opposed. To be sure, this bourgeois notion of respectability did espouse a strong, necessary, and enduring critique of the racist failures of American democracy, but it also "attributed institutional racism to the 'negative' public behavior of their [black] people."[41]

Similarly, the NACW—which consisted of several groups including church clubs, evangelists, and religious workers—believed that America's race problem could only be addressed if the conditions of black women were improved. Historian Deborah G. White argues that clubwomen, as they came to be known, were convinced that "The uplift of women was the means of uplifting the race." Black struggles for equality and progress revolved around improving the images, education, and public behaviors of black women. Informally sharing the NACW motto, "Lift as we climb," both groups explicitly and implicitly operated under an ideological banner that insisted, "a race could rise no higher than its women."[42]

However, in song and aesthetics, blues women articulated a femininity that countered the shared "woman-centered race progress ideology" of the WC and NACW. Blues women, to be sure, did advocate for the advancement of black women. Feminist studies scholar and activist Angela Y. Davis has argued that blues women helped to "construct an aesthetic community that affirmed women's capacities in domains assumed to be the prerogatives of males." Indeed, the songs of female blues singers helped to create discourses and spaces of resistance to gendered, classed, and racial hierarchies; but blues women did so outside the parameters of respectability and Christian piety.[43] Popular race record women, writes Deborah G. White, "sang songs about black women who were fallible, about women who were disgusted . . . sensual women, who enjoyed sex and used it for financial and emotional gain." For example, Bessie Smith's "Young Woman's Blues" bellowed, "I'm a young woman and ain't done runnin' 'round" and "I ain't gonna marry, ain't gonna settle down, I'm gonna drink good moonshine." Similarly, Ida Cox's "Wile Women" proclaimed, "You never get nothing by being an angel child, You'd better change your way and get real wild. . . . . Wild Women are the only kind that ever get by."[44]

Similarly, Ma Rainey's "Prove It on Me Blues" flaunted her purported lesbian relationships. The Paramount artist proclaimed, "Went out last night with a crowd of my friends, They must've been women, 'cause I don't like no men. Wear my clothes just like a fan. Talk to the gals just like any old man." Undeniably, blues women, like the "flapper" amongst white women, publicly proclaimed and affirmed their sexuality and power. As F. Scott Fitzgerald surmised in 1931, the women of the Jazz Age were the first women to openly and unashamedly proclaim "that love was meant to be fun." In doing so, blues women challenged the traditional mores of black club and churchwomen's gendered notions of sexual propriety specifically and racial uplift in general.[45]

An alleged encounter between Langston Hughes and a black clubwoman was exemplary. Hughes recalled in 1926, "A prominent Negro clubwoman in Philadelphia paid eleven dollars (comparable to spending about $700) to hear Raquel Meller sing . . . but she told me a few weeks before she would not think of going to hear 'that woman' Clara Smith." Meller was a Spanish-born international film and theater star while Smith was a top-selling blues woman. Smith recorded over one hundred songs with Columbia. Nicknamed the "Queen of the Moaners" for her suggestive style, she recorded hits such as "Black Women's Blues," "Daddy Don't Put That Thing on Me Blues," and "Got My Mind on That Thing." In the clubwoman's eyes, seeing Meller was worth the large financial expenditure, but Smith was not worth a penny. Paying top dollar to see Meller was a form of cultural politics; a display of black uplift. But the sexual assertiveness of the phonograph recordings of Clara Smith and others was singularly at odds with the traditional "Christian" sexual mores and women-centered race progress of the WC and NACW.⁴⁶

In addition to race record lyrics, the Black Protestant Establishment also opposed race record advertisements. Race record ads often featured stereotypical and racist images and tropes of African Americans (i.e., mammy), exaggerated physical characteristics and tattered clothing and often depicted blacks engaging in lewd and illegal behaviors (murder, theft, alcohol consumption). Okeh, for example, centered their commercials on one principle: "the thing people like best is entertainment and . . . folks love to laugh." Okeh's ads were purposely done in caricature so they would be "so entertaining that everyone will stop and look at it."⁴⁷ Other labels followed suit, adding captions to their racist parodies. A Paramount ad for Ma Rainey added, "Having a phonograph without these records is like having ham without eggs!" A Columbia commercial for Bessie Smith records likewise noted, "Having a phonograph without these records is like having pork chops without gravy— Yes, indeed!"⁴⁸

In Louisiana, Columbia records went a step further, creating a live caricature that played upon the mythology of black criminality. The label hired an African American actor to don a "striped prison uniform" to advertise Bessie Smith's "Jail House Blues." The impersonator simply sat in the window display of the Kaplan Furniture Company surrounded by Bessie's records for the entire day. In exchange, he was compensated with a "union" wage and a couple of race records for him and his "dusky lady." Henry Irwin, the local Columbia field representative and advertising "guru," proudly proclaimed that the "live" advertisement worked well, adding, "It cleaned out the stock of the records . . . . [and] it stimulated record business generally and increased sales in the other departments of the store." The store credited the ad with bringing

Figure 2.1: Political cartoon. Source: *Baltimore Afro-American*, August 15, 1925, A11.

in over $750 worth of business for the day (comparable to $50,000 today).[49]

Uplift groups branded these commercials racist, contrary to bourgeoisie representations of blackness, and therefore a blight to racial progress. Black proponents of middle-class racial uplift believed that the public sphere held the power to shape popular—that is, white—conceptions of African Americans. Such race record ads only served to set black people back. Floyd Calvin, one of the first black radio journalists, noted on the front page of the *Pittsburgh Courier* that he and his friends "frowned" upon race records and their advertisements, which were "extensively advertised in the negro press."[50] Calvin was disgusted by how "certain colored women seem to thrive on salacious notoriety." He saw the popularity of blues women and their ads as "a direct affront to the influence of the churches."[51]

At one point, the advertising manager of Okeh Records asked Calvin if black consumers liked the records and the ads. The college-educated journalist dismissed the question, chiding that he and his cultured and church-going friends did not bother with race records or their ads with "outlandish titles," but preferred the "popular tunes" of Irving Berlin, the Russian-born composer and songwriter of such well-known songs as "What'll I Do," "God Bless America," and "White Christmas." The trailblazing black reporter and his friends distanced themselves from race records and the "dirty work" of their ads and publicly identified with Berlin's cultured ballads, Broadway tunes, and movie scores. But Calvin was not content to just ignore the ads; he strongly believed it was "high time something was done about it."[52]

The editor of the *Half-Century Magazine*, a Chicago-based periodical named to mark the fiftieth anniversary of the Emancipation Proclamation, was also concerned "with the ridiculous blues ads that grace many of the current periodicals." The bimonthly magazine was one of several black publications of the era that was, as Noliwe Rooks notes, "overwhelmingly focused on the significance of consumerism for African American women" in urban locales. In a 1925 editorial, "Widening the Gap," the magazine declared that the majority of blues ads were "an offense and insult to the race." At issue were white perceptions of African Americans. The journal contended that race records and their ads constituted the predominant interactions whites had with African Americans. White Americans would never know of the existence of the pious black professional and middle classes "so long as Colored papers accept these ads that ridicule and the Colored people in general set their seal of approval on them by purchasing these records and singing these songs." Unless the phenomenon was tapered, the editorial concluded, race records and their ads would continue to "do much to increase hatred and widen the breach between the races."[53]

Readers of the magazine agreed wholeheartedly. One reader wrote to the publication, "Why doesn't some uplift organization get busy and try to stop the cartoonist from running such ridiculous cartoons. . . . . Such cartoons are giving the other races the wrong impression of us." If an uplift organization did not step in and make an "outcry," she continued, other races would take the cartoons and ads "for granted that they are true to life and treat us accordingly." "It would be well for us if these cartoons were discontinued." The collective fate of African Americans depended on it.[54]

Nannie Helen Burroughs of the WC and NAWC summed up this viewpoint well in an editorial for the *Philadelphia Tribune*. Burroughs declared that black churches and uplift organizations had a responsibility to patrol black commercials on behalf of the gullible black populace. "The masses are ignorant, thoughtless and credulous. They do not think for themselves." Stereotypical racist depictions of blacks in advertising "gives them the wrong impression of their own race and develops the inferiority complex." Racial uplift necessitated that the black masses see more than just low-down "propaganda." Advertisements should display the progress of blacks since slavery. Such images would reveal to African Americans and the world how in "only sixty five years under the transforming influence of a Christian democracy," African Americans had developed "social standards and high ideals and live up to them."[55]

Opponents of race records even appealed to "medical science". The *New York Amsterdam News* and the *Baltimore Afro-American*, two nationally circulated black newspapers, published a scathing report on the social effects of race records by "noted physician" Dr. E. Elliot Rawlings. The trusted doctor concluded that in the age of Prohibition, race records intoxicated listeners, replacing "whiskey, wine, and beer."[56] Rawlings's findings were reportedly based on a "clinical" study he conducted on a young couple. When left alone in a room listening to classical music on the phonograph, the young couple acted with propriety. However, when the same couple was left alone listening to a race record they were soon dancing and kissing.[57] The physician concluded that such music "overpower[s] the will. Reason and reflection are lost, and the actions of the person are directed by the stronger animal passions." Rawlings strongly believed that church involvement was the only solution to this social vice. "In the social life of the people today jazz music is king and jazz music will reign until a spiritual awakening and reformation sweeps like a whirlwind over the land."[58] Black faith communities agreed, a "spiritual awakening and reformation" was indeed needed to stave off the vicious effects of race records. However, they were divided on how exactly to stoke this much-needed revival.

Creation

The role and work of black Protestant faith communities in urban America was far from a forgone conclusion during the rise of the urban black entertainment industry. When Mamie Smith and other black popular artists began crooning from the phonograph, more than 70 percent of both the black populace and churches were rural—meaning that almost three-fourths of African Americans and black Christian churches were in communities of populations of less than 2,500. Black Baptists were particularly rural, with some 80 percent of their congregations in such communities. Black Christian practices were largely shaped by and encompassed within this rural milieu of habits, expressions, commerce, and entertainments. The development of a black Protestant ministry that could appropriately address the particularities of urban social, cultural, and recreational needs was largely unchartered terrain.[59]

It is no surprise, then, that crafting a philosophy of urban Protestant ministry able to confront the rise of the urban-based black entertainment market was at the heart of one of the earliest known public articulations and sociological analyses of "the Negro Church."[60] In a speech at Hampton Institute (now Hampton University) in July 1897, W. E. B. Du Bois predicted that as the twentieth century dawned, the question of urban amusement was bound to become a central issue in the welfare of black life and black Protestantism. His address, *The Problem of Amusement,* asserted that amusement practices revealed and influenced one's morality, aspirations, and welfare. "The Negro Church" had been the "central organ of the organized life of the American negro" not only for religion and instruction but also for "amusement and relaxation." Du Bois cited fieldwork from his forthcoming 1899 landmark study, *The Philadelphia Negro,* to bolster his point. "The church has been peculiarly successful, so that of the ten thousand Philadelphia Negroes whom I asked, 'Where do you get your amusements?' fully three-fourths could only answer, 'From the churches.'"[61] However, Du Bois prognosticated that the rise of black commercial entertainment would profoundly challenge such dominance. Black faith communities would be forced to reassess the role and mission of churches in black life.[62]

Some believed that the best way to respond to this problem of amusement—to stave off the dire effects of race records and fuel a revival of sorts—was to revitalize church work by, ironically, replicating rural church life. Churches could remain the central purveyor of amusement by creating alternative forms of commercial entertainment; with one exception: the amusements would be bourgeois in style. "Wholesome" amusements, reformers argued, should form a central element of the mission of urban black faith communities. Such church work would support racial uplift and Christian virtue. Dr. George E. Haynes, Secretary of the Commission on the Church and Race Relations for the Federal Council of Churches, spoke for many churchgoers in his 1928 essay, "The Church and Negro Progress." The former Director of Negro Economics in the U.S. Department of Labor urged black churches to recognize their responsibility to provide black migrants with wholesome recreation and amusement. "All his [the negro's] leisure-time activities that condition intellectual development and emotional motivation . . . must find their channel mainly through the principal community agency the Negro has—his church." Haynes lamented, however, that "[p]rogress in this adjustment of the Negro church has been slow."[63]

A 1925 cartoon in the *Baltimore Afro-American* urged the church along the same course (Figure 2.1). The sketch encouraged black churches to create alternative amusement spaces. The cartoon depicted jazz as a reckless automobile that was "ruining the youngsters of today." The drawing urged "Churches" to establish "sane amusements" to counteract secular black entertainments, especially race records.[64] Satisfying black migrant desires for pleasure and entertainment with high-class entertainments was the only way to instill "proper" and Christian cultural values in current and future black generations. Subsequently, churches sponsored, instituted, and hosted commercial amusements such as musicals, operas, race films, and dances. These amusements embodied bourgeoisie aesthetics as a means of uplift.

Reverend Lacy Kirk Williams, pastor of Chicago's Olivet Baptist Church, president of the National Baptist Convention (NBC), and vice president of the Baptist World Alliance, strongly urged urban black churches to take this approach. In a *Chicago Sunday Tribune* editorial, Williams identified black urban recreations of the non-"religious kind" as a major cause of religious decline in black communities. He added,

"The promiscuous mixing, the need of recreation, and the love of pleasure are leading factors in church declension." He encouraged black churches to engage in church work that was "passionately human, but no less divine." Gospel labors of charity and church facilities "equipped for recreation," according to Williams, were of paramount importance to urban black churches. If black churches ignored this mission, he argued, they ran the risk of losing black migrants to other social organizations and, even worse, forfeiting souls to the moral corruption of the black entertainment world.[65]

Jane Edna Hunter, a member of the NACW and founder of the Phillis Wheatley Association (PWA), pursued such work in Cleveland, Ohio. Hunter, a trained nurse and attorney from rural South Carolina, opened the PWA in 1911. The parachurch organization provided housing and education for working black women. As the jazz and blues craze hit Cleveland, Hunter remarked that she considered such black commercial entertainment "a much more dreadful monster" than the wild animals she had encountered during her youth, beasts that always threw her "into teeth-chattering, blood-curdling panic." Hunter's dread was evident when she visited a nightclub in Cleveland. As joyous patrons danced to "Saint Louis Blues" in the jam-packed nightspot, Hunter disdainfully remarked, "The whole atmosphere is one of unrestrained animality, the jungle faintly veneered with civilized trappings . . . the worst that my race has to offer." For Hunter, the only "answer" to such retrogressive activities was to supply "similar recreation under wholesome influences." Hunter decided to add a "recreational hall" to the PWA's educational and residential agenda. The thrifty Hunter, who started the faith-based organization with "a nickel and prayer," rented a barn for ten dollars a month, "put in a new floor, plastered the walls," and began holding biweekly parties. Guests were not charged admission to the heavily chaperoned soirees, but partygoers were screened and expected to conform to a "wholesome" ethos. All remnants of the "unrestrained animality" of black popular music was to be left at the door.[66]

Atlanta's First Congregational Church is particularly illustrative of such thinking in the urban south. Reverend Henry Hugh Proctor, the Fisk and Yale-educated pastor, insisted that the church be an institution that would be as attractive as urban bars, cabarets, and popular concerts. Proctor believed that Protestantism had to alter its notions of church work in order to remain relevant in twentieth-century urban America, particularly as a social and recreational center for black communities. "For ten years I had sat on my porch near the church and seen the people of my race go by the church down to the dive," he recalled. The urban pastor was perplexed. Why were urban migrants choosing to go to saloons, dance halls, and theaters instead of church? Proctor concluded that the only way to address the problem was to reimagine the way churches approached urban ministry. "My church was locked and barred and dark," the pastor stated, "while the dive was wide open, illuminated, and attractive." He vowed, "God helping me, I will open my church and make it as attractive as the dive."[67] Proctor was clear—urban ministry had to engage the entertainment market.

First Congregational established and hosted an annual music festival as well as occasional classical and opera concerts (the church continues to host the musical festival to this today). The annual music festival and the concerts were advertised as wholesome alternatives to the public commercial amusement establishments "in the city that tends to drag down the colored servant." The church advertised that "for a popular rate of admission" both black and white residents of Atlanta could come and enjoy the annual Jubilee Music Festival. The annual festival featured famous acts such as the Fisk Jubilee Singers and classical concert artists such as tenor Roland Hayes and soprano Anita Patti Brown. The annual weekend event also featured plays and drama to compete with Atlanta's vaudeville theaters, especially the 81 Theatre, which often showcased race record artists such as Georgia Tom and Bessie Smith. Throughout the year, amusement seekers could also enjoy classical music concerts in the First Congregational Auditorium for an admission price of twenty-five cents.[68] The church's amusement offerings were aimed at competing with the city's commercial amusements while also fostering racial uplift and religious devotion. If churches could not stop African Americans from listening to black phonograph artists, at least they could promote a "higher class" of black artists.

One Mississippi churchgoer wrote to the *Half-Century Magazine* in 1922 expressing the dire need for such ministry. The magazine, always concerned with urban assimilation, printed the urban southerner's plea for churches to create alternative entertainment for the faithful.

Prohibiting commercial amusement in the church, he argued, deprived "Christians of innocent diversions." The only other option was for Christians to "attend shows and dance halls with sinners." Simply put, he concluded, "I believe the church is the place for Christians to seek their pleasure."[69]

Prominent black ministers continued to advance the idea that the creation and promotion of high-class entertainment for the masses was a constitutive element, perhaps the foundation, of any successful urban Protestant ministry. However, these amusement offerings were largely unsuccessful. They were plagued by low attendance and little support. The uplift-styled entertainments of the church could simply not compete with the superior technology, talent, and resources of the black entertainment industry. For many, the draw and the flash of a new race record, concert, cabaret, or style show were just too great and too appealing to pass up in exchange for a church concert or dance.

Confinement

Fittingly, many urged black faith communities toward a posture of confinement. These reformers insisted that black churches were wasting their time and resources on a losing round of amusement offerings. In a 1922 *Half Century Magazine* editorial entitled "Is the Church Fulfilling Its Primary Objective?" the writer, Langston L. Davis, noted that black people, contrary to popular belief, had not lost their interest in religion nor grown indifferent to the church. The reason church attendance and the church's social influence were on the decline, he argued, was that the church was "failing to fulfill its mission." "The church edifice," Davis declared, "is a place of worship and should be used as such." Davis insisted that hosting commercial concerts and dances and the like went beyond proper church work. The primary mission of the church was to "supply the religious needs of the people," not to condemn or compete with popular music concerts and phonograph artists. Engaging the black commercial entertainment market was not a boon for the church, but actually its undoing. If the church ceased to provide commercial entertainment and focused more on the religious sphere, he reasoned, "the general public would have more respect for churches and things clerical."[70]

Likewise, Du Bois believed that black churches should confine their resources and work to spiritual enlightenment and leave black entertainment to the entertainment industry. He lamented that black life in the twentieth century was characterized in part by "saloons outnumbering churches." But he did not believe that churches should attempt to mimic such spaces and complained that churches were too busy "catering to saloons."[71] Du Bois believed that the solution was clear: "I insist that the time has come when the activities of the Negro church must become differentiated and when it must surrender to the school and the home, and social organizations, those functions which in a day of organic poverty it so heroically sought to bear."[72] In Du Bois's view, the emergence of black consumer culture and black welfare organizations freed black churches to operate a more circumscribed but focused program of church work. Indeed, he perceived the urban awakening of black America—the social, ecological, psychological, and economic changes of urbanity—necessitated a revival of black Protestantism. However, he saw the revival as one in which black churches refocused their efforts from being social centers of amusement, pleasure, and gathering, to one of primarily spiritual instruction and inspiration.[73]

Du Bois was not alone. Reverend David Johnson, an AME pastor in Indiana, heartily believed in this circumscribed mission. In a front page editorial for the *Chicago Defender,* Johnson wrote, "The church is scathingly condemned by many because it does not engage more directly and definitely in things secular and material such as fostering industries and commercial enterprises." However, such critiques were remiss. "The work of the church is to make men, to mold character, and to perpetuate the highest ethical and spiritual ideals. It is the duty of the individuals that are molded and developed by its teachings to go forth and do the work of society in all its branches." The institution of the church, according to Reverend Johnson, had no business in business.[74]

Richard R. Wright, Jr., a special fellow in sociology at the University of Pennsylvania, felt the same way. Wright conducted a study on social work and urban African American churches. Wright, an AME minister and later bishop, asserted that urban migration had challenged the social control of African American Protestant churches on social welfare services. He observed, for example, that saloons were continually open to provide "music, lunch, reading matter, tables, toilet, telephone, pen and ink and many conveniences" that were formerly provided by black churches. Wright therefore urged black churches to cease running on "the small town church plan" and reprioritize their mission according to city life. A theological reorientation toward the black entertainment market was needed. He admonished black religious institutions not to go into the "dance hall, pool room, or gymnasium . . . businesses." Rather, urban black churches should "revise their teaching regarding amusements and adopt not merely a negative but a positive position."[75]

Black parishioners agreed. Eileen Jones, a churchwoman from Cleveland, Ohio, wrote to the *Half Century Magazine*, "the church edifice should not be used for entertainment." She continued, "It should be used for worship and for business meetings of members, pertaining to matters that affect the church directly." Jones believed that the church in urban America should host lectures for the general public that addressed biblical subjects and morality. Such activities should constitute the church's attempts to entertain. She concluded, "But I do not approve of using the church for entrainments."[76]

For Du Bois, Johnson, Wright, and churchgoers like Jones, the development of black commercial entertainment had not only precipitated a change in the programmatic focus of black Protestantism but also in ideology and theology. Churches should not attempt to bring black amusement under the realm of church work. Church energies should be confined and directed toward a deliberate system of teaching, instruction, and inspiration. Establishing "proper" amusements for the masses was the job of black professional men. The commercial sphere, Reverend Johnson surmised, was best left to "specialized agencies and highly trained leaders."[77]

Black Swan, the first black-owned record label, was established in 1921 toward this end. Founder Harry H. Pace projected Black Swan as "the only records made entirely by colored people" and "the only record using exclusively Negro voices." As valedictorian of his class at Atlanta University, Pace invited his former professor W. E. B. Du Bois to join the company's board—an invitation Du Bois accepted. Du Bois announced in the *Crisis* that the phonograph industry was a "tremendous" opportunity to provide wholesome amusement for black Americans, highlight the achievements of the race, and shape public conceptions of African Americans.[78]

In his address "Public Opinion and the Negro," Pace stressed the importance of shaping the public sphere and pointed to the relationship of public representation and ideas of racial progress. "Unless we take hold vigorously of this matter of creating and shaping public opinion itself, all other efforts we may put forth in any line will be useless." Pace advised his listeners that the best way to approach public opinion "is to anticipate Public Opinion and to help mold it and shape it so as to be sure that it does react the way we want."[79] This was, in part, the mission of Black Swan.

In fact, Du Bois explained that the label took its name, Black Swan, from Elizabeth Taylor Greenfield, a nineteenth-century black opera singer whose talent altered public perception of her. Her voice, according to Du Bois, was so "beautiful" and full of "astonishing power . . . and richness" that people called her "the Black Swan." The Black Swan was not "handsome" in her physical appearance. However, her cultured dress coupled with a voice endowed with a "keen searching fire, and penetrating vibrant quality" purportedly led many, including Harriet Beecher Stowe, to amend their assessment of her physical beauty. Once people had heard Greenfield's voice, her true beauty became evident. Similarly, Black Swan Records would showcase a myriad of classically trained black artists whose voices would give the race a makeover via the entertainment market.[80]

From their New York City Times Square office, the label produced "high-class" black musical expressions to counter the "negative" and debased folk singing and images of race record artists. Black Swan stated, "While it is true we will feature to a great extent 'blues' numbers, we will also release many numbers of a higher standard." Du Bois assured the public, Black Swan—unlike Okeh, Columbia, and Paramount—would "preserve and record our best voices," expressions geared toward racial uplift and advancement.[81]

William Grant Still, a member of the Harlem Symphony, was Black Swan's music director and arranger. He gave Bessie Smith a chance to test record for the label. But when she stopped singing in the middle of her test recording and requested, "Hold on, let me spit," William Still declared that she was too "raw" for the label's musical and cultural vision. He rejected the aesthetics and expression of black artists like her. Instead, the label recorded such celebrated concert artists as former

Fisk Jubilee Singer Roland Hayes, noted soprano Revella Hughes, and concert vocalist Carrol Clark. It also made the first recording of James Weldon Johnson's "Lift Every Voice and Sing," which is commonly referred to as the negro national anthem. Black Swan did issue some popular blues. Ethel Waters and Isabelle Washington (who later became the first wife of noted black clergyman and congressman Adam Clayton Powell, Jr.) recorded "dignified" versions of the blues for Black Swan to help the struggling company gain revenue. Ironically, some of the label's "exclusively" black popular music was actually recorded by white artists under "black" pseudonyms such as "Ethel Water's Jazz Masters," "Black Swan Quartette," and "The Creole Trio."[82] Black Swan was resolute in shaping public opinion, no matter the means.

However, the label's primary focus on bourgeois racial uplift and inattentiveness to black popular taste left it in considerable financial trouble. A former employee of Black Swan mourned the company, adding, "If they'd stuck with blues they would have been more successful." The market for black classical music was dwarfed by the desire for blues and jazz. Black Swan lasted just two years. Bankrupt, the label and all its masters were sold to Paramount in 1923. As one Paramount executive baldly put it, "He [Pace] couldn't pay his bills. . . . [W]e made a deal with him and bought him out, lock, stock, and barrel!" Unlike Black Swan, Paramount employed scientific methods (albeit crude ones) to determine if there was indeed a sizeable market for black opera records. Shortly after purchasing Black Swan, Paramount solicited talent suggestions in the company catalog and the *Chicago Defender*: "What will you have? If your preferences are not listed in our catalog, we will make them for you, as Paramount must please the buying public. There is always room for more good material and more talented artists. Any suggestions or recommendations that you may have to offer will be greatly appreciated." Reportedly, 90 percent of the respondents recommended a blues singer. Such overwhelming popularity of black folk music combined with the precipitous collapse of Black Swan all but eliminated the notion that widespread bourgeois racial uplift could be achieved through the phonograph industry.[83]

•   •   •

Ma Rainey's often repeated signature performance embodied all that the Black Protestant Establishment abhorred about the phonograph industry. Rainey began the infamous performance inside a life-size phonograph. A chorus girl would stroll across the stage, place a make-shift record on the "big Paramount Talking Machine," and then crank the handle, signaling the band to begin playing. On cue, a harmonizing Rainey emerged from the oversized phonograph, singing "Moonshine Blues," adorned in her notorious bejeweled gown that weighed up to twenty pounds, gold plated teeth, and a necklace of twenty-dollar gold pieces. As the spotlight hit her, Ma glistened and bellowed, "I've been drinking all night, babe, and the night before . . ." The performance left the audience spellbound every time. "Oh boy," wrote a *Defender* music reviewer, "What a flash Ma does make in her gorgeous gowns." Another awestruck observer added, "Her diamonds flashed like sparks of fire falling from her fingers. The gold-piece necklace lay like a golden armor covering her chest. . . . The house went wild . . . Ma had the audience in the palm of her hand." Whether performing in the black metropolis of Chicago or the towns of the deep south, Rainey's show was emblematic of the race record phenomenon: African Americans were enjoying a new form of commercial recreation and entertainment that praised gaudy adornment, conspicuous consumption, sexual explicitness, folk expression, and drinking during the Prohibition era. And all of it was, figuratively and literally, coming through the phonograph.[84]

The Black Protestant Establishment was deeply concerned about this phenomenon. It viewed the entire race record enterprise as detrimental. The songs were laced with new gender norms, illegal behaviors, and the commercials were guided by racist caricatures. Even a prominent African American artist and repertoire man (A&R)—a combination talent scout, producer, and manager—for race record labels admitted that the ads were largely racist, adding that the industry "wrote the ads definitely from a white man's point of view."[85] The rise of the industry, from this viewpoint, was an affront to racial progress. Something had to be done.

However, black faith communities had limited success in responding to race records and the black entertainment industry via creation and confinement. Race records continued to increase in sales while church-based amusements limped along. Moreover, the fate of Black Swan Records showed the limits of the Black Protestant Establishment's efforts to use the phonograph indsutry for their brand of racial uplift.

In their quest to "win the black lower class's psychological allegiance" to respectability, race record opponents failed to see the appeal of race records to black folk. The aesthetics and content of race records articulated alternative narratives of black life; stories that championed and authenticated folk expression and chronicled black working-class life—not bourgeois experience. Some buyers heard and saw themselves in race records and joyfully embraced the experience, despite the admonishments of the Black Protestant Establishment. While the proponents of the politics of respectability often deemed race records a product of the bankrupt cultural practices of "the folk," many consumers viewed them as rich contributions to black working-class survival and resistance.[86]

The experience of Robert Hayden, the first black U.S. poet laureate, is indicative. Born in 1913, he fondly remembered how Bessie Smith and her songs were "close to the folk . . . close to the soil." However, "Religious people—'church folks,' as we used to say—thought her songs immoral, and my staunch Baptist foster father, for instance, didn't want Bessie's low-down songs played on our Victrola." However, Bessie found her way into the house and hearts of the Haydens. Robert, his aunt, and others identified with Smith and her songs. Like other blues men and women, Bessie did not sing about black middle-class life but rather, as Hayden put it, "about the uncertainties and sorrows of life as poor Negro people knew them." He fondly recalled one of Smith's live performances in Detroit, remembering that her working-class urban migrant tales had "us ghetto folks . . . clapping, shouting, and whistling."[87] Race records, unlike the selective attendance of church amusements and mediocre sales of Black Swan records, spoke the dominant language of the rural diaspora in a manner that resonated with black migrants.

These conditions encouraged black evangelical clergy to attempt a new avenue of revival. Black clergy joined the black entertainment industry and attempted to replicate its most popular product: race records. Historians of American religion have observed that the vitality of urban religious movements, particularly evangelical

Protestantism, has not been solely based on uplift or social service ministries. Rather the buoyancy of urban faith has been directly related to a movement's ability to establish religious practices that replicate popular entertainment and fastidiously utilize aspects of consumer culture.[88]

The evangelical impulse in America has historically distinguished itself in this manner. Evangelical faith communities have modeled themselves and their ministries after the popular forms of commercial entertainment of their respective historical periods. R. Laurence Moore, a historian of American religion, has argued along these lines that "If religion is to be culturally central, it must learn to work with other things that are also central." Accordingly, Christianity in America has found it increasingly necessary "to embrace techniques of commercial expansion."[89] Reverend George Whitefield's utilization of the theater and stage as well as storybooks and magazines during the eighteenth century made him the first clergyman to achieve commercial celebrity in the colonies.[90] In the nineteenth century, Charles Finney argued that God never revitalized Christianity nor advanced the church without the use of "new measures" and new means of proclaiming the gospel. Adopting and copying popular entertainments, commerce, and communication, according to Finney, could and should be employed as the primary means of reviving the church.[91] In the twentieth century, Aimee Semple McPherson and Charles Fuller, among others, founded successful ministries based on their use of radio modeled after popular radio variety shows.[92] Simply put, as historians John Giggie and Diane Winston have argued, "The success of evangelical Christianity in founding and growing urban religious movements is directly related to the creative ability of its leaders to develop spiritual practices based on popular entertainment."[93]

A host of African American clergy during the interwar period followed this evangelical tradition on the phonograph. In their urban ministries, black phonograph preachers did not concentrate on using their own resources and facilities to establish consecrated bourgeois entertainments or on confining their church work from the entertainment market. Rather, these evangelical entrepreneurs joined the titans of the black entertainment industry and modeled their ministries and church work after black America's embrace of the prevailing commercial entertainment of the day: race records.

The logic was simple: sanctify the phonograph and race records for church work. As one phonograph preacher plainly explained to a journalist: "If the Devil could make such success with this popular invention, there is no reason why the Lord can not do the same!"[94] The first two preachers to take this perspective, Reverends Calvin "Black Billy Sunday" Dixon and William White, set the trend and began the practice of selling to the souls of black folk.

Selling to the Souls of Black Folk

The Commodification of African American Sermons

"His sermons," the first phonograph sermon commercial declared, are "given in a spirited evangelistic style!" The Columbia advertisement, complete with an image of the pioneering phonograph preacher Reverend Calvin P. Dixon, promised consumers that the pair of four-minute homilies "get under your skin and are not easily forgotten!" The advertisement for the sermons addressing urban migration and vice was featured in the national edition of the *Chicago Defender* on March 7, 1925. Another newspaper ad praised the intrinsic value of the sermons, promising consumers that the sacred commodity "will inspire you," and adding, "Be sure to buy this record!" (Figures 3.1 and 3.2).[1]

The new product was priced at 75 cents, comparable to about $35 today. The pricey record was marketed alongside ads for a host of branded goods and services, including skin care ointment by the Black and White Co., the Saint Louis Poro Beauty College, the Red Seal Clothing Company, and the Federal Life Insurance Company, as well as the latest records of Bessie Smith, Ma Rainey, and Ethel Waters. The sermon was one of a host of labeled products available for purchase in stores and retail outlets across the country as well as by mail order. African American sermons were now officially a part of the phonograph industry and popular consumer culture.[2]

•   •   •

Reverend Dixon became the first ordained African American clergyman to utilize the phonograph as the basis for his modern ministry.

The South Carolina native was a noted traveling preacher along the east coast. Columbia Records invited "the famous evangelist" to its New York City Columbus Circle studio on Broadway Avenue to record his sermons. On Wednesday, January 14, 1925, Dixon recorded the first of ten sermons for Columbia. From the city known as the "Big Apple," the small-town resident linked black preaching to big corporate business.[3]

Dixon adopted the nickname "Black Billy Sunday" in honor of famed white revivalist Billy Sunday. Beginning in the late nineteenth century until his death in 1935, Billy Sunday barnstormed the country championing a muscular Christianity and moral crusades against the urban "vices" of drinking, dancing, and gambling. The popularity of his revivals established Billy Sunday as both the national restorer of old-time religion and a spokesman of American Christianity in the new century.[4]

Dixon's moniker was apropos. Black Billy Sunday achieved a status similar to that of his muse within black Protestantism, even drawing the praise of his namesake. Black Billy Sunday used the phonograph to trumpet his voice across the country and establish himself both as a reviver of traditional black Protestantism and a progenitor of modern black church work.[5]

The inaugural ads for phonograph religion, like all commercials of the day, were objects of modernity—announcements and declarations of the latest trend in black religion. The ads heralded two new and important developments within black religious practice. First, the ads tell of a new form of black church work and norm for urban ministry: black clergy utilizing the medium and resources of the black popular entertainment industry as a basis of ministry. Innovative African American clergy used the production and marketing of phonograph sermons as a new measure to revive and sustain black Protestantism in an urban context that was increasingly centered on the phonograph and black consumer culture. Mass media ministries, these preachers believed, were best suited to influence the moral and cultural habits and practices of modern black life.

Second, and closely related, the sermon advertisements reveal the emergence of black sermons as a modern commodity. The emergence of America's modern marketplace was founded on the production of cheap standardized goods, omnipresent national advertising that linked consumption with self-actualization, and nationwide distribution.[6]

Recorded sermons were manufactured, advertised, and distributed accordingly. Ads for the mass-produced spiritual commodities were seemingly ubiquitous in black urban America. The thorough marketing of phonograph religion explicitly and implicitly promised consumers that the consumption of recorded sermons was a balm for all that ailed modern black life in the city. Record labels employed national distribution networks to make the sermons available to all, regardless of location. Simply put, phonograph preachers pioneered the tradition of selling to the souls of black folk.

Recording the First Sermon

Recording and selling a sermon by an ordained clergyman was unchartered territory. However, by 1925 the overwhelming success of race records seemed to guarantee that recording any form of black popular expression would be profitable. Yet there was little methodology in race recording, let alone recording a black sermon. An executive of one leading race record label admitted that most labels were simply guided by trial and error. He confessed that he conducted his entire race record enterprise "by the seat of my pants." Hoping to discover a hit, labels aimlessly made test records by various race artists who had been discovered by A&R executives or recommended by artists and dealers. Race record leader Paramount, for example, made as many test records as possible every day. Labels would listen to a single verse of every test song and decide whether they wanted to sign up and record the artist. Another white phonograph executive admitted, "We would sit around and listen to them [sample recordings] and make our observations . . . and try to figure out the potential hits against the duds. . . . and sometimes we were right, and sometimes we were wrong. It wasn't a scientific operation. We never had a theory."[7]

This lackadaisical approach was often guided by racist and simplistic conceptions of black music and consumers. A music reviewer for the popular weekly magazine *Collier's* considered the sound of many race records "unearthly," adding, "There are colored numbers so strictly African and special that nobody but a Negro could understand them or appreciate them." Such music "make[s] no sense whatever to the untrained white mind." Indeed, Ralph Peer, recording director for

Okeh, swore that Mamie Smith's trailblazing record was "[t]he most awful record ever made." Baffled but proud, Peer commented sarcastically: "and it sold over a million copies."[8]

Moreover, some executives believed that black consumer tastes were incomprehensible. H. C. Speir, a profitable record storeowner and freelance talent scout (he went on to sign several preachers), claimed it was impossible to predict which artists or recordings would be a commercial success. In fact, Speir claimed that white race record execs "didn't know a thing except for sales, if it didn't sale they knew that, if it made money then they knew that too! That's the only way you can talk about this blues business, ya understand." The plan was widespread and basic: record as many artists and new talent as possible and to "keep moving, hoping something would happen!" Speir's expansionist vision included aggressively recruiting black talent across the south. On more than one occasion, white sharecroppers ran him out of town, convinced his tales of stardom only led to the disappearance of their black labor force. Speir described his haphazard approach in simple terms: "Sometimes you miss it, sometimes ya hit!" In reality, anticipating a hit could have easily been accomplished had Speir taken note of black consumer demand. However, the white supremacist admittedly refused to heed black consumer demands or requests, no matter how costly. Instead, he simply signed the black artists he favored.[9]

Thus, with little direction or structure most labels simply flooded the market with race records in the hope that they could continue to reap financial returns from the thriving race record market. A Paramount executive summed up the industry's perspective of black consumers: "These people were simple people. They sang and played the way they lived and thought." Selling records to "simple people" did not require great thought, research, or effort.[10] Recording a hit record, let alone a sermon, was not strategic; it was, in many ways, a shot in the dark.

However, Black Billy Sunday had a clear direction and strategy for his ministry when he was invited to preach on wax. The revivalist was known for his aggressive campaigns against modern thought and black commercial amusement. He complained that ministers of the day had accepted new scientific knowledge and doubted the validity of biblical literalism, particularly miracles, healing, and bodily resurrection. Sunday argued that ministers were more eager to display "intellectual ability" and "aptness" than they were to convey "what the Bible says and really means."[11]

Around 1922, the popular revivalist settled in Newport News, Virginia, and established the Black Billy Sunday Tabernacle. His opposition to black commercial amusement quickly gained the favor of churchgoers and the ire of black amusement proprietors. His congregation grew quickly while the local black entertainment market, according to the local paper, considered him an "inveterate foe." The black proprietor of a jazz and blues dancehall in Newport News complained to city hall that Black Billy Sunday had "knocked the bottom out of my business." He lobbied city officials, arguing that the crusading evangelist was bad for business. If Black Billy Sunday was forced out of town, he told them, black amusement proprietors and their partners could "make a lot of money."[12]

Despite such opposition, Sunday's traveling ministry flourished along the east coast, particularly in Virginia, Maryland, North Carolina, Baltimore, Washington, D.C., and New Jersey. His revivals, including a 1923 meeting held in a tobacco warehouse in North Carolina, reportedly drew interracial crowds of two to three thousand people. Sunday was so popular that he eventually established his own denomination, the Evangelical Christian Church. Dixon was elected the first senior bishop of the Church. The entrepreneurial evangelist established and oversaw churches along the eastern portion of the country from Atlanta to Philadelphia, and continually packed out churches, warehouses, and even courthouses.[13]

Such recognition caught the attention of Columbia Records. Labels often signed up new talent based on such popularity. Frank Walker, the famous Columbia A&R associated with such acts as Bessie Smith and others, visited black theaters and black churches solely for the purpose of finding new talent.[14] Like many evangelical clergy before and after him, Black Billy Sunday was deeply concerned with spreading his traditional gospel message to a swiftly changing world by the most efficient and popular means. In black America, the phonograph was the best means for the task. Columbia, on the other hand, simply aimed to capitalize on Sunday's widespread public acclaim, telling an industry journal it expected the preacher's sermons to "enjoy a large sale." The preacher's evangelical orientation and Columbia's desire to expand the race record genre were a perfect match. On January 10, 1925, the *Norfolk Journal and Guide* proudly announced that the noted local revivalist had been summoned to New York City to record sermons for Columbia Records. The *Talking Machine World* announced, "Nationally known Evangelist Preaches Sermon to be released on a Columbia Record."[15] Dixon's mass media ministry was born.

Dixon's time in the studio pulpit was emblematic of his evangelical orientation to black popular entertainment and the roaring twenties. The stately evangelist was set to record at Columbia's Broadway studio right after Bessie Smith and Louis Armstrong finished their historic recording session, which produced eventual blues classics such as "St. Louis Blues" and "Reckless Blues." In the former, the superstar blues woman tells the sad tale of traveling to St. Louis to find her estranged lover who had left her for the material riches of urban America, where the women have "diamond rings" and "store-bought hair." The popular song was eventually turned into a short film, featuring Bessie in the role of the drunken heartbroken lover. In "Reckless Blues" Bessie proclaimed her sexual assertiveness, bellowing, "My mama says I'm reckless, my daddy says I'm wild." Together, Smith and Armstrong, both urban migrants, told a story of urban migration that featured the allure of wealth and new sexual mores.[16]

Bessie Smith and crew finished their recordings, gathered the moonshine that was known to accompany recording sessions, extinguished their cigarettes, and filed out of the studio. Black Billy Sunday then entered the studio and prepared to ignite a counternarrative on wax. The speakeasy atmosphere morphed into a studio pulpit. He approached the mouth of the two-foot wide recording horn, the red recording light flashed, and Sunday uttered the first words of black religious broadcasting: "My text will be found in Deuteronomy, the third chapter and the eleventh verse." Then he announced the title of his sermon, "As an Eagle Stirreth Up Her Nest."[17] The magnitude of the moment must have rattled Dixon. He cited the wrong verse. Dixon's intended verse, Deuteronomy 32:11, compares God's care and activity to an eagle that purposely disturbs the nest of her eaglets in order to compel them to fly. Dixon assured his listeners that since the days of the apostles, God had always "stirred" up or destroyed the nest of his followers until they were willing to "emigrate to new quarters . . . or change their localities." The sermon depicted God

Two inspiring sermons
by
CALVIN P. DIXON
(Black Billy Sunday)
"The Prodigal Son"
and
"As an Eagle Stirreth Up Her Nest"
on Columbia Record 14057 D

These two sermons, written and delivered by the great evangelist, Calvin P. Dixon (Black Billy Sunday), will inspire you with their power and originality of thought. As you listen to this remarkable record you realize how this gifted preacher holds the congregations of great tabernacles spellbound. Be sure to buy this record—it is one you will always value in days to come.

COLUMBIA PHONOGRAPH CO.
1819 Broadway   New York

Columbia
PHONOGRAPHS   RECORDS

Figure 3.1: Black Billy Sunday sermon advertisement. Source: *Chicago Defender*, March 7, 1925, 2.

as allowing or causing disarray in order to compel his followers to greater things. The preacher continued, "We can never move to a new locality without breaking our relationship to the present locality. We can never go into a better climate without disrupting from the climate we are in." His metaphor was not lost upon the millions of urban migrants who dubbed cities such as Chicago and Harlem simply as "the Promise Land." Urban migration, the preacher said, must be understood as a divinely orchestrated act undertaken to enhance one's spiritual state, not to revel in the amusements and consumerism that dotted the urban landscape. Dixon's sermon was a rebuttal to Smith. He did not name Bessie or any other race record artists in his sermon—he did not have to.[18]

Following suit, the other side of the wax sermon warned against urban vices. Black Billy Sunday was particularly concerned about the newfound wealth and leisure income of urban migrants. The sermon centered on "the Prodigal Son," based on Luke 15:18. The biblical parable is about a son who requests his inheritance from his living father, and then moves "into a far country, and there wasted his substance with riotous living . . . and harlots." The text provided a striking contrast to Bessie Smith's "St. Louis Blues." Dixon used the scripture to warn the expanding black working, middle, and professional classes against the evils of urban America and their newfound wealth and social mobility. Indeed, God had compelled the urban migration to bless migrants with the opportunities of urban America. However, inhabitants of the "promise land" should be careful not to squander God's blessings on sinful living and the urban vices of cabarets, dances, and the assortment of material objects and beauty products Bessie sang about. He proclaimed, "Many of the educated, rich, honorable, and hopeful as you, have assumed and possessed much and yielded to temptation and lost all! Let sin alone!" Dixon's recorded sermons inaugurated a modern form of church work. The phonograph amplified his brand of traditional black Christianity across the country. The *Baltimore African American* praised the black evangelical media ministry, claiming that Black Billy Sunday had become "known throughout the country . . . as a phonograph record star."[19]

Black Billy Sunday was not alone in the nascent phonograph ministry. Reverend William Arthur White, an evangelical Baptist, made his own recording a few months after Black Billy Sunday. The second black phonograph preacher focused his media ministry on the influence of modern thought and new knowledge in black Christian practice. Evangelical black clergy were deeply concerned with the way new scientific knowledge was shaping black faith. Scientific discoveries and ideals of the era, most notably the theory of human evolution, called literal interpretations of the Bible into question. In faith communities, the debate over evolution became a cultural and institutional struggle between evangelical fundamentalists who rejected any scientific theories that countered literal interpretations of the Bible and Protestant liberals/ modernists who embraced such new knowledge.[20]

White, a preaching prodigy since his youth, signed up with Paramount Records two weeks after the close of the infamous *State of Tennessee v. John Thomas Scopes* case. The July 1925 lawsuit, which came to be known as the Scopes Monkey Trial, came to typify the fundamentalist-modernist debate in American Protestantism. Public school teacher John Scopes was charged with violating Tennessee's prohibition of any theory that denied divine creation. In the national cause célèbre, noted conservative evangelical and three-time presidential candidate William Jennings Bryan was chosen as the special prosecutor in the case. Clarence Darrow, famed defense attorney and leading member of the American Civil Liberties Union, represented John Scopes. Evangelical fundamentalists saw the trial as a harbinger for the moral and cultural direction of the nation. Convicting Scope would serve as an affirmation of biblical literalism and its rightful place in guiding societal norms. An acquittal, however, would signal a national embrace of the authority of modern science over the Bible. In the end, Scopes was found guilty and the ban against teaching evolution was upheld by the court. Bryan and the evangelical fundamentalists won the case; however, they lost in the court of public opinion.

Fundamentalism was ridiculed everywhere. In addition to the mainstream white press and the work of influential journalists like H. L. Mencken, leading black newspapers denounced the decision and fundamentalism. They deemed Christian fundamentalism a hindrance to black social progress and modern Christian practice. William N. Jones, editor of the *Afro-American*, argued that even if African American Christians could not completely reconcile evolution with the Bible, they certainly should not accept the fundamentalist "Christianity of William Jennings Bryan." He assured his readers that "Real Christianity will survive" fundamentalism, "as it has survived all other human misconceptions." The *Pittsburgh Courier* agreed. According to the *Courier*, the trial did not set religion against science. Rather the contest was actually between ignorance and science. The *Courier* concluded, "We hope science wins!"[21] According to some in the black press, fundamentalism was an unenlightened and outdated form of Christianity.

CALVIN P. DIXON
(Black Billy Sunday)

WRITER, Student, Evangelist and Preacher. We doubt if there is anyone among the Race folks today who is doing better and more forceful work than "Black Billy Sunday." His sermons, written by himself and delivered straight from the shoulder, are given in a spirited evangelistic style that gets under your skin and is not easily forgotten. His records do him justice—they should be in everybody's home.

14076-D—The Handwriting on
75c   the Wall
        Clean Out Your
        Wells—Your Water's
        Muddy
14061-D—Who Is Your God?—
75c   Part I
        Who Is Your God?—
        Part II
14057-D—The Prodigal Son
75c   As An Eagle Stir-
        reth Up Her Nest
14089-D—Dry Bones in the
75c   Valley
        Parts I and II

Figure 3.2: Black Billy Sunday sermon advertisement. Source: *Chicago Defender,* January 30, 1926, 7.

Figure 3.3: Reverend W. A. White sermon advertisement. Source: *Chicago Defender,* September 26, 1925, 7.

For Reverend White and black evangelical clergy, it was clear: a war was being waged for the soul of the church and the nation. Mainstream black newspapers and black public opinion all seemed to embrace the modernist turn in biblical interpretation and theology. Fundamentalists and evangelicals in turn attempted to establish their own urban institutions and religious media to combat Protestant liberalism. Moreover, according to one black Baptist minister, they vigorously enlisted "colored Christians for campaign purposes throughout the country, to help save the world from the doctrine of evolution."[22]

Chicago's Reverend White joined the fight by signing up with Paramount Records. It was an ideal partnership. True to his evangelical ethos, Reverend White sought to harness the popular medium in the service of promoting traditional Christianity. Paramount in turn employed Reverend White as an answer to Columbia's Black Billy Sunday. The Scopes trial had proven lucrative. Columbia's retelling of the trial was one of the top-selling story records of the era. Both Reverend White and Paramount in their own ways desperately wanted to engage the firestorm between Christianity and evolution.[23]

The crusading minister linked his ministerial efforts with the phonograph industry at Paramount's rented studio located on Chicago's Loop, the downtown commercial district. Ma Rainey and her Georgia band (which included Louis Armstrong and Thomas Dorsey) preceded White in the non–air conditioned, cramped twenty-square-foot studio. On this swarming hot August day, Ma Rainey's melodic tales of sex ("Night Time Blues") and utilizing a fortuneteller to locate a lost love ("Four Day Honory [sic] Scat") were of secondary importance to White. The preacher was set to sear the public's conscience against evolution.[24]

"Divine Relationship of God to Man," was a staid but stern sermon opposing evolution and the black embrace of it. "And in these days of Evolution that we read so much about," White lectured, "if the thought would come to us: Has God not ordained that man should be in His own likeness and His own image?" If so, White concluded, "[t]here would not be any evolution in our minds at this hour!" White was clear that authentic Christianity necessitated a belief in divine creation. He went on to record other titles along the same lines, including "What Is Man?" a didactic sermon championing divine creation. White's sermon corpus militantly opposed evolution and defended literal interpretations of the Bible. For White, using mass media to express such definitive religious positions was pivotal to the urban black church.

Dixon and White used the phonograph industry to establish modern ministries. The pioneers of phonograph religion attempted to utilize the medium of black popular entertainment as a means to sway the habits and practices of modern culture toward traditional black Protestant piety and beliefs. Indeed, Dixon and White deliberately recorded sermons that addressed what they believed to be the pressing issues confronting black faith communities: the black entertainment industry, migration, urban life, and the theological and cultural changes that accompanied such socioeconomic shifts. The talking machine offered their moral and theological treatises a mass media platform for a public that was enamored of the medium. Recording sermons was the first stage in modernizing their ministries. Making those sermons consummate modern commodities was the second.

Manufacturing

When Dixon and White delivered their respective sermons into the studio's acoustic recording horn, their voices traveled down an eight-foot-long path to the needle of a stylus, which converted their homilies into sonic grooves on a master disc. The three-inch wax "mother" discs were packed in dry ice to prevent melting or warping, and shipped to record-pressing factories. From here, black preaching joined the commercial world of cheap mass production and consumption. The rise of new technologies such as electricity, machine manufacturing, and the assembly line led to an unprecedented growth in mass production during the 1920s. From 1910 to 1920, U.S. industrial production rose 12 percent, but from 1920 to 1930 it increased 64 percent. The routinization of production supplied the nation with an ostensibly endless supply of standardized goods, all of which were made by the most inexpensive means possible to maximize profit.[25] Phonograph religion made such corporate standardization and profit a major aspect of black preaching.

Paramount manufactured its records in Grafton, Wisconsin. The four-story complex was an old knitting factory that was converted in 1917 into what the *Talking Machine World* called, "a modern talking machine record plant." The "daylight factory" was in operation six days a week, with one shift from 7 a.m. to 5 p.m. During the summer months, as labels stocked up for the holiday shopping season, the plant ran until 9 p.m. Once the master copy of the sermon was delivered to the factory, it only took four to five days to reproduce it for the masses.[26]

The highly regimented bulk production process consisted of several stages divided up among the factory's floors. The sifting of the clay and shellac material for record pressing was done on the second floor, the wax was heated and flattened in the basement, and the records were mechanically pressed on the first floor. The 40 to 50 foot automated record pressing machines were heated by steam drawn from a water wheel on the nearby Milwaukee River. The steam-powered presses each produced about 500 records per day. More than one hundred Paramount employees filled the steaming factory. They toiled in temperatures upwards of 100 degrees during the winter and at least 115 degrees during the summer. For their grinding labor, employees made between 45 to 52 cents an hour (about $5 to $6 an hour today). The steam-powered factory had a peak capacity of about 25,000 records per day at a manufacturing cost of less than a $1.50 per hundred records.[27] The modern evolution of mass production made it possible to quickly and cheaply produce White's antievolution sermon.

Dixon's sermons were pressed at Columbia's Bridgeport, Connecticut, fully automated and electrified factory. The mammoth facility housed about 60 state-of-the art record presses. The mechanization worked at more than twice the speed of Paramount, producing records at the staggering pace of two records per minute. In the course of a minimum eight-hour workday, the plant turned out about 35,000 records.[28]

The factory's output was impressive, but conditions inside were shameful. John Hammond, famous for producing the likes of Fletcher Henderson, Billie Holiday, and later Bob Dylan, toured the record-pressing factory under the pseudonym Henry Johnson. He profited handsomely from his music career, but hated the conditions of the industry. He called the factory a "sweatshop." The undercover journalist described Columbia's factory as "the hottest and dirtiest place I had ever seen." The combination of the "distasteful smell of the hot shellac" and the company's refusal to install air conditioning in the factory made it "so hot it was barely possible to breathe." Black soot from the shellac mixture covered the floor, making for hazardous conditions. The state's labor board cited the factory for fifteen regulatory violations, including minimum wage statutes, allotted working hours, and sanitary conditions.[29] Dixon's sermons against urban vice were ironically produced in near criminal-like conditions.

Once the sermons were pressed, they were inspected, polished, placed in record jackets, and then packed in wooden crates in increments of forty. The boxes of sacred commodities, along with the label's host of other race records, were loaded onto trains to be sent to wholesalers. Paramount sold their recorded sermons to vendors for 27.5 cents per record, netting about 25 cents profit per record (comparable to about $17 today). Columbia's electrified manufacturing process produced a better-sounding record at a cost of about 7 cents a record. Columbia sold its phonograph sermons to wholesalers for about 37 cents a piece (a profit of about $20 today). Black sermons were undeniably enrolled in the genre of standardized production and corporate profit; and Paramount and Columbia were poised to make handsome revenues.[30]

Advertising and Marketing

Mass production necessitated persistent mass advertising. Columbia and Paramount utilized their corporate networks and resources to inject the new black spiritual commodities into the bazaar of national advertising according to prevalent marketing trends. Black Billy Sunday and Reverend White's sermons rode the wave of mass advertising and baptized black preaching into national marketing.

Prior to the 1920s, the phonograph industry, like most American businesses, approached advertising haphazardly. In 1922 the *Talking Machine World* criticized the phonograph industry for approaching advertising as "a matter of mood rather than sound business practice." The trade journal pleaded with the phonograph industry to recognize the "fundamental truth . . . that advertising is the greatest possible factor in achieving business success to-day."[31] Robert R. Udegraff—famed business consultant to such companies as General Foods, Kellogg, and John Hancock—agreed. Modern times, the business sage often chided, required consistent advertising. "The businessmen of 1900–1914," Udegraff said, "could afford to sail slowly, choosing his own rate of progress and electing to advertise or not as he saw fit." However, "[t]he stream of life in America has become swifter since the [First] World War." Americans "are quicker to . . . sample new products, to test new services—but quicker also to toss them aside if they do not suit us." He advised American businesses that successful enterprises in the new America required a new order of marketing: constant advertising. Similarly, President Calvin Coolidge, known as "Silent Cal," being a man of few words, put it succinctly in 1926: "In former days, goods were expected to sell themselves." However, modern business "constantly requires publicity."[32]

Businesses listened. In the decade following America's entrance into World War I, newspaper advertising more than doubled and national magazine ads increased more than 600 percent. By the end of the decade, the national advertising volume had increased from roughly $600 million to almost $3 billion. One journalist of the era predicted, "When the historian of the twentieth century shall have finished his narrative, and comes searching for the subtitle which shall best express the spirit of the period, we think it not at all unlikely that he may select

'The Age of Advertising' for the purpose." Indeed, national advertising began bombarding the American public following World War I.[33]

Ubiquitous advertising was particularly important in black life. Jim Crow discrimination often barred black shoppers from entering stores. Others limited black patrons' ability to explore, examine, listen, or try on products before purchase. In addition to learning about products through word of mouth, black consumers therefore often made purchases on the basis of advertising campaigns.[34]

Black newspapers emerged during the age as one of the most extensive forms of advertising in black communities. According to one study of black urban life, circumscribed access to radio made black weekly and daily periodicals "by far the most important agencies for forming and reflecting public opinion" in black America. Except for crime reports, mainstream papers across America mostly ignored black life. In response, by 1930 there were 114 black newspapers, which made it a point to highlight the accomplishments, triumphs, movements, and the latest products of and for the race.[35] The most prominent of these periodicals reached across the country with national editions. The *Baltimore Afro-American* became the most widely circulated black newspaper along the Atlantic coast. The *Pittsburgh Courier* circulated as far west as Texas. The *Courier* even boasted bureaus in Atlanta as well as New York City. The *Chicago Defender* claimed a nationwide circulation of more than 200,000 by the outbreak of World War I. By the outbreak of World War II, the *Norfolk Journal and Guide* ranked fourth in circulation behind the aforementioned papers. All had a larger out of town circulation than they did locally, establishing black newspapers as a major form of national communication in black life. Simply put, as one black university professor reflected in 1925, black newspapers "scattered throughout the country wield[ed] an immense amount of power in molding the opinions of the Negro masses to which they appeal."[36] Advertising was a major aspect of these papers. Their wide circulation made them ideal sites for advertisers. A three-month study of five black weekly newspapers by the University of North Carolina in 1925 is telling. The interwar study, which examined sixty issues, excluding classified ads, contained approximately 50,000 column inches of advertising. Black newspapers covered the news, but financial necessity led them to be riddled with commercials. Economics professor Paul Edwards concluded that the majority of African Americans came into contact with standardized products via such ads. In fact, Edwards found that brands that were otherwise known across the country but not advertised in the black press, were largely unfamiliar to black shoppers. He concluded that a "high percentage" of black families were "absolutely ignorant of the existence of some of the most widely advertised brands of types of consumer products" simply because they were not advertised in the black press.[37] In black life, nationally circulated black newspapers constituted *the* nationwide venue for advertising and marketing.

Columbia and Paramount rigorously advertised their new phonograph sermons in this national marketplace. Columbia placed at least one sermon advertisement in every weekly edition of the *Chicago Defender* until the depressed economy brought an end to such ventures in 1932. Moreover, Paramount's race record business relied solely on the Chicago paper for national commercial promotion. A survey of a national edition of the *Defender* conducted during the 1920s revealed that the paper contained almost 1,100 consumer advertisements. Almost 20 percent of them were for phonograph records like Black Billy Sunday and Reverend White (Figures 3.1–3.3).[38]

Likewise, a three-month analysis of the *Norfolk Journal and Guide* revealed that approximately 12 percent of its national advertisements were for race records and recorded sermons. Fittingly, in 1927 the *Pittsburgh Courier* ran a front-page investigative story on the profusion of such ads. According to the *Courier*'s New York City correspondent Floyd Calvin, the paper's national readership wanted to know the origin of the recorded sermon ads that were "so extensively advertised in the Negro Press!" Black sermons were a pronounced hallmark of the national black marketplace.[39]

In addition to the national black press, sermons were also heavily advertised in local stores and record label catalogs. The windows of local record shops were plastered with colorful posters, cards, and handbills of recorded sermons. The size of these cards and posters ranged from 11 by 14 inches to as large as 14 by 22 inches, assuring versatility. The commercials were usually sent to dealers across the country once a month. They came complete with display instructions about how to arrange the posters in the most attractive and effective manner. Stores also disseminated race record catalogs to store patrons and mailed them to potential customers. In addition to the respective label's jazz and blues selections, these small booklets advertised the company's sermons as well. Record catalogs coupled with local store advertisements gave recorded sermons a prominent place in community advertising. One southern migrant was amazed at the barrage of phonograph advertising in the black neighborhoods of Saint Louis in 1926, noting, "They used so much publicity . . . fly sheets, advertisements, throw-aways and all types of displays."[40] Advertisements for black sermons were ubiquitous.

The inescapable advertisements for sermons featured modern sales patter aimed at pitching the sacred products not as nonessential novelties, but as must-have commodities. Prior to the twentieth century, marketing strategies were fixated on product attributes. The ads celebrated the real and exaggerated properties, quality, and usefulness of products. However, during the 1920s advertisers reduced their emphasis on product attributes and began focusing on establishing a seamless connection between branded products and status. The socioeconomic context of the roaring 1920s facilitated this trend. The era witnessed the hardening of class lines, declining opportunities for social mobility, specialized labor, and the anonymity of city life. Ad men exploited such conditions by purposely developing "strategies for transforming their clients' products into plausible solutions" to such modern problems. Ad men were bent on presenting the consumer marketplace as chock-full of answers to life's modern problems.[41]

F. H. Massman, vice president of the National Tea Company grocery chain, one of the largest chains in the Midwest at the time (now a part of the Schnucks supermarket chain), spoke of such advertising bringing about the "enlightenment" of the public. Coolidge also bore witness to the phenomenon, asserting that modern advertising was "the most potent influence in adopting and changing the habits and modes of life, affecting what we eat, what we wear, and the work and play of the whole nation." More than this, advertising, Coolidge affirmed, was a "part of the greater work of the regeneration and redemption of mankind." Advertising in the 1920s began the process of presenting consumption not as a frivolous endeavor, but as a necessity for personal flourishing and self-actualization.[42]

Advertisers particularly used symbolic images of people to accomplish this purpose. The technological developments of the era enabled a gradual incorporation of people and representative images into advertising messages. The images were not necessarily of real people, but rather were representative of people who possessed or stood for the latent desires and dreams of consumers. They depicted happiness, authority, and self-fulfillment as well as the reigning social values of the day, particularly indicators of "status differentiation." The era witnessed the shift in advertising away from product attributes toward campaigns that focused on the benefits of consumption and the drawbacks of not participating in consumer culture.[43]

Phonograph preachers fit well into this advertising schema. As Du Bois and other scholars of the era recognized, black clergy represented status and authority in black communities, especially those who were accomplished. The ads for trailblazing phonograph preachers featured their image and listed their mass-produced spiritual wares. The ads used their images to indicate how the spiritual commodities contributed to personal flourishing and distinction in modern life. The image of the black preacher represented modern success through Christian piety. For many Protestants, such values were at the core of their faith.

In a press statement, Okeh records, a Columbia subsidiary by 1926, argued that the pathos of their advertising images "influence more people than the lengthiest editorial." Miss A. M. Kennard, an advertising manager for the company, believed that visual integration was key to its marketing success. The former textual ads were inconspicuous and at times too bookish. "We can't give them too much high brow stuff," the white executive cautioned. However, brief but catchy phrases and conspicuous images were ideal for reaching black and white consumers. She declared that the label had to use images "chock full of human interests and a smile" to advertise its records in order to "keep it down where they can get it." The objective of the new strategy was simple: make the ads "so entertaining that everyone will stop and look at it." The philosophy was fruitful. As Kennard told a black journalist, race record sales indicate that "[t]hey all love it."[44]

Black Billy Sunday's ads noted his socioeconomic status and the consumer benefits of the spiritual sermons. By today's standards the ads seem unrefined. However, to consumers of the day the ads were in line with marketing trends. Sunday was lauded as the "gifted preacher [who] holds the congregations of great tabernacles spellbound." The "power" of the sermons, "[w]ritten and delivered by the great evangelist, Black

Billy Sunday, were assured to "inspire you" (Figure 3.1). Likewise, another advertisement showed a well-dressed preacher declaring that Black Billy Sunday was a "Writer, Student, Evangelist, and Preacher. We doubt if there is anyone among the Race folks today who is doing better and more forceful work than Black Billy Sunday" (Figure 3.2).

The connections were explicit to consumers of the era. Black Billy Sunday exemplified self-actualization and mobility. He was educated, whereas more than three-quarters of black ministers were not. He wrote and read his sermons at a time when more than a fifth of the black population could not read or write. Moreover, he was a towering figure in "race" work and uplift. He captivated black America's burgeoning urban churches and "great tabernacles." It was apparent to readers of the ad that Sunday, a small-town migrant from South Carolina, had not only climbed to the lofty heights of black Protestantism but that he had also gained fame in corporate America. Purchasing his spiritual commodities, advertisers suggested, would rouse and "inspire" consumers toward the same accomplishments. Therefore the sermons of the accomplished preacher "[s]hould be in everybody's home" (Figure 3.2)[45]

Paramount pitched Reverend White in a similar fashion (Figure 3.3). The label's race record division outsourced its advertising. Henry Stephany, a young white employee of the Wisconsin Chair Company (Paramount's parent company), drafted the ads with no input from the artists or A&R. The outline was then sent to an advertising agency in Milwaukee for illustration. Mayo Williams, the label's only black A&R, occasionally arranged for a *Chicago Defender* reporter to take pictures of his black artists, occasionally outfitted in clothes chosen by the label. He did so for Reverend William Arthur White's evolution polemic. The newspaper commercial presented a debonair and scholarly White in suit, tie, and spectacles. White's attire and clean-shaven appearance set him apart as an established man of wisdom and means. "Now in his great Paramount record," the ad announced, the learned preacher "*solves the question of evolution*—the great religious topic that so stirred the country just a few weeks ago." The ad thus tried to convey a pivotal message: the spiritual products of the urbane preacher provided much-needed authoritative wisdom on the question of evolution. Reverend White's sermon was a must-have for faithful Christians seeking to navigate the treacherous waters of modern thought.[46]

Phonograph sermons made black Protestantism a modern commodity. Phonograph religion standardized the production of black sermons and thrust African American Christianity into the marketplace anew, alongside a host of standardized products; all of which promised to provide answers to some temporal and/or spiritual dilemma of modern-day life. Purchasing recorded sermons, advertisers maintained, was essential to black flourishing.

Distribution

National advertising demanded national distribution. Widespread advertising of the sermons helped to create a national demand for the new sacred commodities. Columbia and Paramount made certain that the sermons were readily available across the country. The labels distributed and sold them throughout the nation in a number of ways. First, local department store chains sold phonograph sermons. These corporate retail outlets rapidly replaced independent stores and brands during the 1920s. Between 1920 and 1932, the number of department and grocery store chains increased 500 percent from 30,000 to an incredible 159,638 stores, the highest number in American history. By the close of the 1920s, chain stores comprised 10 percent of all retail stores but accounted for 22 percent of total retail sales, that is, approximately 20 cents of every dollar spent in American retail went to the country's growing assortment of chain stores. Chain stores and the branded merchandise they sold became insignias of modern consumer culture.[47]

Recorded sermons were a feature of these mammoth stores. Harry Charles, a Paramount salesman in charge of selling race records in Virginia, Georgia, North and South Carolina, Tennessee, Mississippi, and Louisiana, had great success in the region's department chain stores. Charles, who recruited and recorded several "colored preachers," religiously set up a Paramount record counter alongside the miscellany of corporate retail merchandise. The stores advertised Paramount's stock by playing the label's sermon and blues records over the department store loudspeaker. Charles even arranged a live daytime performance by Ma Rainey at an Atlanta chain store. During the hour-long show, Charles reported that the chain store "was selling them records as fast as they could hand em out." The city's chain stores were a sweet spot for

Charles, reportedly grossing an average of $6,000 in Paramount pho-
nograph and race records sales per week. In the midst of appliances,
clothes, and domestic wares, Paramount's record kiosk of blues and
sermons assured shoppers that they could meet their sacred as well as
mundane needs and desires in the department store.[48]

Patrons who did not have access to department stores could rely on
the trendy service of mail order shopping. Montgomery Ward established the first modern mail order catalog of standardized products in
1872, tagging it "A Department Store in a book . . . an urban shopping
experience at your finger tips." Mail order commerce offered rural and
small-town residents access to modern goods that had formerly been
exclusively available to urban centers. The expansion of the U.S. postal
service made the phenomenon a routine part of the American shopping
experience. City postal delivery service grew by almost four times from
1900 to 1930, expanding from 796 cities to 3,098 cities. Free rural postal
delivery also grew at an astonishing pace during the period. Nationwide
service was instituted in 1898, and expanded from 1,259 to 45,318 routes
by 1930. Subsequently, by 1930 the average individual received about
twice as much mail compared to the beginning of the previous decade.[49]

Mail order catalogs and the growth of postal services expanded the
urban shopping experience across the country. The *Half Century Magazine* praised the commercial dimensions of extended postal service. The
delivery of an assortment of urban-based goods and services to rural
America aided the progress of the race. "In short," the magazine concluded in 1925, "the letter carrier is the medium that has transformed
the once secluded inhabitant of the rural district into a cosmopolitan
citizen."[50]

The urban-based labels and dealers pounced on the opportunity. In
the *Chicago Defender*, Paramount utilized Reverend White's picture to
entice mail orders. The ad and order form announced, "You All Know
'Preacher White.'" It continued, "Send No Money. If your nearest dealer
hasn't this Paramount record, check no. 12302 on the coupon below.
Send no money! Pay the postman 75 cents for each record plus a small
C.O.D. fee when he delivers them" (Figure 3.3). Paramount charged
about 8 cents postage per record ($5 out of an average income today).
In an effort to shore up multiple unit sales, the label assured customers,
"We pay postage and insurance on orders for more than one record."

The official order form made such purchases convenient for retailer and shopper both; however, the printed document was not required for procuring the sermon. Alfred Schultz, a longtime Paramount employee, recalled that the label often received requests scribbled on paper scraps. The local post office "often got letters and wondered what it was." Once the postman figured it was a mail order request, he delivered it to Paramount, leaving the employees to "turn it at all different angles" to ascertain the content of the order. One determined customer even sent in an order request on the back of butcher's wrapping paper. Whether consumers used the official order form or makeshift stationary, Paramount made certain to deliver the sermons.[51]

The *Chicago Defender* alerted shoppers of other mail order companies as well. Chicago's Kapp Music Company pledged to deliver Black Billy Sunday's sermons to the doorstep of any consumer. Kapp paid the postage charge. Fans of the revivalist only had to pay the cost of the sermon, 75 cents, and a 15 cent (roughly $9 out of an average income today) cash-on-delivery charge. To further capitalize on Black Billy Sunday, Kapp also attempted to package Black Billy Sunday's recorded sermons with a written "series of sermons in pamphlet form." The music store and mail order record retailer saw great profit potential in the preacher's sacred wares.[52]

Pittsburgh's Goldman and Wolf, the self-professed "Largest Exclusive Race Artists' Music Store," sold both Sunday's Columbia sermons as well as White's on Paramount. The mail order company assured customers that regardless of their location, their favorite race record or sermon was "as near to your home as your mailbox." Consumers did not have to send any money, only complete the order form in the national edition of the *Pittsburgh Courier* and "tear [it] out and mail [it] today." The mail order company also offered consumers "a big free catalogue" from which to order. Moreover, shoppers could also write their orders to Goldman and Wolf as a letter. No form of contact was rejected. Either way, all consumers had to do was simply "pay the postman when he delivers the records to your door."[53]

The F. W. Boerner Company enjoyed a great deal of success in the race record mail order business. Maurice Supper and his brother-in-law Frederick Boerner, both former Paramount employees, established the mail order company in January 1925 with the promise that they would always offer the newest "Blues, Spirituals, and Sermons." In addition, the company offered patrons free phonograph needles and records for customer referrals. The Port Washington, Wisconsin, company grew quickly, gaining a mailing list of upward of 25,000 names from Alabama to California. The success of Boerner's voluminous mail order commerce reportedly caused the small town post office to be upgraded from a Class 3 to a Class 1 facility, a designation usually reserved for postal services in large cities. Boerner stayed in touch with customers by sending them a monthly catalog that offered the latest releases by Columbia, Paramount, and a host of other race record labels. Boerner, on average, shipped four records per order. Such sizable orders came with a C.O.D. fee as well as a 35 cent postage charge (approximately $23 out of an average income today).[54] For the right price, spiritual consumers could have a sermon of their choice sent to them, no matter their location.

The Colored Music Shoppe attempted to best all the other mail order companies. The exclusive Paramount dealer marketed its business the same way as other mail order firms—with one exception: the Colored Music Shoppe took phone orders. This innovation was very popular with willing but illiterate consumers. "We are as near to you as your mailbox or telephone," declared the company advertisement. Moreover, the Colored Music Shoppe not only covered the postage, but also guaranteed that it would replace any sermon broken during transit free of charge. "Postage paid on all orders for two or more records. C.O.D fee $0.15. Records Broken in the mail are REPLACED FREE OF CHARGE" (emphasis in original). Customers could order Reverend Sunday's or White's newest sermon release and have it delivered to their doorstep, all with one quick phone call.[55]

Local dealers also sold recorded sermons, and black newspapers directed consumers accordingly. The *Afro American*, for example, alerted consumers that Baltimore's Lauren's Music Company on Lauren Street had Black Billy Sunday's sermon. Likewise, the Kapp Music Company of Chicago's Madison Street advertised "Sermons by Calvin P. Dixon." Pittsburgh's Goldman and Wolf music store sold Black Billy Sunday's sermons as well as those by Reverend White. Black and white music stores across the country did the same.[56]

In addition to department store chains and music stores, recorded sermons were available in a number of other commercial venues across the country. Publishing firms like Michigan's R. L. Polk and Company promoted countrywide commerce by compiling business and retail directories. By 1925, Polk and Company offered 8,000 different databases including retail, postal, and banking directories. Labels could purchase lists at a rate of $7.50 (comparable to about $500 today) per thousand entries. One list contained nearly 25,000 retail furniture stores and dealers. Such home décor stores were particularly useful to the phonograph industry because they avidly sold phonographs as home furnishing and records as well.[57]

Columbia had great success with one such store in Atlanta: the James K. Polk Furniture Company. Polk C. Brockman convinced his grandfather and father that the family business needed a phonograph department. Eventually profits from phonograph and record sales were higher than those from the furniture operation. The family had to remodel its Atlanta warehouse and hire more staff to accommodate the volume of its phonograph commerce. By 1926, the business had changed its name to Polk Music Supplies and was solely a phonograph and music concern. By the close of the decade, Brockman estimated the company was doing about $2 million (about $120 million today) worth of business. The company became one of the largest phonograph and record distributor and wholesalers in the country, operating branches in Cincinnati, Dallas, Memphis, New Orleans, and Richmond. All its shops carried the latest phonograph sermons. Brockman's network of stores offered consumers the latest styles in modern furnishings as well as black ministry.[58]

For its national distribution Paramount Records connected with the Saint Louis Music Company, which claimed to be the "World's Largest Distributors of Race Records by Mail." In 1925, the firm merged with the Artophone Corporation, a larger Saint Louis wholesaler. The consolidated company shipped records throughout the midwest and the south including Saint Louis, Dallas, Kansas City, Memphis, and New Orleans, as well as parts of southern Illinois, Arkansas, and Mississippi. The widespread distribution placed recorded sermons in a variety of stores. As a Paramount salesman recalled, "Any kinda [sic] store'd [sic] sell 'em [sic] sometimes, you couldn't tell." Similarly, Artophone vice president Herbert Schiele recollected, "Now of course, your music stores and department stores were your biggest outlets, but there wasn't any

standard place." The company utilized almost every commercial channel, selling Paramount's sermons in jewelry stores, shoeshine parlors,
confectioners, pharmacies, and dry goods stores. Ray Kornblum seized
every opportunity for a potential sale. The scrupulous Paramount executive made it a practice to place spiritual and sermon records in funeral
parlors to comfort the bereaved or to be placed in the coffin of the
deceased. Apparently the venture was profitable. Kornblum bragged,
"They got 'em dead or alive."[59]

Similarly, Earl Montgomery, an executive who joined Artophone's
Memphis branch, also seized upon unusual retail outlets. In addition
to selling records to furniture stores and general stores, the executive of
Paramount distribution in the deep south also sold a good many records
to plantation commissaries and country stores in the Mississippi delta.
No venue was left untapped for sale of the new commodities.[60]

Finally, record labels also employed the traditional technique of
door-to-door salesmen to sell recorded sermons. Art Satherley, a longtime Paramount executive, was one of the company's earliest traveling
salesmen. The salaried purveyor covered territory ranging from "Nova
Scotia to Florida." Satherly attended county fairs, country dances,
house parties, funerals, and religious services, usually armed "with
twenty-five [records] in each hand," noting, "I had no trouble of dis-
posing them . . . they were eaten up." If a pastor or church was resis-
tant to such overtures, Satherly made it a practice to "give the pastor a
donation of five or ten dollars" in exchange for the opportunity to make
sales announcements or at least announce his presence in town. Such
offerings were often a boon for sales, as the compensated and converted
pastor "would tell other pastors and he would tell other pastors and the
word spread!"[61]

In addition to official employees, Paramount also solicited informal salespersons to sell its records. One such overture in the *Chicago Defender* was headlined, "MAKE BIG MONEY EASY." The label
assured potential employees that the job was rewarding. Paramount
even promised to supply each employee with a "free salesmen's out-
fit." Doorknockers only had to "take orders from your friends and
relatives . . . just show them the lists and let 'em choose." Salesmen in
turn were promised "a big commission on every sale." Agents simply
had to buy ten or more records at 45 cents each, plus postage. Peddlers

were free to sell the records to the highest bidder. "Our agents," Paramount's commercial beamed, "make big money." The venture was very successful. A Paramount employee recalled that the company's request for door-to-door salesmen resulted in "[h]undreds of people sending in that they wanted to become agents," partcicularly "clergymen [and] black people who had little grocery stores." Sales pitches for sermons arrived on doorsteps, mailboxes, family gatherings, social events, church services, grocery stores, and street corners—wanted or not.[62]

Railroad employees often functioned as unofficial salesmen. Black Pullman porters took orders from across the country during their travels, especially throughout the south. In the case of Paramount, porters stocked up on records at the office of Mayo Williams, Paramount's only black executive, located on Chicago's black commercial district known as the "Stroll." Williams recalled that customers would see ads like that of Reverend White in the *Chicago Defender* and promptly petition porters "The next time you go to Chicago pick me up this record." The entrepreneurial carriers would come to Chicago with "orders for 'em and would pay for 'em, the wholesale price (about 45 cents)." The porters would gather the requested records and then return to southern small towns and stations where "they'd sell 'em both to dealers and private persons . . . sometimes for a dollar a piece, as much as the traffic would bear."[63]

Columbia records benefitted from enterprising black Pullman porters departing New York City's Grand Central and Penn Stations. Journalist and novelist Kyle Crichton observed, "It seemed that Negro Pullman porters on trains going south invariably left New York with as many as twenty five records apiece under their arms."[64] The faithful, whether by department store, mail order, local retail, or salesmen had access to the newest recorded sermon(s). Black preaching could seemingly be bought and heard anywhere.

•　　•　　•

In 1926, famed ad agency N. W. Ayer and Son confidently predicted the revelatory role of mass advertising. "Historians of the future will not have to rely on meager collections of museums, will not have to pore over obscure documents and ancient prints, to reconstruct a faithful picture of 1926." Rather the agency, noted for several groundbreaking advertising campaigns (Morton's Salt's "When It Rains It Pours," Camel cigarettes' "I'd Walk a Mile for a Camel," and later De Beers's "A Diamond Is Forever"), declared that advertisements alone would provide future historians with sufficient data to chronicle any historical moment. "Were all other sources of information on the life of today to fail, the advertising would reproduce for future times, as it does for our own, the action, color, variety, dignity, and aspirations of the American Scene." Similarly, a year later *Printer's Ink*, the first national trade magazine for advertising, asked: What kind of narrative will the American historian "in 2001 A.D." write "if the historian . . . bases his information on some of the advertisements clipped from 1927 publications?"[65]

One major finding of such an analysis is the emergence of African American preachers teaming up with the entertainment industry to make black Protestant sermons a modern commodity. Evangelical black clergy did so in an attempt to modernize and revitalize their ministries in light of the popularity of the phonograph and modern consumer culture in black life. The phonograph provided a mass medium through which they could reach the masses, while the marketplace offered a powerful sphere in which they could shape the cultural and moral habits of urban America. The sanctifying of the phonograph and mass cultural industry made black Protestant sermons a prominent fixture of America's national marketplace.

Despite their mass production, trendy marketing, and nationwide publicity and availability, the new sacred commodities did not match the staggering sales of their secular competitors. The labels pressed about ten thousand copies of the respective sermons. While the precise sales figures on the sermons are not known, the short-lived mass media careers of the preachers are indicative of their relative lack of success. After recording ten sermons for Columbia in January 1925, Black Billy Sunday was never invited back to the studio pulpit. His mediocre sales did not warrant additional recordings. Sunday, turned bishop, concentrated his efforts on his new denomination. As bishop he was chauffeured across the country, overseeing his growing movement.[66] White's sermons were presumably slightly more popular. Paramount's parsimonious policy restricted multiple studio sessions to black artists who sold out of their initial pressing of ten thousand records. The policy was straightforward: if an artist "sold real good," Speir recalled, "Paramount brought 'em back!" White had four studio sessions. He recorded a total of eight sermons. Nevertheless, White's popularity faded. His mass media ministry spanned just two short years. In the end, neither preacher came close to the highly profitable six-figure sales numbers of phonograph stars. Because they did not produce a large profit for their respective labels they were both dropped. Race records were a business, and as one Paramount executive put it bluntly, if an artist ceased to be profitable "we couldn't afford to record 'em."[67]

Aesthetic differences account for the less than stellar sales. Race records gained mass appeal in part because the records were grounded in forms of black vernacular and spoke to quotidian concerns. The inaugural phonograph sermons, on the other hand, were delivered in formal language and primarily addressed erudite theological issues. The pioneering phonograph preachers adopted the medium of black popular entertainment, but not the style.

The evangelical black clergy who followed Black Billy Sunday and Reverend White likewise viewed the phonograph as a new and necessary means to preach the gospel to the black masses. However, they deliberately fashioned their sermons after the folk expression and format of popular race record artists. As a result they popularized recorded sermons and created the first and enduring model of popular black religious broadcasting.

Apostles of Modernity

*Phonograph Religion and the Roots of Popular
Black Religious Broadcasting*

G. K. Korn, a Columbia record dealer in Newark, New Jersey, quickly sold out of his initial shipment of Reverend James M. Gates's first recorded sermon. Likewise, the Broad and Market Music Company, one of Korn's local competitors, also swiftly sold out of its stock of a thousand copies of the black vernacular sermons by the Atlanta preacher. In an attempt to beat out his competitor, Korn astutely placed a rush supplemental order to Columbia's New York City warehouse. He was convinced that "Death's Black Train Is Coming" was a hit. However, to his chagrin, the popular record was already out of stock at Columbia's warehouse. Korn was told he would have to wait until a new stock could be pressed and delivered from Columbia's Bridgeport, Connecticut, record factory. Korn retorted that he "was unable to wait . . . the demand was so strong." Undeterred, he made the eighty-mile drive to the grimy Bridgeport factory to personally pick up the latest pressing of the sermon; no small feat given the "blazing" speed limit of 35 MPH. Korn was bent on cashing in on the sermon. He was not the only salesman to recognize the writing on the wall. One phonograph magazine reported, "Wholesalers were deluged with orders by telephone and telegraph for quantities of fifty and in some cases as high as 500 of this one record."[1]

The craze extended to the south as well. The *Baltimore Afro-American* noted that the sermon had "taken Baltimore by storm." A local dealer in the city reported that he sold over six hundred copies of the sermon in two days. Kaufman's, another Baltimore dealer, decreed the record was "THE GREATEST SERMON." Likewise, the city's Jazz Shop pronounced the sermon "[t]he Greatest religious record ever made," stating, "Nothing like it has ever been heard on records before. We have sold hundreds already."[2]

Westerveldt Terhune, manager of Columbia's Atlanta branch, visited the label's New York City corporate offices to discuss the "exceptionally good summer" his division had in record sales. The twenty-year industry veteran promptly informed company executives that Reverend Gates's 1926 debut sermon ranked first among his best sellers.[3] Local competitor Joe Luttrell sold three thousand copies of the local preacher's recorded sermon in three weeks. "Never before in the time that I have been connected with the phonograph business," he reflected, "has there been such a demand for a record. It is impossible for us to keep in stock!"[4]

The 75 cent sermon cost almost twice the average hourly wage, comparable to more than $30 today. But the cost did not matter. Streams of religious consumers rushed to buy it. To the industry's surprise, the record flew off the shelves. The *Talking Machine World* reported, "No one guessed this record would sell as well as it did until suddenly colored people began to swarm into dealers' stores." America's black rural diaspora heard the familiar in the preaching of Reverend Gates. For willing listeners, hearing and experiencing the "downhome" folk sermon was priceless.[5]

Reverend Gates was the first to record a hit sermon. He blazed the way toward a fruitful and popular mass media ministry in black Protestantism. The phonograph industry in turn recognized the lucrative potential of black preachers and their sermons. Together these discerning media preachers and the entertainment industry created popular black religious broadcasting.

•   •   •

After the mediocre sales of Black Billy Sunday and Reverend White, a host of phonograph ministers drafted a formula for success. These popular phonograph preachers—all born in the rural south a generation or so after slavery—eschewed the urbane, didactic, and stoic sermons of Reverends Sunday and White. Instead, they preached their homilies in black vernacular expression, that is, in the form of the folk sermon.

Their preaching was marked by metaphor, simile, double descriptors (high-tall, low-down, kill-dead, more-better), and the use of verbal nouns such as "funeralize." The sermons were also chanted, beginning with conversational prose and then transitioning to a "metrical, tonal, and rhythmic chant." A staged and primed studio congregation joined these folk sermons with singing, clapping, shouts of affirmation, and popular music. For many black listeners, this homiletic formula constituted authentic black Protestant preaching. As Zora Neale Hurston discovered in her interwar fieldwork, a good many African Americans deemed the folk chanted sermon the only true form of preaching; anything else, according to them, was "lecturing" or worse, trying to sound like a "white man." Moreover, these antiphonal sermons avoided scholarly theological discourse. Instead, they employed black dialect, idioms, and memes to preach on topics such as Christian piety, racism, and popular cultural events: everyday black life. Essentially, these phonograph preachers delivered an extended folk sermon introduction, followed by a climatic and demonstrative chanted close. They preached black "vernacular homilies" to the tune and pace of the jazz and blues era.[6]

This formula catered to a religious need. An interwar study of black Protestantism conducted by the Institute of Social and Religious Research (ISRR) reported that some "faithful church people" from rural and small towns "suffered moral and religious shipwreck" when they migrated to the cities. Many urban churches refused to adjust their worship practices to the expressive folkways of the rural diaspora. Some faith communities even prohibited "shouters" from attending or joining the church. During the 1920s, for example, scores of black Baptists near Savannah, Georgia, had their church membership rescinded or were outright banned from some faith communities. The shared crime: their worship practices of jumping, shouting, and clapping were deemed "too noisy" and improper. Understandably, one rural migrant lamented to the ISRR, "a large number of southern people desire a church similar in worship to the churches in the rural south."[7]

Phonograph preachers helped to fulfill this desire. To be sure, urban migrants established house and storefront churches where they could engage in expressive worship. However, popular phonograph preachers condensed the common facets of black evangelical worship to fit the limited time parameters of a record and packaged it for easy consumption. Simply put, they re-created the African American evangelical worship experience on wax. As an unfamiliar aural and aesthetic urban religion swirled around the rural diaspora, phonograph religion captured an expressive religious sound and experience that was familiar; one that could be repeated on demand seemingly anywhere, any time. As one black minister reported from Atlantic City, New Jersey: Every time one churchgoer listened to a Reverend Gates recorded sermon, "she gets 'happy' at home and neighbors have to come in and hold her!" The *Afro-American* summed it up best: churchgoers seeking a revival experience no longer had to risk being ostracized, nor did they have to travel and brave the elements and crowds; they could simply "sit home by the warmth of their firesides and get their gospel by the process of gramophone [phonograph] reproduction."[8]

This brand of phonograph religion enjoyed much success, rivaling, and at times surpassing, the sales of leading blues artists. Such acclaim left a lasting template for widely accepted black religious broadcasting for years to come: mostly male clergy preaching in common and simple vernacular, replicating popular entertainment, and placing an emphasis upon personal expressive worship. The collective innovations of these old school phonograph preachers made them apostles of modernity in black Christianity.[9]

Folk Style

Phonograph religion helped to satiate the rural diaspora's yearning for folk preaching. Reverend James M. Gates met a demand. The urban migrant from rural Georgia forsook the polished delivery of his predecessors, instead recording sermons in emblematic folk style using improvisation, tonal modulation, and rhythmic chanting. He became the first phonograph preacher to achieve widespread success. His attention to and retention of the folk ways of his upbringing and migrant experience transmitted the ethos and pathos of nineteenth-century evangelical religion on wax. Gates was an innovator of popular black religious broadcasting.

James Gates was born in the rural Georgia black belt community of Hogansville, Georgia, in February 1884. Around 1913, Gates and his wife Nellie migrated to Atlanta. The coupled settled in the city's Summerhill neighborhood. Summerhill was situated near several train stations. The location made it a popular settling ground for the city's black and white urban migrants and immigrants. The masses arriving at the nearby train platforms brought their rural cultural practices with them. One disgusted urbane visitor even called the urban neighborhood "the picture of a country town." Most of the small homes in the neighborhood lacked flooring and running water. The migrants' clothes seemed singularly inappropriate for city life. The men wore overalls, the women lacked stockings, and children went without shoes. Given the small, overcrowded accommodations and limited opportunities for recreation, residents congregated and gathered on street corners for conversation and leisure. Neighbors exchanged pleasantries and discussed private affairs in rural dialect out in the open. James and Nellie Gates lived in a folk paradise in the midst of Atlanta.[10]

The neighborhood provided an oasis of folk expression for migrants like James and Nellie in a city that was otherwise hostile to such expression. Martin Luther King, Sr., for example, also migrated from rural Georgia to Atlanta in 1913. When he went outside the haven of his immediate neighborhood, people derided him for his cultural expressions. "My first few months in the city were often discouraging," King remembered. "I couldn't say anything, it seemed to me, without someone laughing or correcting my speech." Urban America had prescriptive forms of speech and habits which migrants like Martin were not used to. "All I knew," he recalled, was that "[d]own at home, in the country, everybody I ever heard sounded something like me. I never knew how we were mangling the language."[11]

Migrants were especially reminded of their backward ways in Atlanta's established black churches. King recalled preaching at a black Methodist church full of "city people, not transplanted country men and women." In his emotive "country" sermon, King described Jesus carrying the cross to the urban congregation, bellowing "'Caintcha see him totin' it?'" [sic]. King recalled that he was "so rural that my speech style just ran the English language ragged." Such language and volume were inappropriate and not found in what King referred to as "Atlanta's vocabulary" of racial uplift and propriety. The cultured congregation "just turned up their noses and fanned themselves a little harder," and "the church choir muffled its laughter" during his sermon. King was ashamed. He felt that his "dusty, un-creased clothes" and "rough country style of speaking" signaled that he was an "uneducated farm boy" who had not been reformed and assimilated to the new urban setting. He was, in his own mind and perhaps in the view of the congregation, nothing more than an embarrassing relic of the rural life many blacks despised, or at least had attempted to leave behind and forget. "They didn't need any reminders from preachers or anybody else, of what they'd left behind." Martin King desperately tried to relinquish his folk speech patterns, but found it difficult. "Oh, I tried hard enough, imitating all the smooth talkers I heard around town," he remembered. He used mimicry and eventually higher education to avoid ridicule and embarrassment and to obtain respectability and acceptance.[12]

Migrants like James Gates, however, relished their folk religious practices. He joined Mount Calvary Baptist Church in the city's Rockdale Park neighborhood, a migrant church that had been founded in 1900 by seven black women. The church was determined to continue its folk practices in the city despite public disapproval and meager resources. The group established an open-air church in the clearing of a neighbor's backyard. Mount Calvary brought evangelical revivalism to the city in the form of an urban hush harbor congregation.[13]

The combination of James and Nellie's neighborhood, informal street gatherings, and his faith community facilitated the continuity of their folk practices. It allowed them to dress, congregate, and express themselves in ways that were familiar to them in native rural Hogansville, Georgia. The survival of black rural culture and forms of expression in the city proved to be characteristic themes in Reverend Gates's mass media ministry.[14]

Gates became pastor of the migrant congregation after his predecessor resigned and headed north to pastor a larger church in Detroit. James Gates remained pastor of Mount Calvary from 1916 to 1942. During his tenure, the church grew to capacity and eventually expanded, building a brick edifice with stain glass windows, pews, indoor plumbing, and a baptismal pool. Mount Calvary made the transition from a rural to a modern church. However, the worship stayed the same, especially Reverend Gates's much-celebrated folk preaching style. A journalist who set out to study Mount Calvary was impressed. "The church was crowded to capacity," he remarked. He reflected on the preacher's black folk evangelical penchant for starting his sermons slowly, only to bring the sermon and the congregation to a chanted, emotional, and demonstrative climax. Reverend Gates "eases off at the start but after he gets his congregation in the 'swing' the sermon seems to touch you from its own momentum." Reverend Gates led his growing migrant congregation in the celebration of folk religion in the midst of the cosmopolitan city.[15]

Gates's reputation as a stirring old-time preacher came to the attention of Polk Brockman. Brockman operated Atlanta's Polk Music Supplies, Inc., one of the largest record wholesalers and distributors in the country. In addition, he served as a popular talent scout. On a weekly basis, he visited the city's 81 Theatre, musical gatherings, and local black churches looking for new folk talent. He found many popular artists in this manner. He arranged the recording of Fiddlin' John Carson for the first blockbuster hillbilly/country record, Lucie Bogan on the first blues record recorded in the south, and the widely recorded African American comedy team of Butterbeans and Susie. Brockman's visits to black churches and the like were not an expression of his personal fondness for folk music. Unlike other race record executives, he was not guided by personal preferences, but simply by the market, "I don't ever look at a thing [record] as to what I think about it," he declared. "I always try to look at it through the eyes of the people I expect to buy it. My personal opinion never enters into anything I ever [sic] have anything [sic] to do with when it comes to merchandizing." He continued, "I never thought about it from any other angle except how much I could make." For Brockman it was simple, "Ya gotta have good record sense!" His wife confirmed such, stating the only sound her husband was interested in was "the sound of the cash register." And when Brockman heard the sound of Reverend Gates preaching, he heard a profit.[16]

Brockman had a plan to make Reverend Gates a star. In another departure from his contemporaries, he did not simply hope an artist would produce a hit record. Rather, he got actively involved. He arranged the recordings, set up the technology, and even contributed lyrical content. "We had a program all laid out ahead of time," he recalled of his studio sessions. "[W]e knew exactly what we's [sic] gonna [sic] do. It wasn't any hit or miss to it at all." Reverend Gates's desire to spread his folk ministry and Brockman's shrewdness for profit converged on a Saturday evening on April 24, 1926 when Brockman arranged for the preacher to record for Columbia records in Atlanta.[17]

Reverend Gates's first recording had the benefit of cutting-edge technology. Columbia was the first of many labels to purchase Western Electric's electric recording system. Pioneering phonograph preachers Black Billy Sunday and Reverend White had recorded their sermons using acoustic recording which channeled all sound through a recording horn. All sound performance was treated and recorded equally with little thought for catching or removing studio noise. The process demanded that voice and musical performances produce their own power and amplification. Recording quality, then, depended on the distance of the sound from the recording horn as well as the force of the sound. This cumbersome process made it challenging to record more than one person with consistent quality. Moreover, acoustic recording was plagued by mediocre sound, especially for on location recordings.[18]

Electric recording replaced the recording horn with carbon microphones. Microphones produced superior sound and made it possible to increase the audio frequency range of the recording. The microphone captured and amplified central sound performances and attenuated others. Emily Thompson, a historian of science and technology, observes, "Microphones freed the musicians in the studio from the cramped spatial arrangements that acoustic recording had necessitated. Now, electrical amplifiers ensured adequate sound intensity. An appropriate balance between instruments was achieved not through the awkward placement of musicians, but through the use of multiple microphones and mixing consoles in which the signals from those microphones were blended and balanced electrically" from the control booth. The new technology not only made it easier to record groups, but it also netted superior sound quality "with higher fidelity." Simply put, the revolutionary recording process "made a record sound more like a live performance." Columbia is said to have paid $50,000 (comparable to spending more than $3 million today) and a percentage of recording royalties for the groundbreaking innovation. The label believed it was worth every penny.[19]

The company recorded Reverend Gates in Atlanta with its innovative recording technology. Unlike his preaching-on-wax predecessors who recorded their solo lecturing voices in the rigid confines of recording

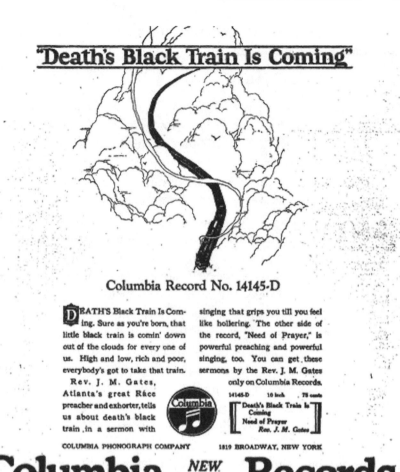

Figure 4.1: Reverend James M. Gates sermon advertisement. Source: *Chicago Defender*, August 21, 1926, 8.

studios, the Baptist minister had the benefit of preaching his recorded sermon in the familiar surroundings and comfort of his own church in the presence of his congregation. Several members of his migrant congregation were on hand for the landmark occasion. True to the black preaching tradition, the microphones transformed them from spectators to participants. This time, Columbia captured a recorded sermon that not only had superior sound quality, but also had the contextual benefit of a migrant church sanctuary and the accompanying rituals.

Columbia's recording of Gates thus captured a black evangelical worship service. Reverend Gates and Mount Calvary, with the help of Columbia's microphones, recorded five sermons during the session. The first release, "Death's Black Train Is Coming," was put on sale on July 20, 1926. It packaged and transmitted the folk worship of Reverend Gates and Mount Calvary across the country.

The sermon began with perhaps the most significant words of black religious broadcasting and certainly of Reverend Gates's ministry: "I want every sinner in the building to come to the anxious seat and bow and accept prayer." The anxious seat or bench was a ritual that developed in nineteenth-century evangelical revivalism. Ministers invited spiritual seekers to the anxious seat—usually in the front or center of the sanctuary—to ponder their spiritual state, seek the counsel of ministers, and eventually have a conversion experience. Revivalist Charles Finney made the ritual famous. Finney championed the introduction of such "new measures" into preaching in order to arouse new fervor for the faith. The anxious bench, as evident in Reverend Gates's record, became a prevailing practice of evangelical Christianity. In the spirit of Finney and evangelicalism, Reverend Gates believed the ritual of the anxious bench was necessary for conversion. Gates used the phonograph as a "new measure" within black evangelical Christianity to inject the culture with new zeal for an old faith.[20]

Gates brought this evangelical expression to phonograph religion not just in ritual but also in form and content. After Reverend Gates's brief appeal to the anxious seat, he led the congregation in singing the title track. "Death's Black Train Is Coming" was a folk favorite composed sometime in the late nineteenth century. Gates was the first to make a commercial recording of it. The song was based on the biblical story of the impending death of King Hezekiah in 2 Kings 20. In the story, the prophet Isaiah tells Hezekiah to get his affairs in order because he is sure to die. The folk song situated the train, not the prophet, as the omen of coming death. Reverend Gates bellowed, "Oh the little black train is coming get all your business right. You better set your house in order for the train may be here tonight!" The microphonic congregation joined in, creating a syncopated folk song.[21]

The black vernacular song was grounded in the African American cultural practice of utilizing aspects of the railroad as religious metaphor. The train was a popular symbol of social and spiritual transformation and deliverance for African Americans during the Great Migration. In fact, the African American religious imagination of train travel was so pervasive that some trains in the south destined for urban areas simply carried the chalked message, "Bound for the Promise Land." The centrality of the train to black modern life, especially in the twentieth century, contributed to the flourishing of chanted songs and sermons centered on the aural and visual metaphor of the train. Because of its significance, African American writers, artists, and preachers could assume that their audiences were familiar with train travel. The *Atlanta Daily Word*, the nation's first black daily newspaper, even compared Reverend Gates's preaching to the train. "You who have not heard Reverend Gates," it said, "will have to hear him to appreciate him." The paper promised its readers that Gates executed his sermons like "the veteran engineer of a heavy freight train."[22] Thus, in his sermon Gates elucidated a prevalent experience and theme in African American life: the train as a transformative entity. This metaphorical usage of the train drew upon the experiences of the masses of African Americans who boarded trains to America's urban cities in the belief that the train was an instrument in a divinely orchestrated sojourn from rural disenfranchisement to purported urban prosperity and freedom.

Gates's utilization of black folk expression and the cultural meme of the train made the release the first phonograph sermon to receive wide acclaim. Like the European immigrants who requested phonograph recordings in their own common speech, African American migrants were especially interested in Gates's phonograph sermon. Gates articulated black Protestant faith in a familiar manner, one that reflected rural and southern forms of black expression. Contrary to the decorous and reserved recorded sermons that preceded him, Gates's religious expression included antiphony, black vernacular, and emotion. The *Chicago Defender* advertisement promoted both Columbia's electrical recording process and the demonstrative nature of "Reverend Gates' powerful sermon." In addition to Columbia's "new process" of electrical recording and the declaration that "You can get these sermons by the Reverend J. M. Gates only on Columbia Records," the ad announced: "Reverend

J. M. Gates, Atlanta's great Race preacher and exhorter, tells us about death's black train in a sermon with singing that grips you till you feel like hollering!" (Figure 4.1).[23] Black religious broadcasting would never be the same.

Reverend Gates's religious transmission was a hit across the country. The *Talking Machine World* declared, "The colored evangelist Reverend J. M. Gates has been given a great reception by record fans."[24] Indeed, in Atlanta the sermon eclipsed all of Columbia's race record sales. Columbia record dealers quickly placed a supplemental order for the popular sacred commodity. The label reported that it was unable to keep pace with the demand. The *Atlanta Daily World* declared that the release of the sermon made the preacher's "fame as a revivalist circulate over the country."[25]

A visiting journalist to Cleveland, Ohio, testified to the preacher's extensive popularity across the nation. The reporter recounted that he first heard Reverend Gates's premier sermon while traveling through the city's black neighborhoods. The sermon echoed throughout the black enclaves of the city as house after house blasted their devices from open windows and doors. Moreover, the preacher's amplified voice permeated the thin walls of the shacks and tenement housing in the black community. The journalist recalled that as he passed through black Cleveland, it seemed as if he could hear "the record made by Reverend Gates in nearly every home."[26] The city's black migrant population may have experienced staid and high-class worship in the city's established black churches, but Reverend Gates made it possible for them to go home, or to a neighbor's house, barber shop, brush arbor congregation, or any other place with a phonograph, and immediately experience worship in a style that resonated with their migrant experience.

Columbia Records recognized the preacher's money-making potential and released another record that fall. In "I'm Gonna Die with the Staff in My Hand," Gates once again used the aural and visual metaphor of the train. In this recording, the preacher refers to "that train that runs to glory" and has "Jesus as the captain and he always makes his time." The record sold well. Exact sales were rarely reported or announced to the public prior to 1945. Labels considered such data private and publicity about it an intrusion on their business dealings. However, order numbers are available for some records. Such figures indicate anticipated popularity and sales. From a label's standpoint, a race record artist, especially a new one, was considered a profitable success if he or she sold over ten thousand records. Reverend Gates's second record had an initial order of 34,025 copies on October 10, 1926. The record sold quickly, causing a supplemental order of another 20,000 the very next month, totaling 54,025 copies. The numbers were staggering. Given the size of the industry and consumer public in 1926, an order approaching fifty thousand copies is arguably the equivalent of a platinum (one million copies) selling artist today. Such figures made him the most successful recorded sermon preacher to date.[27]

Reverend Gates's record-breaking sales occurred alongside releases by some of the industry's most popular race record artists. However, the preacher's sales eclipsed those of the leading entertainers in the country. His orders of over 50,000 topped Columbia's requests for 17,400 copies of famed blues artist Ethel Water's "Take What You Want/We Don't Need Each Other Anymore" and 21,325 copies of Bessie Smith's "Lost Your Head Blues/Gin House Blues." In fact, orders for all four of Bessie's latest releases totaled 53,000. Reverend Gates was not only attracting the masses with the gospel, he was also rivaling and surpassing the sales of some of the most notable names in black popular entertainment. Traditional black Protestantism, it appeared, was not dead. Sale numbers indicated that it was thriving in urban America. And Gates was its leading spokesman.[28]

After the lucrative success of his first two releases, Gates was bombarded by a host of record labels seeking to record him. He quickly capitalized on his bursting stardom in two incisive ways. The first astute move was securing the copyright of "Death's Black Train Is Coming." According to Mayo Williams, a good number of race record artists "didn't know anything about copyrighting." Instead, many artists "sold their compositions outright for a flat proposition. They didn't want to wait and see what they might earn on royalties. They'd say, 'give me $50–$75 or $100' and forget about it." Whether or not talent scouts and record executives actually found or managed an artist, they banked on artists not being familiar with the inner workings of the record industry. Music copyrights positioned men like Mayo and the companies they worked for to receive all royalties and "to make a lot if another company made a record using that composition." Joe Davis, a white singer, promoter, and executive with the Triangle Music Publishing Company of the famed Tin Pin Alley, attempted a similar feat with Reverend Gates and "Death's Black Train Is Coming." Davis—who worked with famed artists such as Mamie Smith and Ethel Waters, and later helped to launch the music career of evangelical stalwart Anita Bryant—alerted *Billboard* magazine that he had "made arrangements whereby he has secured all rights to Death's Black Train is Coming." Davis predicted that the publishing sales would exceed that of the famed multimillion selling hit "The Wreck of the Southern Old 97." However, Gates beat him to the punch. The shrewd preacher filed for the copyright of the record as well as a host of his other recordings. Gates owned the traditional folk song outright and stood to collect royalties from sales and any label that attempted to record the composition.[29]

Second, Gates broke with most race record artists' tradition by not signing with a label. Successful artists such as Bessie Smith and Ethel Waters recorded almost exclusively for one label. Phonograph preachers did the same. However, Gates only signed with an agent. Polk Brockman seized the opportunity to sign Gates when he noticed that the preacher's sermons were "going over very well" with the public and that Columbia had failed to sign Gates to an exclusive contract. Brockman tracked Gates down at his tenement home in the Summerhill neighborhood one evening and the two negotiated throughout the night. Gates hesitated to sign with Brockman, asking the impatient agent for a day to ponder the arrangement. However, the twenty-seven-year-old Brockman was audacious with the preacher, almost twice his age, recalling, "I stayed 'till about two o'clock in the morning." The late-night dealings came to a close when Brockman laid $200 on the table. Brockman remembered the moment: "I laid ten $20 bills down on the table with the green side up" and straightway told Gates, "Well it's just best to get this off my mind tonight, here you take this [money] and sign this agreement." The money, which is equivalent to about $13,000 today, was certainly a small fraction of what the preacher's budding media ministry was actually worth. However, the cash advance was about half of what most black families in Atlanta made in a year. For this reason, in the wee hours of the morning, Gates "signed it and took the two hundred dollars." The preacher became a bona fide phonograph star and the shrewd Brockman his agent. It was quickly becoming evident that Gates's style of black religious broadcasting was not only effective in reaching the masses; it was also proving to be a well-paid enterprise.[30]

The professional relationship was mutually beneficial. In line with industry practices for agents and talent scouts, Brockman received a finder's fee in the range of $50 to $100 for each label that recorded Gates. Brockman was not only well connected in the phonograph industry, he was also known as a hit maker. An artist associated with Brockman was accepted into most studios, no questions asked. Labels respected his opinion when it came to popular recordings. The professional agreement offered Gates an unprecedented opportunity for his ministry. Having ties to an agent and not a label afforded him the opportunity to record widely and utilize the phonograph industry to spread his ministry far and wide without restriction. Gates could record for any label that desired his services.[31] To capitalize on the arrangement, Brockman set Gates up with an unprecedented recording excursion in New York City. In the late summer of 1926, the well-connected agent and the top-selling preacher boarded a train for the recording capital of the world with the freedom to record with the highest bidders.[32] It proved to be a highly rewarding trip for both.

Gates did not have to share studio time with other artists during the recording crusade, unlike Dixon and White. Labels cleared their studio schedules on the days Gates was recording. All-day recording sessions provided the space and time to maximize his production and profit. As a result, Gates recorded approximately fifty titles for several different labels. He preached sermons for mail order labels like St. Louis-based Herwin records, a subsidiary of Paramount, owned and operated by the major record distributor Saint Louis Music Company. He recorded for race record pioneer label Okeh as well as industry giant Victor. Victor rarely recorded folk artists, preferring to stick with the high-class music of artists like Caruso. Brockman recalled that Victor believed folk artists were "beneath their dignity." However, Reverend Gates's popularity and potential for profit as well as Victor's shrinking sales motivated the label to break with old patterns and relinquish its notorious "Victor Attitude" to record Gates. Gates went from being a black belt farmer to a featured preacher on the largest and most successful record label in the world.[33]

A European label also took notice. Gates recorded for the French Pathe Actuelle label during the New York recording marathon. The company had operations in its home base of Paris as well as London, Milan, Moscow, and New York. Gates also recorded several sermons for a host of inexpensive chain store labels while in New York. The Kress chain store company recorded him on its exclusive Romeo brand, while McCory's chain of dime stores recorded him on Oriole. Eventually Gates recorded for both Bluebird, a discount Victor label that was exclusively featured in Woolworth's chain of stores, and Montgomery Ward's label of the same name. The deeply discounted ($0.35 to $0.25) records of these "dime store labels," as they become known, proved particularly popular during the economic woes of the Great Depression. Gates's recording tours spread his ministry far and wide, from Europe to America's string of chain stores.[34]

Gates was very deliberate in the studio pulpit during the month-long recording visit to New York. Brockman recalled that Gates was a very mild-mannered man. However, he was delighted to see that when the microphones were turned on, Gates really "put it on." He never failed to deliver the evangelical fervor that made consumers rush to purchase his sermons and dealers bombard label warehouses for more copies. Gates's media savvy personality extended beyond style. He recorded under the aliases of Reverend M. J. Walker and Reverend Sam Hall Jones as well. This shrewd move permitted him to record the same sermons for different labels and perhaps pocket the finder's fee that would have otherwise been paid to Brockman.[35]

However, not every major record label was impressed with the new celebrity preacher. Thomas Edison took note of Gates during his 1926 wax revival circuit. Edison noticed that Gates's profit potential had convinced even his New Jersey neighbor Victor to break with its tradition of only issuing "respectable" and "high-class" records. Edison considered doing the same. But when Gates made a stop at Thomas Edison's studio in Orange, New Jersey, on September 10, 1926, Edison was not moved by what he heard. The father of the phonograph, known for thinking that blues and jazz was music "for the nuts," refused to sign the preacher. He wrote of Reverend Gates in his talent file, "This fellow might be a wonder, but I can't use him." Gates's black vernacular preaching, while popular, was deemed by some as a "lower" class of expression, a form Edison continually rejected in his recording lists.[36]

Nevertheless, Gates recorded over ninety sermons in 1926, more than all previous sermon recorders combined. Gates went on to record over two hundred sermon titles by 1941, making him the most recorded preacher of the era. His sermon corpus avoided intricate biblical exposition. Instead he addressed the gamut of daily life, offering listeners encouragement, advice, and admonishment on such topics as gender, Jim Crow, the New Deal, war, consumer culture, President Roosevelt, and sexual propriety. His penchant for incorporating aspects of popular entertainment even led him to name some of his sermons after trendy blues tunes and to adopt radio's style of using serial characters. "These Hard Times Is Tight Like That," for example, was a direct riff on his friend Thomas "Georgia Tom" Dorsey and Hudson "Tampa Red" Whittaker's 1928 sexually laced blues hit "It's Tight Like That." Gates used the popular title for an antiphonal sermon featuring a staged conversation between himself and Deacon Davis and Sisters Jordan and Norman, "members" of his congregation, about the effects of the Great Depression.[37]

Gates's popularity stemmed from his folk style and the innovations he brought to black religious media. He preached sermons that grappled with everyday life situations and avoided explicit theological discourse. His creative sermons addressed the sacredness of the mundane in daily life, all modeled after popular black entertainment.

Gates went from being relatively unknown to being a famous religious broadcaster. Polk Brockman, although he was responsible for several wildly successful artists who sold well over 200,000 records, attested that Gates was his biggest and most lucrative recording star. Unlike many phonograph preachers and race record artists, Gates's popularity survived the Great Depression. Race record issues significantly decreased after 1931, dropping from a peak of ten new blues and gospel releases per week during the 1920s to a low of less than three a week in 1933. These new records had an average initial sale of little more than a thousand records. As a whole, record sales dipped from over 100 million in 1927 to 6 million in 1932. The labels that survived these lean times did so in part by exclusively reissuing records of phonograph stars on dime store labels. Industry leader RCA-Victor repackaged Gates's 1926 sermons on its Bluebird label for sale at Woolworth's. Labels cautiously resumed production as the industry slowly climbed to an eventual all-time high of 127 million records sold in 1941, releasing an average of roughly five new blues and gospel records per week. Labels recorded only the most popular artists during this resurrection, those sure to turn a profit. As RCA-Victor rebounded, it made sure to record the unfailing Reverend Gates on several occasions from 1934 until government restrictions on shellac stopped most recording in 1941.[38]

Whether the industry was experiencing prosperous or meager times, Gates's sermons were a fixture in the marketplace. His sermons were featured in department stores and retail venues across the country as well as the nation's burgeoning chain stores. Furthermore, a host of mail order services and catalogs would swiftly deliver his sermons to any doorstep or mailbox. For those who preferred to shop with locally owned businesses, the sermons could be purchased in record shops, furniture stores, pharmacies, and a host of other retail outlets. His sermons entered homes, barbershops, churches, and any place that would accommodate a phonograph, garnering a national congregation of followers, listeners, and admirers. Reverend Gates had a nationwide media ministry.

Although Gates was not afforded the same mainstream news coverage as iconic white religious broadcasters of the day, he is just as notable as they in the development of American religious history. The phonograph preacher significantly shaped popular black religious broadcasting. He blazed the trail of urban black church work that was not based on traditional notions of community mobilizing, organizing, or classic forms of racial uplift. Rather, Gates's ministry was rooted in a religious culture of mass media, consumer culture, and spiritual commodities produced in the form of popular entertainment.

Popular Music and Expressive Worship

Gates built his popular mass media ministry by channeling the folk expression of race records. However, he neglected one aspect: musical instruments. The majority of black Baptist ministers during the era only used pianos in worship. Reverend Gates's record "Reverend Gates' Song Service" is a perfect example. The recording features Gates and his congregation singing to the accompaniment of a lone piano. Black Baptists (and several Holiness groups) tended to view the use of drums, horns, and guitars as theologically inappropriate for worship. Such instruments were considered secular in nature, belonging to the realm of jazz and blues, not sacred song. As one black Baptist minister remembered, "The Baptist Church didn't allow us to play music in church when I was coming up. Anything besides the piano was considered to be the music of the devil."[39] Another black Baptist minister decried the use of jazz and swing instrumentation in church as contrived and irrational, leading to a state of inebriation. The Morehouse and Harvard trained cleric wrote to the *Pittsburgh Courier* declaring that such music "plays upon the emotions of the innocent, but illiterate portions of our people. This music has no appeal to the rational reflection . . . it intoxicates." Moreover, such music only reminded the faithful of "the things which they come to church to get away from. . . . [T]his sort of music is a detraction from worship rather than being a working part of worship itself. It should be destroyed and forgotten."[40] It would take the protracted adoption of gospel music beginning in the mid-1930s to turn the tide of black Baptist churches toward such music.

However, Pentecostal faith communities viewed the use of black popular and commercial cultures, especially music, as an integral aspect of worship. Black Holiness and Pentecostalism often get lumped together, the primary distinction being the Holiness refrain from speaking in tongues. Yet there is another significant difference in discourse that is often overlooked: many black Holiness churches were founded in part on their refusal to speak the language of the market. Black Holiness groups established themselves by their disdain for all forms of popular commercial traditions, especially music and consumer culture. Pentecostals, on the other hand, began making full use of consumer culture and black popular music very early on. They utilized bass, guitars, tambourine, cymbals, cornet, trombone, and drums in worship and packaged such expressions for the market. The emphasis upon personal piety within Pentecostal faith, then, should not be confused with being otherworldly or ascetic. Rather, Pentecostalism has been very pragmatic regarding such matters. "For the saved and sanctified performer," religion scholar Cheryl Sanders has written, "the selective synthesis of sacred and secular elements in the music proceeds according to the principle 'in the world, but not of the world'—what matters here is not the sacred or secular origin of the particular style or technique being used." Intention is paramount. At stake is whether or not the music or performance is projected to invoke the aims of sanctified worship: "emotional release, spirit possession, shouting, and conversion." Individuals, instruments, musical styles, and even popular culture can be sanctified for the service of the church. This approach appealed to churchgoers seeking a worship experience that integrated popular rhythms and practices, especially urban migrants. "People need to feel the rhythm of God," a Baptist turned Pentecostal minister explained, and Pentecostalism "put rhythm into the church because the people wanted it."[41]

A critical mass of black Pentecostal ministers applied this "secular" embrace to the culture industry, becoming phonograph preachers. Church of God in Christ (COGIC) bishop and evangelist Reverend Ford Washington McGee was the most successful Pentecostal minister to employ this formula on wax. The addition of popular instrumentation to his folk preaching made him one of the most influential sermon recorders of the era. In just three years, from June 7, 1927 to July 16, 1930, McGee made forty-six recordings for RCA-Victor, many of which were advertised and sold throughout the Depression and into the 1940s.[42]

F. W. McGee was born the third of ten children on October 5, 1890 in Winchester, Tennessee, to the musical family of Will and Mary McGee. The "mulatoo" or racially mixed family migrated to Hillsboro, Texas, about an hour outside Dallas, when Ford was a child. The McGees bought a home in a black working-class neighborhood on Third Street in Hillsboro. Will McGee worked for the railroad, Mary stayed home with the large family, and young "Fordy," as the family called him, managed a restaurant. Music was the family's primary leisure activity. Will learned to play several instruments. Music and religion kept the family's spirits lifted, especially during their persistent economic woes. In fact, Ford recalled that the family proudly gained the reputation of being the first African American family in Hillsboro to own a piano.[43] Music was central in the McGee household and it would be seminal in McGee's ministry.

After Ford graduated from college in Oklahoma, he and his wife Annabelle bought a home in the small farming community of Little River, Oklahoma. Ford became a high school teacher. However, he left the teaching profession after attending a Pentecostal worship service where he encountered what he called "some unusual power working within." He was convinced that Jesus was baptizing him "with the holy ghost and with fire." The young convert joined the ministry of the COGIC, the first legally chartered and incorporated Pentecostal faith community in the United States. McGee was attracted to the expressive worship and music, and the beliefs of the denomination, especially healing. Faith healing, he recalled, "was a gift I had," a gifting many Baptists did not embrace. McGee admitted that he "was hardly aware" of his gift, but once he joined the Pentecostal faith community he "had great success in healing sick people."[44] He became a popular traveling healer, preacher, and singing evangelist.

The successful evangelist established the COGIC in Des Moines, Iowa, in one campaign. Before his arrival, the church had a membership of two people. McGee and a few musicians he garnered showcased their demonstrative worship and attracted a host of new members. He recalled that people "came from all over to hear me, they came on wagons, and horses, even on cots!" Law enforcement had to be called to help direct the large crowds. After the fruitful campaign, the COGIC made McGee bishop of Iowa. As a bishop he had two aims: to grow the COGIC in Iowa and to dispel stereotypes about the denomination. McGee believed that established urban black churches purposely perpetuated the stereotype that the animated worship of the COGIC was the antithesis of racial progress and respectability. He believed the established black churches tried to stigmatize such worship practices because churches such as the COGIC were increasingly attracting parishioners away from them. He declared, "They could no longer say the Church of God in Christ was for the ignorant once I, a college man, took command."[45]

In 1925, McGee set his sights on black Chicago to further prove his point. He set up his "gospel" tent in Brownsville, on the corner of 33rd street and Prairie Avenue, about one block east of Pilgrim Baptist Church. The location was strategic. Pilgrim, one of the city's largest black congregations, was known for its decorous worship (Thomas Dorsey did not introduce the congregation to gospel music until February 1932). Like many established black churches in urban America with a trained clergyman, Pilgrim regarded reserved worship practices and standard church music as tools for and expressions of racial uplift

Figure 4.2: Reverend F. W. McGee sermon advertisement.
Source: *Chicago Defender*, October 1, 1927, 8.

and progress. James Mundy, director of Chicago's first black opera, led music at Pilgrim. The classically trained musician led the congregation in worship that consisted of classical music such as Bach's Cantatas and Felix Mendelssohn's *Elijah* accompanied by a twenty-seven-piece orchestra. This form of religious practice was seen as a sign of progress and respectability. As one established black Chicago minister remarked, such worship was truly the hallmark of "intelligent folks" as opposed to those who do "a lot of hollering and so forth and carrying on."[46]

One block away, however, McGee and his music band echoed the folk expressions of blues singers and led the faithful in the ecstatic worship practices of "hollering and so forth and carrying on." McGee's "secular" musicians, such as pianist and Okeh recording artist Arizona Dranes, led worship with blues styled bass, guitar, drums, trumpet, and trombone. The revival attracted large crowds. McGee recalled the excitement surrounding the tent worship, noting, "The whole church was something new, it was like a circus." McGee's self-proclaimed novelty is perhaps overstated. Ecstatic worship was not new to black Chicago. However, his popularity brought a windfall to the local COGIC. Bishop C. H. Mason, founder of COGIC, rewarded the sanctified rainmaker by removing the state's bishop and appointing McGee bishop of Illinois.[47]

McGee made certain that all his worship services featured lively music as opposed to what he saw as the sedate "waltz-time" worship music of Pilgrim Baptist. The "secular" instruments and popular music style were vital tools for dancing, shouting, congregational singing, and ecstatic conversion: evidence of "real" Christianity. As one black Baptist turned Pentecostal recalled, "I thought I was saved before that, but I really wasn't." The Chicago migrant testified that he really became a Christian at a Pentecostal service. The experience was so outstanding that it was stamped in his memory. "I got saved at 11.40 a.m.," he reminisced.[48] Indeed, as historian Anthea Butler observes, such rituals were more important in the Pentecostal tradition than bourgeois notions of decorum and shaping white opinion. Rather, the COGIC derived its notions of respectability from the Bible and the desire to live "right." McGee brought this religion, often relegated to revival tents and storefronts, to the forefront of African American religious broadcasting.[49]

Arizona Dranes introduced F. W. McGee to several recording executives following his successful tent revivals. Ralph Peer, a talent scout working for Victor, signed McGee to an exclusive contract. Peer hoped McGee would be the label's exclusive answer to the profitable but freelance Reverend Gates. McGee used Victor's Gold Coast studio on North Michigan Avenue in Chicago to re-create the sanctified worship experience on wax. The migrant preacher recorded his down-home religious expressions, complete with his band and chanted antiphonal sermons, in the midst of one of the nation's wealthiest urban neighborhoods.[50]

Fittingly, McGee's first studio session was sandwiched between Clifford Hayes and the Dixieland Jug Blowers—a jazz and blues band featuring instruments such as a jug, banjo, guitar, fiddle, saxophone, trombone, piano, and clarinet—and Laura Smith and the Wild Cats' recording of "Mississippi Blues"—an ode to the Mississippi River flood of 1927. Like his studio mates, McGee used an assortment of instruments in his recordings. His sermons typically began with a scripture verse followed by a song and a celebratory close accompanied by shouting and music. Sermons such as "My Wife's a Holy Roller," "Jonah in the Belly of the Whale," "The Crucifixion of Jesus," and "Resurrection of Jesus" well exemplify his style.[51]

McGee laid out the reasoning for this approach in his two-part recorded sermon series "Three Ways." He used Ephesians 5:19, "Speaking to yourselves in psalms, and hymns, and spiritual songs, singing and making melody in your heart to the Lord," to declare how the faithful should worship. Accompanied by a trombone, guitar, piano, and jazz percussion, he used an upbeat song and a chanted sermon to display the "privilege" of singing and worshiping not just with the Psalms (verbatim or paraphrased) or the classical hymns that characterized established black churches, but with real "spiritual songs," compositions that expressed the contemporary experiences and musical styles of the saints. Such songs incorporated black human experience and culture into liturgical practice. According to McGee, those who neglected such spiritual songs forfeited their own experience with the divine, a vital and required aspect of faith. Those who lacked or ignored such experience were bereft of true spiritual enlightenment. McGee's records re-created this "spirit-filled" worship experience on wax.[52]

Aptly, a Philadelphia record store and mail order commercial in the *Chicago Defender* exhorted, "Rev. F. W. McGee and congregation offer two sermons that ring with genuine religious fervor." The ad assured consumers that the sermons were authentically Pentecostal in flair, add-ing, "They make you feel that you're right in the church. You hear it all just as it actually happens. The preacher's burning words . . . spontane-ous shouts from the congregation . . . and the low pitch hum of musical instruments as the message is turned into wonderful harmonies [*sic*]" (Figure 4.2). The advertisement described the "frenzy" of Pentecostal worship: the musical accompaniment, the expressive worship of the congregation, and the chanted sermon all merged to create an ecstatic worship experience. Pentecostals believed this brand of euphoric expe-rience was a must for true Christian experience. Profits from the media ministry indicated that many consumers agreed.[53]

Although exact sale figures are not available, McGee's contract is illustrative of his popularity. Beginning in 1927 he was paid $25 per ser-mon, which amounts to approximately $1,500 per sermon today. How-ever, McGee demanded a contract renegotiation once he realized the popularity of his sermons. McGee, far from being satisfied with the assurance of receiving his treasure in heaven, refused to record with Victor until the label agreed to more than double his pay. He demanded $100 per sermon, convinced that his sales warranted the pay increase. The label agreed. McGee's new salary amounted to more than $6,000 per sermon in today's dollars. This was more than what the overwhelm-ing majority of race record artists made. Only artists such as Bes-sie Smith and Duke Ellington made more per title. The profits from McGee's record sales convinced Victor that he was well worth it.[54]

McGee established a pattern in both black religious broadcasting and Pentecostalism. His forty-six titles were very popular. Although black mainline churches rejected his style of worship, black consum-ers embraced it. Pentecostal worship with its emphasis on personal expressive worship and the sanctification of "secular" instruments and culture proved to be effective in helping the nascent denomination transmit its gospel to the black masses. In addition, McGee's success proved that broadcasting and selling black Pentecostal worship could be a well-paid enterprise. As Bishop of Illinois, F. W. McGee's media ministry, embrace of consumer culture, and the subsequent lucrative financial reward ceased to be an exception to the norm in Pentecostal-ism. Rather, as a Bishop in the young denomination, McGee emerged as a model and standard of potent urban black ministry and salesman of Pentecostalism. Black Pentecostalism, often dismissed as retrograde and ascetic, was actually a pivotal tradition within modern black religious commodities and broadcasting.[55]

Gender

Male clergy dominated the studio pulpit as they did in the church. However, the period of rapid urbanization did witness a rise in black female preachers. According to U.S. census data, the number of female clergy increased over 600 percent (from 68 to 494) from 1910 to 1926. By the end of the decade, black female clerics comprised about 2 percent of ordained black Protestant clergy. This increase in black women preachers was a constitutive element of what historian Wallace Best calls "the new sacred order" of black urban America. Black women were slowly rising in the ranks of Protestant ministry, finding ways to make their voices heard not just through activism, social welfare, and parachurch organizations, but also from the pulpit. Phonograph sermons reflected this numerically small but culturally significant trend.[56]

Seven black women recorded their sermons on wax, comprising about 7 percent of phonograph preachers. Reverend Cora Hopson was the first. Little is known about Hopson's background. She broke the gender barrier in phonograph religion sometime in May 1926 at Paramount's Chicago studio. Having learned its lesson with the staid sermons of Reverend White, the label moved to recording folk sermons. However, Paramount was apprehensive about the profitability of recording a female preacher. For good measure, the label recorded Hopson preaching a composition with proven appeal: Paul Laurence Dunbar's 1896 poem, "Antebellum Sermon," a black dialect "sermon" highlighting the double entendre and irony of the Exodus story in slave preaching. In a two-part recording, Reverend Hopson chants the acclaimed and controversial sermonic verses without the aid of any accompaniment. While Hopson did not preach a self-authored sermon on her only trip to the studio pulpit, she did interject the practice of recording a multipart sermon into phonograph religion, a novelty male phonograph preachers would later adopt.[57]

Six black women followed Hopson over the next two years. On March 16, 1927, "The Lady Preacher" Evangelist R. H. Harris recorded

RECORD No. 8486

10 in., 75c

REV. LEORA ROSS

*and The Church Of The Living
God Jubilee Singers*

This record is as clear and powerful as if
you were face to face with this preacher.
A great sermon—worth hearing many times.

"DRY BONES IN THE VALLEY"

"A GAMBLER BROKE IN A
STRANGE LAND"

C OKeh Phonograph Corporation, 25 West 45th Street, New York City

Figure 4.3: Reverend Leora Ross sermon advertisement. Source: *Chicago Defender*, August 27, 1927, 3.

for Gennett Records, a label based in Indiana. Missionary Josephine Miles followed suit a year later. Sister Erna Mae Cunningham's media ministry got started with Paramount Records. Reverend Sister Mary Nelson teamed up with Vocalion, while Evangelist Anna Perry recorded two sermons, but never had her sermon released. All came from the sanctified church tradition. To be sure, some Pentecostal and holiness groups prohibited women from preaching because of their interpretation of biblical gender norms. However, some faith communities in this tradition looked past gender toward a single requirement: religious experience. Nevertheless, black women were rarely permitted to pastor congregations unless they established their own sanctified churches and denominations, as Elder Lucy Smith (All Nations Pentecostal Church, 1918) and Bishop Ida B. Robinson (Mount Sinai Holy Church of America, Inc., 1924) elected to do. The COGIC and Pentecostal Assemblies of the World, for example, still prohibit women pastors. Many sanctified churches continue to recognize the giftedness of black women preachers. Pastoring, however, is another story.[58]

The sermons of black women phonograph preachers, which included titles such as "Jesus Is Coming Soon," "Sign of Judgment," God's Warning to the Church," and "Holiness" (Parts 1 and 2) were focused on sanctified notions of Christian piety. They did not explicitly address gender discrimination in the church; however, their presence at the microphone was itself an overt challenge to established gender norms in black Protestantism. The simple visibility of these female pastors, evangelists, and missionaries in the studio pulpit and in black consumer culture challenged strongly held conceptions of gender and religious leadership and ability.[59]

Reverend Leora Ross was the most prominent black female preacher of the era. Her eight sermons made her the leading female preacher on wax. Ross was born around 1890 in Missouri. She migrated to Ohio in the early twentieth century. Ross and her husband, Reverend Marcellus, settled in Cincinnati. The ministerial duo was educated. Ross was a high school graduate while Marcellus was college educated. They bought a sizable home on Carlisle Avenue, an all-black neighborhood of factory workers, cooks, private servants, hotel porters, and barbers. The neighborhood residents were all renters, making the Ross family the only homeowners on the block. They were the proud owners of a radio set, one of two on the entire block. The coveted radio gave the Ross family access to the latest in media entertainment, including cutting edge religious radio programming such as fellow female broadcaster Aimee Semple McPherson.[60]

It is unclear how Ross was discovered by the phonograph industry. Perhaps the radio success of Pentecostal counterpart McPherson or McGee's lucrative phonograph ministry inspired her and Okeh. Nevertheless, on Wednesday May 4, 1927 Leora, accompanied by her Church of the Living God Jubilee Singers, gathered in Okeh's Chicago studio and, following blues recordings by famed singer and actress Hattie McDaniel (the first African American to win an Oscar), asserted her place in the world of black religious broadcasting.[61] Ross's husband was conspicuously absent from her recordings. Ross and her group of unidentified female singers made their media ministry an all-female affair. Ross's spiritual commodities, like Reverend McGee's, began with a song. She followed up with a chanted sermon, complemented by the moaning and humming of her all-female cast. The climaxes of her sermons were followed by another song. Ross's demonstrative worship and chanted sermon followed the proven pattern for success on the phonograph with one exception—it was an all-female ministry.

Reverend Ross addressed several biblical themes in her media ministry, including Ezekiel's vision of the valley of the dry bones. In her first recording, "Dry Bones in the Valley," Ross elaborated on the prophet's vision of human bones reassembling and coming back to life on account of Ezekiel's words. Ross used the metaphor as a springboard to admonish "dead" sinners to come to be reborn and to come to life through salvation in Jesus Christ. The sermon did not mention blues women, but the sermon advertisement made the implication clear (Figure 4.3). Her sermon ad featured a picturesque flapper: a woman with her hair cut short in a "Ponjola" bob, a plain dress that was short sleeved, form-fitting, and revealed her stockingless legs and high heel pumps. The flapper, who eschewed traditional morality by listening to jazz and dressing in a "revealing" way, is pictured stranded in a dry valley surrounded by death. She is stuck in the proverbial valley of sin. Her only salvation is a feminine angel descending from the sky. The sermon commercial proclaimed that the trailblazing female evangelist's homily was "as clear and powerful as if you were face to face with the preacher.

A great sermon—worth hearing many times."[62] Ross's sermon was marketed as an antidote to the culture of blues women and flappers.

The female broadcaster was also the first phonograph preacher to record a sermon that specifically covered a current event. In "God's Mercy to Colonel Lindbergh," she addressed the pilot's unprecedented and historic solo flight across the Atlantic. The phonograph industry attempted to capitalize on the moment. In June of that year, Victor used a total of fifteen records to record a live radio wiretap of Lindbergh's reception and ceremony. Okeh Records did not depict the event live, but they did ask Reverend Leora Ross to explain its biblical significance to all those who were interested. Following the song "He's a Prayer Answering Savior," Ross preached from Job 5:19: "From six troubles He will deliver you. Even in seven, evil will not touch you." Her sermon declared that God's mercy had enabled Charles Lindbergh to complete his historic nonstop trans-Atlantic flight. Encouraged by the shouts of the Church of the Living God Jubilee Singers, the preacher encouraged "the church" to remember that they prayed to the same God that "carried him across the ocean." Ross's innovation of titling and preaching her sermon on a current event brought a new style of preaching to the studio pulpit.[63]

Leading phonograph preachers followed her lead and preached several similar sermons. Reverend Gates's "Baptist World Alliance," for example, addressed the international religious meeting in Atlanta. "Joe Lewis Wrist and Fist" was recorded just a few days before the championship boxer defended his title.

Although Ross's media ministry was trendsetting, it was short-lived. Neither Okeh nor any other label invited her back to the studio. Consumers and the phonograph industry embraced and lauded blues women and later black female gospel singers. However, black women preaching on wax did not receive the same reception. To some, black women preachers were the consummate representatives of the skewed womanhood of the decade. This "new woman" of the 1920s, Deborah Gray White has written, "held a job in the expanding job market, made decisions based on her own wants and needs, and generally embodied the spirit of individualism." Such women migrated to the city and shed old notions of femininity, including the need to "choose between a career and marriage." Women were everywhere men were, including the ministry and the sacred studio to broadcast their sermons. Singing was acceptable, perhaps even expected of women. Preaching, however, was largely seen as a man's role.[64]

Black scholars and leaders of the era bemoaned this "encroachment" of black women upon the black male professional sphere. Leading black sociologist E. Franklin Frazier told the 1926 gathering of the National Urban League that "the larger freedom of women" and the rise of "bread-winning women" in urban America was integral to the "disorganization" of black family life. Women were out in the public sphere performing the duties that rightly belonged to men. The remedy rested in the acquisition of black male "education" and "technical skills." When black men acquired such "socialization," black women could retreat from the workplace and the black home could become a "functioning social unit." For Frazier, black social progress depended on gender essentialism. Likewise, Marcus Garvey's UNIA newspaper, the *Negro World*, declared, "Let us again place our women upon the pedestal from whence they have been forced into the vortex of the seething world of business." Black women, it averred, should depart from the masculine public sphere of business, politics, and preaching and once again act like "true" women. A letter, or perhaps written prayer, to the editor of the *New York Times* at the close of the roaring 1920s summed up such longing: "Dear God, give us back our Women!"[65]

Even the leading figure of phonograph religion was opposed to female preachers. Reverend Gates's sermon, "Manish Women" exemplifies his stand. The sermon, like Ross's, was released on Okeh. Perhaps Gates feared Ross's competition. His chanted sermon, accompanied by female affirmations, declared that women were "trying to do everything they see or hear of a man doin'." Women were "getting everywhere," including, to the preacher's dismay, "up in the church!"[66]

Phonograph preachers and consumers alike embraced the homiletical and marketing genius of Hobson's sermon series and Ross's topical sermons on current affairs, but they did not welcome the bearers of such innovation in the studio pulpit. As late as 1947, a national poll revealed that 47 percent of Americans still believed that women did not "make as good a minister as a man." The roaring twenties may have significantly fractured America's gender norms, but the stained glass ceiling, in and out of the studio pulpit, remained largely intact.[67]

•   •   •

When a music reviewer accounted for the meteoric success of Bessie Smith in 1924, the critic could just as well have spoken about the prominence of Reverends Gates, McGee, and the host of male preachers that followed their example. Smith's records, the commentator noted, possessed the "old" sounds and expressions of black life. The southern-born Smith enjoyed wide appeal precisely because she strove "constantly to retain those qualities which many a colored entertainer has lost beyond recall through a mistaken desire to take on a so-called metropolitan polish."[68] Similarly, the cadre of successful phonograph preachers were all born in the rural south a generation or so after slavery. When they migrated to different "metropolitan" parts of the nation they did not attempt to take on the urbane homiletical style of established urban churches. Instead, they all retained some aspects of their rural religious ethos and preached it on wax.

In the short span from Calvin Dixon in 1925 to Leora Ross in 1927, a total of thirty black ministers signed contracts to embark on their own mass media ministry. Those with the largest followings were the men who replicated the models of Gates and McGee. The chanted sermons of Baptist evangelist Reverend J. C. Burnett sold very well. Burnett, as one journalist of the day put it, recorded "good old-fashioned sermons in the manner made famous by the Reverend J. M. Gates." The native of Mobile, Alabama, joined the ministry around 1911 and recorded his first sermon, "The Downfall of Nebuchadnezzar," with Meritt, a small Kansas City label founded by entertainer and music store owner Winston Holmes. The small label had limited resources. Holmes primarily advertised out of the trunk of his Apperson sports car and virtually pressed records on demand. The sagacious and self-taught Burnett, who proudly claimed he had "never spent a day in school," successfully peddled his recorded sermon while preaching on the gospel tent circuit of Louisana, Mississippi, and Texas. The herculean self-promotion paid off. In the fall of 1926, Burnett was "discovered" by a Columbia talent scout. Columbia, unrelenting in its desire to lock down a folk preacher who could replicate Gates's success, inked a deal with Burnett while he was still under contract with Meritt. The *Defender* reported that Holmes responded with a lawsuit against Columbia in the Kansas City Circuit

Court. The small label owner was apparently no match for the corporate giant, as Columbia went on to record Burnett preaching the same sermon under the same title. It was a blockbuster, much to Holmes's chagrin, eventually receiving upward of 90,000 orders. The Holmes store and label folded in 1929, while Burnett went on to a rewarding media ministry. Burnett recorded forty-five sermons during the interwar period and continued to record after the war.[69]

Chicago's Bishop D. C. Rice felt led to start his media ministry after he heard Gates and McGee. The entrepreneurial Pentecostal preacher and his ten-person band including tambourines, cymbals, guitars, cornets, trombones, and drums approached Vocalion records for an audition armed with the same blueprint as McGee. Initially Vocalion rebuffed Rice. Executive Jack Kapp told Rice point blank that he did not think Rice and crew were worth "a nickel." Apparently Victor's success with McGee changed Kapp's tune. The label went on to sign Rice for $75 a sermon (comparable to approximately $5,000 today). His Pentecostal media ministry consisted of thirty-nine recordings.[70]

Baptist minister Reverend W. M. Nix (Nix's recordings are listed under A. W. Nix) was also a favorite. Similar to Gates, the Birmingham, Alabama native recorded chanted sermons on quotidian matters and popular events. As a member of the National Baptist Convention music committee—whose goal was to address the "urgent demand for real inspiring and adaptable music" in the Baptist church—he integrated popular music into his sermons. The adroit minister was a master marketer. His "Black Diamond Express to Hell, Parts 1 through 6" not only extended Hopson's sermon series innovation, it also came with a map of the Diamond Express Train's route. The train with "Sin [as] the engineer . . . Pleasure as the headlight, and the Devil as the conductor" made stops at Liars' Ave, Stealing Town, Drunkardsville, Fightstown, Gamblers' Tower, and Dance Hall Depot on its way to the eternal terminus. Nix recorded over fifty such sermons during his illustrious media ministry.[71]

What emerged was a predominantly male-centered template for popular black religious broadcasting: preaching in the common and simple vernacular, replicating popular entertainment, and emphasizing personal expressive worship. This recipe appealed to the rural black diaspora that was moving into America's cities. Migrants were able to grab hold of and lay claim to their heritage and religious practices, even in the strange lands of urban America. These consumers heard "home" every time the phonograph needle was placed on a sermon by Gates, McGee, Burnett, Rice, Nix, and the preachers that followed.

In all, by 1941 approximately one hundred black ministers had embarked on a mass media ministry using the phonograph, issuing more than seven hundred sermonic titles.[72] These enterprising apostles of record evangelism set a new standard for ministry. African American evangelical clergy and churchgoers adopted the idea that potent church work could be accomplished via the phonograph industry and black consumer culture. Evangelizing the nation and having a ministry with widespread influence were possible if the gospel was preached through a popular mass medium and packaged according to prevalent black cultural tastes. With sales competing with those of the best blues singers, corporate America woke up to the idea that black preaching could be a significant moneymaking enterprise. The die of popular black religious broadcasting was cast.

Yet, this newfound visibility and market success made phonograph preachers more than just modern religious broadcasters. They also became commercial icons.

A New Preacher for a New Negro

Phonograph Religion and the New Black Social Authority

Reverend James M. Gates and better known minister Reverend Martin Luther King, Sr. (1899–1984) epitomize the two primary ways in which black clerical authority was remade in the twentieth century. Both King and Gates relocated from rural Georgia to Atlanta in 1913 in the pursuit of a better life. Education at the Atlanta Baptist Institute (ABI) at 533 Auburn Avenue was the first measure the two migrants pursued. The elementary, secondary, and industrial educational institution had an enrollment of roughly two hundred students and a faculty of nine. It was supported by the state and local Baptist conventions as well as Wheat Street Baptist Church. The school's first principal was Sylvia Bryant, vice president at large of the Woman's Convention, Auxiliary of the National Baptist Convention (WC), and wife of Wheat Street Pastor Peter Bryant. Martin Luther King, Sr., began attending the school in 1920 at the age of twenty-one. Despite his rural junior high education, King tested into ABI's fifth grade. He initially refused. How, King wondered, could a grown man sit in a fifth grade classroom? However, he was comforted by the presence of older men like James Gates (fifteen years older than Martin King, Sr.) who were also placed in lower grades. The two rural migrants attended the same school, sat in the same rented classrooms on Auburn Avenue, took the same remedial courses, and perhaps even studied together. However, the similarities ended there.[1]

In 1926 King graduated from ABI and married Alberta Williams. The socioeconomic state of the black clergy made King reconsider going into the ministry. By the 1920s, the cloth, once a stalwart vocation of black leadership, was losing ground socially and economically to the new black urban professional class. "I began thinking," King recalled, "that I should consider again whether to stay in the ministry or go on out into the business world." King was convinced that wealth and social influence were swiftly shifting from the ministry to other white-collar professions. Prodding from his college-educated bride persuaded King to bring such professionalization to his ministry. He enrolled in the religious studies degree program at Morehouse College. Morehouse was one of the many black educational institutions founded in the south by Christian missionary societies following the Civil War. Most of these schools trained their ministers to eliminate cultural memes and practices seen as hindrances to the assimilation of bourgeois culture. Morehouse, supported by the Northern (later American) Baptist Convention, fit the bill perfectly. During this era, it became increasingly identified as an emblem of the new black middle class. As a student from the era proudly recalled, "Morehouse in its outlook, its composition, and its atmosphere" was "*the symbol*" of a new and rising black middle class of lawyers, physicians, teachers, businessmen, and clergy. King's professionalization included classes in systematic theology, biblical exegesis, Christian education, homiletics, and psychology. Morehouse was the place where ministers like King could shed all the cultural and aesthetic vestiges that made them "country bumpkins," as King put it, in order to become members of black America's nascent urban professional class.[2]

Martin King completed his bachelor of theology degree at Morehouse in 1930. Shortly after graduation, he commenced his career as pastor of the noted Ebenezer Baptist Church. By 1932, he was far removed from the days when Atlantans ridiculed him for his "dusty, un-creased clothes," and his "rough country style" of speaking and preaching. King rid himself of what he called the "whole uneducated green farm boy personality." Reverend King, the self-proclaimed "best paid negro minister in the city," enjoyed "great respect" in black and white society.[3] Indeed, by the end of the decade King owned a large home on the city's storied Auburn Avenue valued at $4,000, more than twice the median home value of black-owned homes, and ranking in the ninetieth percentile of black home values. And King's reported salary of $2,500, comparable to a six-figure salary today, was almost three times that of the average black urban minister. King's life and salary

were commensurate with those of many African American professionals.[4] He had definitely moved up in the world.

King's new status gave him access to the civic organizations and
social circles of the black elite. He rubbed shoulders with people such
as John Wesley Dobbs, the grand master of the Prince Hall masons and
the "mayor" of Auburn Avenue; Morehouse president Benjamin Elijah Mays; A. T Walden, legal counsel for the NAACP; and C. A. Scott,
publisher of the *Atlanta Daily World*, the nation's first daily black newspaper. From this position, King became an influential black leader in
Atlanta. He mobilized and organized black Atlanta for several causes,
including equal pay for black teachers as well as voting rights. King
used his specialized education and organizational affiliations to intel-
lectually, socially, and financially join the new black professional class.
He became a new preacher for a new era in black life.[5]

Reverend James M. Gates, on the other hand, did not establish his
social authority through such formal channels; rather, Gates's prestige
was based on the sphere of life phonograph preachers saw as the most
influential: consumer culture. In 1926, when King stepped foot on the
hallowed grounds of Morehouse to study systematic theology, exegesis,
evangelism, and the proper mechanics of preaching, Gates stepped into
Columbia's venerated studio and commenced his widely popular commercial ministry. Gates became a celebrity preacher: a minister who
enjoyed extensive fame, wealth, and social influence based on the success of the spiritual commodities he produced and promoted. Gates's
commercial ministry, as one black newspaper declared, made him an
influential minister "acclaimed throughout the nation."[6]

Celebrity status anointed Gates with noted social standing. He did
not rely on associations with career and organizational elites to lift him
to prominence. Rather, he befriended black celebrities such as Thomas
"Georgia Tom" Dorsey. Such connections, coupled with his wealth from
his commercial success, propelled him up the socioeconomic ladder.
Local black newspapers changed their perspective of the unschooled
folk preacher. Suddenly he was "stately and grand" and, along with the
city's rising black middle class, counted among Atlanta's "Who's Who."
His social arrival was announced: "Rev. J. M. Gates—Known in nearly
every home in the United States. He rode in singing 'The Little Black
Train Is Coming' on the Victrola." Indeed, Gates rode the wave of fame

into the hearts and spaces of the black elite. Members of the city's rising black middle class jockeyed to have Gates leave his migrant congregation at Mount Calvary in order to pastor their churches. C. S. Cox, the well respected owner and founder of the oldest black-owned funeral home in Atlanta, and Roosevelt Flannangan, manager of the pioneering and lucrative Auburn Avenue Service Station, lobbied successfully. During an elaborate installation service, they praised their new celebrity pastor, "known throughout the nation through the medium of the many phonograph records that have been made of some of his hard to forget sermons," as a sophisticated and urbane "Business Pastor."[7]

Some in the black community resented Gates's use of the marketplace, as opposed to an educational pedigree or institutional endorsements. Moreover, the existence of a black clergyman, especially a folk preacher, as a commercial icon was considered anathema to respectability. However, others saw Reverend Gates's ascension to celebrity preacher status as a badge of honor for the race and black Christianity. A black journalist aptly proclaimed, "You may say what you may, but all races have celebrities among them and can boast of them, so the Negro race has a celebrity in the person of Rev. Gates." Further, he viewed Gates's commercial success as the new mark and standard of excellence in ministry, adding that the celebrity preacher "has no peer as a sought for minister."[8] King and Gates were thus two ministers who represented two different clerical channels to leadership and prominence in black life.

•   •   •

Historically, black clergy have based their authority and status on two interrelated grounds. First, the very status of "minister" or "pastor" commanded special esteem in black communities. Clergy headed the church, one of the earliest autonomous institutions in the black experience. The church was the social, political, and religious center of black life and the minister oversaw it all. This "charisma of office" led Du Bois to describe the black preacher at the turn of the century as "[a] leader, a politician, an orator, a 'boss,' an intriguer, an idealist—all these he is, and ever, too, the centre [sic] of a group of men." Closely related to this, ministers also enjoyed leadership status because of the "charisma of person" or the belief that ministers have been endowed with supernatural gifts. Clergy received a "call" from God to be the divine representative and provide communities with biblical interpretation and ethical and moral guidance.[9]

These established norms of leadership were significantly contested during the period of mass urbanization. A research committee convened by President Hoover in the late 1920s noted the shift, concluding, "The most fundamental change in the intellectual life of the United States . . . is the apparent shift from Biblical authority and sanctions to scientific and factual authority and sanctions."[10] In black life, this challenge was particularly pronounced during the New Negro era. This phase of black history, argues cultural critic Gerald Early, can be roughly dated from 1915 to 1940. The period saw the rise of the "first modern and modernist black elites, that is, professional cadres of trained black people in artistic, bureaucratic, commercial, and academic circles."[11] Indeed, by 1930 the total number of black college graduates produced in the twentieth century was four times greater than in the entire previous century. Fewer than 5 percent of these graduates, however, were considering the ministry as a profession.[12] An interwar survey of urban black ministers found that 61 percent had an education ranging from high school to no formal schooling at all. The black population was growing increasingly educated during the interwar period, the ministry was not.[13] As Dr. Horace M. Bond, noted education scholar and later the first black president of Lincoln University, observed in 1925, there were striking intellectual developments among leaders in the fields of black journalism, literature, politics, institutions, and education, but "no like development of leadership can be seen on the part of the Negro Church."[14] Instead, the rising tide of college-educated African Americans pursued other white-collar professions. From 1910 to 1930 the number of black professionals more than doubled.[15] In the process of progressively occupying greater positions of influence, this budding company of black civic and social elites remade the criteria of distinction and leadership in black life on the basis of educational credentials, institutional connections, and income.

Clergy claims to authority based on the office and divine calling had less traction during the New Negro era. The new black intelligentsia contested the status of black ministers as the default embodiment of

political, social, cultural, business, and moral leadership. A black minister of the time commented incisively about the changing status of his
vocation, declaring in a front-page editorial of the *Chicago Defender*,
"We live in an age of specialists. The day of the proverbial 'jack of all
trades' has passed."[16] The new black professional class was educated in
its respective fields. However, black clergy had fallen largely behind.
The expertise of the New Negroes in law, medicine, social service, and
business as well as their affluence gave them equal claims on race leadership. A new culture of black professional leadership came to the fore
and the minister was no longer the focal vocation.

The Institute of Social and Religious Research summed up the
decline of old forms of black clerical authority in a 1933 study of black
Protestantism. "Formerly, the fact that a man belonged to the ministerial profession gave him a standing in the community that no other
man could command." However, a minister is now "required to take his
place along men of other professions and win leadership by achievement, and not by virtue of his profession."[17] The New Negro era forced
black ministers to reimagine how they would establish the respectability of the ministry and make claims to their right to exercise social
authority alongside the new black professional class.

Two primary traditions of New Negro clergy emerged. Ministers
such as Martin King, Sr., won influence and respect by modeling themselves after the culture of black professionalism. Such clerics laid claim
to race leadership through their focused and specialized education,
scholarly sermons and publications, denominational positions, and
connections to elite societies. This cadre of ministers sculpted themselves as professionals and public intellectuals.

Reverend Gates, on the other hand, initiated the tradition of black
clergy gaining authority through the commercial marketplace. The New
Negro era was shaped not just by the rise of trained black professionals,
but also by trends in black consumer culture. The cultural import of
the marketplace was just as significant as the traditional networks and
mediums of professionalization, particularly for African Americans
who lacked access to—or simply did not desire membership in—black
professional life. In this world, the marketplace functioned as the realm
where political and cultural ideals were expressed. In this "marketplace
intellectual life," the consumer market served as the arbiter of esteem

and clout, not the world of letters. And in this world, Reverend Gates was crowned the people's champion.[18]

Thus the spheres of black professionalism and the marketplace both offered clergy a pathway to distinction and a renewed sense of influence during the New Negro era. The black literati had their own rubric by which to choose their clergy of renown, even as the black consumer marketplace anointed its own. Much has been written about the former, little about the latter. Reverend James Gates is emblematic of this understudied tradition. He became a preacher for the New Negro era by patterning his ministry and lifestyle not after black professionals, but after the "intelligentsia" of the marketplace: black commercial celebrities.

Publicity

Publicity in the black press was a key component of the stature of New Negro clergy. Educated black clergy used the positive exposure of the black and white press to bolster their status alongside the commonly publicized accomplishments of New Negroes in business, education, politics, entertainment, and art. When black ministers engaged in "respectable" uplift, the black press commended them, helping to sustain the status of clergy as important and relevant race leaders and members of the African American professional class. Reverend Adam C. Powell, Sr., of Harlem's Abyssinian Baptist Church was fully aware that the "flattering publicity" of the press enhanced his influence. The Yale educated clergyman spoke for many ministers in his autobiography when he pointed to the press's role in lifting him to prominence. "[The press] has kept my work before the public. If I am well known all over the U.S. and Canada, it is not because I am brilliant but because the newspapers of both races have thought well of my work." The professional classes and learned societies regarded Powell and his ministry as being aligned with black professionalism: a New Negro Clergyman. Fittingly, Powell was awarded a 1929 Harmon Foundation Award for Distinguished Achievement among Negroes, joining the ranks of educated black professionals and race leaders such as Theodore Lawless, physician and foremost black dermatologist; Harry Freeman, composer of the first black opera; and John Hope, the first black president of Morehouse College.[19]

Figure 5.1: Okeh Records Christmas advertisement. Source: *Pittsburgh Courier,* December 24, 1927, 15.

In addition to racial uplift and social welfare work, ministers also looked to pen and pad to bolster their public persona. "Much has been done by the living voice to train and lead the people," argued the *Negro Baptist Pulpit,* "but the time has come when the pen must also be employed. Our trained leaders must write." Baptist minister Sutton E. Griggs, author of five novels and several religious tracts, concurred,

"To succeed as a race we must move up out of the age of the voice." The seminary-trained preacher predicted in 1916 that when African Americans were "capable of being moved to action on a large scale by what they read, a marked change in the condition of the race will begin instantly and will be marvelous in its proportions." A host of New Negro clergy wrote and published their sermons. These discourses were often printed in black newspapers and cited and quoted as speaking for black people, even as they were debated in black intellectual circles. Such ministerial contributions embodied what Reverend Reverdy C. Ransom called the work of "the New Negro." In his 1923 poem of the same name, Ransom characterized such men as "bearing rich gifts to science, religion, poetry and song." Pen and pad, not the voice, established clergy as black professionals in tune with the intellectual ethos of the New Negro era.[20]

Reverend Gates, however, could not depend on black high society and newspapers for complimentary publicity or for affirmation of his ministry. The black literati did not offer rosy opinion pieces on his brand of folk religion. It was too loud, demonstrative, and did not cohere with the literary intellectual climate of racial progress and respectability. Moreover, the orality and aurality of Gates's religious expression were rooted in a bygone era, one that black professionals believed was best left to the past (or made into a written tradition, as in James Weldon Johnson's *God's Trombones*).

The consumer market, then, not glowing editorials or the recognition of the black literati, offered Reverend Gates and his ministry affirmation and publicity. Black periodicals and their journalists often despised his commercials, but black newspapers published the ads because they desperately needed the advertising revenue. And the consumer market, judging by sermon sales, was just as influential in reaching the black masses as the channels of the black literati. By the 1920s even Reverend Sutton Griggs conceded as much. The published Baptist minister and advocate of the written word tried his hand in the studio pulpit in 1928, recording a staid sermon for Victor. Griggs's aversion to black popular tastes in favor of a lectured styled sermon doomed his sermon sales. He was never invited back to the mic.[21]

Popular black religious broadcasters such as Reverend Gates, however, took all their cues from black popular culture. In addition to their preaching, they also fashioned their public exposure and persona after the culture of black commercial celebrity. Gates received and pursued a similar brand of advertising as top billed black entertainment celebrities, often appearing alongside them. One mail order advertisement for Christmas shoppers in 1927 declared, "Merry Christmas! Give Records!" Reverend Gates's deliberately pointed sermon topic, "Will the Coffin Be Your Santa Claus," an admonition to remember Jesus during the holiday, was prominently featured alongside the latest releases of artists Louis Armstrong and Duke Ellington. (Figure 5.1). Like Armstrong and Ellington, Gates was a commercial icon, selling a profitable commodity, particularly during the Christmas holiday season. Similarly, race record catalogs, such as the 1929 RCA-Victor catalog, marketed Gates in the same manner as Duke Ellington. The sales booklet, labeled "Vocal Blues, Religious, Red Hot Dance Tunes, and *Sermons*" prominently features pictures of the two top-selling artists and celebrities alongside their respective bevy of records (a digital copy of the sales booklet can be viewed at the Library of Congress, http://hdl.loc.gov/loc. mbrsrs/amrlr.lr03). Such marketing helped to secure and reinforce Reverend Gates's place as a noteworthy figure in black life. According to consumer culture, Gates was among the black rich and famous: worthy of iconic status, public adulation, and emulation. Such popular publicity led one consumer to conclude that Reverend Gates was "the greatest preacher there is, I reckon."[22]

The marketing of Gates's prolific media ministry was not only shaped by black celebrity culture, it also gave him more media exposure than many black superstars. From 1926 until 1932, when the Depression curtailed phonograph advertising, Gates's name, likeness, and image were in constant view of the national populace. In the *Chicago Defender*, for example, Gates and his spiritual commodities enjoyed greater face time than record advertisements for jazz and blues greats Duke Ellington, Flethcher Henderson, Sara Martin, Charley Patton, Ethel Waters, Clara Smith, and Victoria Spivey. In all, the volume of Gates's ads equaled those of Ma Rainey. Gates's fame was equal to that of leading black entertainers. The commercials regularly described him as "Atlanta's great race preacher" and "the well-known race preacher." The *Atlanta Daily World* credited Reverend Gates with being "known all over the United States."[23] While professional journalists and the black literati championed New Negro ministers like King and Powell; black consumer culture, however, crowned phonograph preachers like Gates.

As opposed to denominational leadership and elite channels, the phonograph industry and consumer culture provided Reverend Gates with an organizational apparatus to coordinate and promote his work. As they did for leading black entertainers, labels alerted the black press to Reverend Gates's travels and appearances. These tours, again echoing the practice of black entertainers, were used to further promote and sell his latest sacred commodity and reap the harvest of his fame. For example, the *Pittsburgh Courier* announced Bessie Smith's tour of Birmingham, Alabama. When Smith performed at the Frolic Theatre, the paper reported that the streets were blocked off and "hundreds and hundreds [were] unable to gain entrance to this performance." Moreover, according to the *Courier,* copies of Bessie Smith's "Gulf Coast Blues" were sold during the intermission. When artists such as Bessie Smith, Armstrong, and Ellington went on such tours, Reverend Gates went on revival.[24]

When Gates traveled to preach in Chicago, the label alerted the *Chicago Defender*. The paper heralded Reverend Gates's arrival. Four years after his groundbreaking release of his copyrighted "Death's Black Train Is Coming," the *Defender* announced, "Author of 'Death's Black Train' Is Here!'" The newspaper wrote that during his revival tour of the city, the celebrity cleric "preached to record-breaking audiences at Friendship Church" and the "Metropolitan Church." During a revival in Cincinnati, Ohio, Gates was lauded as a "Victor" recorder and a "leader in the field of song and gospel." The paper assured the public that the icon would not only be "heard" on his records but also "seen" in the city for a ten-day revival tour. Despite, a "six-inch snow blanket," the Cincinnati faithful came out in droves to see Gates. They had heard Gates on the phonograph and seen him in the marketplace, but not even inclement weather stopped them from finally seeing the celebrity in the flesh.[25]

In another Ohio revival, the preacher made appearances in migrant cities across the state, including Cleveland and Akron. Gates also spent two days at the Reverend J. H. Burke's church in Columbus, Ohio, reportedly the largest church in the state. Reports declared that the celebrity preacher was so popular that the city's black churches had invited him to stay for an extended revival tour. Likewise, in Chatta-nooga, Tennessee, "white and colored alike" tried to get the preacher to extend his stay. Churchgoers were reduced to standing room only to see and hear Gates. "He is too big for any church in this city," the reporter noted. If Gates prolonged his tour, religious leaders vowed to try to reserve "the city auditorium for him so that the people can be seated." Gates declined both offers. Purchasing his sermons would have to suffice for the Columbus and Chattanooga faithful.[26]

Gates's forays into selling the gospel made him a well-known minis-ter and famous figure in black life. Indeed, the front page of the *Pitts-burgh Courier* declared that thanks to phonograph religion, "There is the now celebrated Rev. J. M. Gates of Atlanta."[27] His celebrity and influence were not steeped in education and institutional connections or pedigree; rather they were based on his commercial success. Gates did not seek the respectability and status of black elites but the wide-spread recognition of consumer culture. This was the sphere that con-ferred social authority upon Reverend Gates and his ministry. New Negro clergy had to distinguish themselves and their ministries amidst a growing and diversified culture of black professionalism. Commercial celebrity provided one means to such distinction.

Wealth

On February 25, 1928, the cover of the *Pittsburgh Courier* reported that Reverend Gates "preached his way to wealth through the phonograph!" His Christmas sermon "'Will the Coffin Be Your Santa Claus,' brought the big royalty checks flying in!" Reverend Gates's commercial celebrity brought him considerable wealth. Gates's income as a minister, as the front-page coverage indicates, was significant during the New Negro era. At the turn of the century the socioeconomic status and quality of life of ministers began to significantly trail other professional occupa-tions. By the 1920s, there was a pronounced decrease in the real earn-ings of ministers. The typical annual salary of a clergyman had the pur-chasing power of about $574 at the end of the nineteenth century. By 1928, it had fallen to $522.[28]

The common salaries of white-collar professionals surpassed the earnings of the ministry. Ministers made about $1,400 annually. African

American ministers averaged even less. As late as the mid-1930s, over a third of urban black clerics were still receiving less than $1,000 in annual compensation (the percentage of white ministers in this salary bracket was 4 percent). Rural black clergy led several churches to scrape up a salary of about $500 a year. However, physicians, college faculty, and public school teachers netted between $1,800 and $9,000 annually. Salary workers in manufacturing and the railroad industry, as well as federal employees, ranged from $1,700 to $2,500 a year.[29]

Ministers not only trailed other professionals, but they also made less money than many working-class wage earners. By the close of the 1920s, the average minister's salary was less than those in the automotive, iron and steel, and the paper and printing industries. This economic turn was particularly pronounced in black communities as the number of black automotive workers increased by almost 2,800 percent between 1910 and 1930. The rising classes of urban laborers were economically superior to the ministers in their communities.[30]

The *Homiletical Review* deplored the fact that wage laborers made more money than ministers. The editors declared that "the splendid men whose hours of labor in the parish and pulpit exceed those of any other class" should be paid a higher salary, one that permits them to "live on the plane which their position demands." Likewise, a Presbyterian minister, a denomination whose clergy salaries were among the highest in the country, argued before the Presbyterian General Assembly that the failure to compensate clergy in the fashion of other professionals was "an economic and moral crime." Such economic and social decline led one frustrated minister to confess that he had left the ministry precisely because he "could no longer endure the degrading experience of looking down from my six hundred dollar pulpit into the faces of people to whom I was forced to owe money."[31] The ministry, especially in black communities, was once a consummate professional vocation, but by the 1920s ministers were quickly slipping out of the professional class.

Du Bois observed that the economic slippage of ministers would result in a shift in leadership in the black community. "The habit is forming of interpreting the world in dollars," he lamented. In this world, "The old leaders of Negro opinion . . . are being replaced. . . . [N]either the black preacher nor black teacher leads as he did." Rather, "all those with property and money" were rising as the embodiment of leadership in black communities.[32] Upward economic mobility, not tradition, constituted the new rubric of race leadership.

The New Negro era established a trend: the average black Protestant minister was no longer guaranteed the lifestyle, privileges, income and status of the black professional classes. New Negro clergy were confronted with a sliding pay scale and a culture that was increasingly equating income and upward mobility with social influence and authority.

Phonograph preachers used their income from selling the gospel to shore up their socioeconomic status. To be sure, the wealth of American celebrities (black or white) often pales in comparison to corporate CEOs. However, the visibility of celebrity, as opposed to the relative invisibility of the bosses of commerce and industry, inclines the broader public to identify celebrities as the standard bearers of affluence and status. Such recognition helped celebrity clergy stake claims to respectability.[33]

Reverend Gates received a $200 cash advance from A&R Polk Brockman. This income instantly catapulted Gates up the local black socioeconomic ladder. As late as the 1930s, the median annual income for black families in Atlanta hovered around $615, with 83 percent of black families only making about $476 a year. Gates's advance, then, was significant. His late night negotiations with the determined record executive garnered him almost half what the average black family in Atlanta made in an entire year. Agreeing to sell the gospel facilitated the migrant preacher's immediate ascension to economic respectability.[34]

Reverend Gates's total income from his fifteen-year media career is not completely clear. However, the compensation practices of the industry offer some insight. By the middle of the 1920s race record labels such as Okeh Records negotiated royalty agreements with many of their leading artists. In general, these agreements guaranteed artists between 1 and 2 cents per record sale (today artists receive about 7 to 10 cents per download and 0.5 to 0.7 cent per stream). Leading artists prospered through this arrangement. Victoria Spivey, for example, testified that her first royalty check from Okeh Records for "Black Snake Blues" was in the amount of $5,000. Jazz pianist and prolific songwriter Clarence Williams reportedly garnered about $10,000 a year in royalties during the 1920s.[35]

At 2 cents a record, Gates would have earned roughly $1,200 in royalty payments for his first two recorded sermons alone. In economic terms his royalties were twice the median income of black families in Atlanta and placed him squarely among the black elite. Gates's royalties were about half of Reverend King, Sr.'s annual salary and certainly more than what the average black preacher made. His royalty income was equal to the general annual salary of Atlanta's black schoolteachers, the highest compensated black teachers in the state.[36] Gates's royalties from his first two recordings also equaled some faculty salaries at some of the city's esteemed black colleges. Benjamin Elijah Mays, for example, joined the faculty and administration at Morehouse College after graduating from the highly regarded Bates College. As a full-time faculty member at Morehouse from 1921 to 1924, Mays was paid an annual salary of $1,200, the same as Gates's initial royalties.[37]

The selling of recorded sermons therefore enabled Gates to establish the same kind of socioeconomic lifestyle as the city's black professionals, something the overwhelming majority of black preachers could not do. Although he did not have the education of the teachers and professors, he had the salary. When the royalty checks starting "flying" in, as the Pittsburgh Courier put it, Reverend James Gates and his ministry were elevated to a different plane.

In addition to royalties, exclusive artists also received flat rate payments. In the heyday of the 1920s, top-selling exclusive artists received between $75 and $200 per recorded side or $150 to $400 per record.[38] Reverend Gates probably received about $100 per sermon or $200 per record. Here again the salary of Benjamin Mays provides an illustration. Mays, in addition to being on the faculty at Morehouse, also served as pastor of the nearby Shiloh Baptist Church. The 125-member church paid him a monthly salary of approximately $100, from which he paid the "choir director twenty-five to forty dollars a month." Gates stood to make more money recording one sermon than Mays's entire monthly salary as a pastor.[39]

In view of this situation, Gates amassed significant wealth at the outset of his career. In 1926 alone Reverend Gates released over ninety sermons. This output likely amounted to $9,000, which was what top-rated white physicians earned during the 1920s. In current terms, the flat payments amounted to more than half a million dollars.[40]

Gates did not have to pursue specialized education or join distinguished black organizations to rub shoulders with New Negroes. He established himself economically and socially among the nation's urban professionals by virtue of the marketplace. Social authority based exclusively on the ministerial office was on the wane. Conversely, authority based on upward mobility and wealth stood on solid ground during the New Negro era. Few ministers exemplified this more than Gates.

Automobiles

Reverend Gates used his car as the primary means of authenticating his status. During the New Negro era, virtually no other item had greater cultural and social value in black life than automobiles. Cars have been a significant cultural and social signifier in America since their invention. Car ownership, the *New York Times* wrote in 1922, "implies higher individual power . . . and [a] potentially higher social state." The *Atlanta Constitution* added that in cars "there is life, health, happiness." The thrill of car ownership expanded rapidly during the 1920s. In 1920 there were 9 million cars in use across the country. By 1922, the number had risen to 11 million, comprising 83 percent of the world's cars. Over the course of the decade the number of car registrations in the nation more than doubled, rising from 9 million to more than 23 million. Accordingly, the *New York Times* advocated that the word "automobility" be added to the nation's dictionaries. "Truly," the paper wrote, "we are an automotive or an automobile people."[41] In black communities, vehicles took on even greater significance in light of the Jim Crow laws of public transit. These laws prohibited African Americans from boarding streetcars or buses until all white passengers had been seated and mandated that black riders enter and exit from the rear and never under any circumstances sit beside or in front of white passengers.[42]

Cars provided a means of circumventing such laws. The *Negro World*, the weekly newspaper of Marcus Garvey's UNIA, avidly supported black car ownership, declaring that cars enabled African Americans "to enjoy personal liberty and to go from one city or state to another unrestrained."[43] Writing for the Urban League, Alfred Edgar Smith, a member of President Franklin D. Roosevelt's "Black Cabinet," stated that

black car ownership and driving were "good for the spirit." The quality, speed, and appearance of one's car were irrelevant. All that mattered,
Smith thought, was that cars gave African Americans the ability "to just
give the old railroad Jim Crow the laugh."[44] Journalist and author George
Schuyler expressed similar sentiments in H. L. Mencken's popular magazine the *American Mercury*. Schuyler argued that the infamous troubles
of the biblical character Job were "trivial" compared to the plight of African American travelers. He instructed "all Negroes who can do so, purchase an automobile as soon as possible in order to be free of discomfort,
discrimination, segregation and insult. This is a gesture of manliness and
independence." Car ownership was seminal to the black experience of
emancipation. It offered African Americans aspects of civil and human
rights that were otherwise legally and violently denied. In a sense, "automobiles supplied one significant means to measure the distance travelled
toward political freedoms and public respect."[45]

The cultural value of cars coupled with their mass production made
vehicles more common across socioeconomic strata. Yet cars remained
a seminal object of distinction in black life. Branded wares such as
clothes and timepieces, for example, could be easily forged. A fast, distinguished, and pricey brand name vehicle, however, left little room for
class piracy. For this reason, black professionals purchased high-class
cars. Black celebrities, in particular, disproportionately invested in luxury cars. The black famous were deprived of many of the appurtenances
of their celebrity status. No matter how famous and wealthy black icons
suffered the same sting of segregation and discrimination as the black
populace. Unlike white icons, they were legally denied accommodations that were commensurate with their stature as well as the acceptance of high society. Black celebrities, unlike their white counterparts,
would never find their names on the White House guest list. A luxury
car, then, was more than just a means of transportation or symbol of
citizenship and class for black celebrities. It was a means by which black
celebrities set themselves apart from everyday people. An extravagant
vehicle was one of the few conspicuous canvases on which black icons
could depict and proclaim their celebrity for all to see.[46]

Black newspapers signaled the importance of such purchases by
chronicling them often. One black periodical openly debated who was
"Harlem's Best Car Owner," detailing and comparing the owners of

luxury cars in the city. Another gave front-page coverage to elite vehicle purchases across the country.[47] Although black icons could not enjoy all the trappings of their white celebrity counterparts, they could at least drive like them.

Duke Ellington recalled the period as a time when he and his fellow black entertainers "were all crazy about automobiles." By the 1920s, Ellington was sporting a Chandler motorcar. These luxury vehicles, ranging in price from roughly $1,800 to $3,000 (comparable to about $100,000 to $180,000 today) were highly regarded for their reliability and speed.[48] Ethel Waters did not know how to drive, but she demanded that Paramount purchase her a convertible Locomobile in exchange for recording four songs for the label. Locomobiles, according to one car historian, were "exceptionally fine and very expensive cars." They featured glass lamps designed by Tiffany & Co. and elegant interiors devised by Elsie De Wolf, arguably the country's first professional interior decorator. The namesakes of the Wrigley, Carnegie, Wanamaker, and Vanderbilt families all had Locomobiles. Fittingly, the company's advertising slogan declared it to be "Easily the Best Built Car in America." Waters had to have it.[49]

In 1926, Bessie Smith purchased a Cadillac convertible right off the showroom floor for her husband. The white car salesman was in the process of graciously asking the black phonograph star to leave the dealership when Bessie informed him she wanted to buy the custom car. The salesman attempted to dissuade her by telling her the showpiece cost $5,000 (comparable to spending $300,000 today or the base price of a Maybach). Bessie flipped up the front of her dress, reached into her underlying overalls, retrieved the small fortune, and paid cash for the car. The white salesman, Bessie happily recalled, nearly fainted. As they drove the car off the showroom floor, Bessie reveled in the compensatory nature of shopping and cruising on the same terms as the nation's white elite.[50]

Reverend Gates modeled himself after this celebrity car culture. As Duke, Ethel, and Bessie sported luxury cars, Gates also rolled in style. A black journalist in Atlanta witnessed Reverend Gates driving a luxury car and proudly wrote, "Stately and grand Reverend J. M. Gates, the nationally known pastor glides down Auburn in his Hupp Car."[51] The Hupp Motor Car Company in Detroit, Michigan maintained a relatively exclusive clientele. In 1930, the company ranked seventeenth in automotive sales, right

The new
low cost of luxury
and distinction

The extremely low prices of these wonderful new Century Hupmobiles is no barrier to their entree into circles of wealth and strict discrimination, where good taste is a supreme criterion of motor car ownership and value. ¶ It is good taste to own a Century Six or Eight no matter where you live or what your income. In design these Century models possess a correct and dignified distinction. In performance they are a complete embodiment of the Twentieth Century's best. ¶ 42 body and equipment combinations standard and custom, on each line. Six of the Century, $1800 to $2190. Century Eight $2470 to $2870. All prices f. o. b. Windsor

HUPMOBILE 1929
CENTURY
SIX AND EIGHT

Figure 5.2: Hupmobile advertisement. Source: *MacLean's Magazine*, October 1, 1928, 41.

behind Bessie's beloved Cadillac. In 1930, the price of a Hupmobile averaged about $1,900, which amounts to over $100,000 today. These prices were significantly higher than the average price tags of Chevrolet (about $500) and Ford (about $800), the top two selling U.S. automobile brands in the 1930s.[52] Gates's Hupmobile was far from an average car.

Hupp marketed its cars as scions of "luxury and distinction." The company claimed that its cars provided an "entree into circles of wealth and strict discrimination." Hupmobiles were known for the sheen of their plush mohair interiors, uniquely colored paint combinations, aerodynamic design, sloped windshields, chrome wheel discs, and relatively high speeds. Accordingly, the company made distinctive appeals to the sexes. "The style-conscious woman" would unmistakably recognize the "smartness and modernity" of a Hupmobile just as easily as she would spot "the latest gown by the Paris Grande Couture." The combination of style and speed made the Hupmobile "Her car for its dash; his car for its deeds!" (Figure 5.2).[53]

The Atlanta news reporter's reaction, and later boast to his readers that he got "a lift in Rev. J. M. Gates [sic] Car," indicates the social significance of Reverend Gates's luxury vehicle. Even as late as 1936, only 17 percent of Atlanta's black families possessed an automobile, compared to 63 percent of the city's white families. In black Atlanta, possessing a car made a statement. Possessing a luxury car made an even more emphatic statement. Moreover, being "spotted" driving on Auburn Avenue was a jackpot of social capital. The "Ave," as one black journalist characterized it, "is to Atlanta what Seventh Ave. is to New York, Wylie Ave. is to Pittsburgh, Beale Street is to Memphis or Ninth Ave. is to Chattanooga." Auburn Avenue was the center of the black social world in Atlanta. Being seen on the Ave with the latest accouterments was sure to make one the topic of social chatter and gossip. The preacher's Hupmobile and its high price tag and lavish features, then, were an outward manifestation of the commercial celebrity he had become, all put on display on the all-important Auburn Avenue. The Hupmobile was the first in a line of luxury cars for the preacher. The *Atlanta Daily World* even joked that every Christmas Gates probably told Santa Claus, "I got a new automobile . . . throw a paid in full note or two in my stocking." In an era when the professional status of the ministry was unstable and car possession was a status symbol of freedom for some and celebrity for others, Gates's standing was apparently only as distinguished as the car he drove. He lacked the pedigree of the establishment clergy as well as the growing classes of black professionals. However, his commercial celebrity and his ostentatious automobile enabled him to traverse the famed Auburn Avenue, the city, and region, in the exclusive manner of the professional and celebrity classes.[54]

Residence

Gates's luxury car solidified his celebrity, but when he purchased a home in a majority-white neighborhood he laid claim to respectability and

social mobility. Home ownership did not have the same cultural significance in black celebrity life. Bessie Smith, for example, was reportedly making $2,000 a week, half that during the Depression (roughly
$100,000 to $70,000 a week by today's standards). Yet the constantly
touring Smith rented modest residences—a cozy apartment in New
York City and a humble home on Webster Street in Philadelphia.[55] In a
neighborhood of black laundresses, porters, and waitresses, Smith paid
about $18 a month for her home in the city of brotherly love, almost
twice the median monthly rental cost of black homes.[56] Duke Ellington's home on Harlem's Edgecombe Avenue, a neighborhood known as
Sugar Hill, was more affluent. Living in the "citadel of stately apartment
buildings and liveried doormen," soaring over the rest of Harlem, cost
Ellington five times what Bessie Smith paid; but Ellington also rented.[57]

However, black home ownership was characteristic of the black professional class. Two landmark studies noted the trend. Black economist
Paul Edwards's study of black consumer practices and sociologist E.
Franklin Frazier's diagnosis of the black middle class both concluded
that black home ownership had become a standard mark of the black
bourgeoisie.[58] The bigger the better. Buying a home in a white neighborhood had even more cachet. President Hoover's national inquiry
into housing revealed that when possible African Americans tended
to move into predominantly white residential areas to signal their
increased income and higher class status. Proximity to whites was not
the main reason for this. Rather, a majority-white neighborhood gave
one access to better homes and city services.[59] Cars were flashy, but buying a home, and in a white neighborhood no less, was a pronounced
status move, one that signaled upward mobility.

When Gates and his wife Nellie arrived in Atlanta in 1913, their abys-
mal living conditions were emblematic of postbellum southern cities.
Many black residents lived in small tenement houses tucked into alleys.
According to a 1908 study of African American families, the majority of these homes were a crowded cluster of one- to two-room cabins
consisting of siding with "unfinished boards running up and down; no
ceiling or plastering, no windows, no paint, and an open fire space" for
cooking and heating. All this was "set directly on the grown, without a
cellar or foundation." Six to eight people or several families often shared
each adjoining home.[60]

James and Nellie shared such a small home with at least one other family. In addition to having a dirt floor, the home also lacked running water. The majority of Summerhill residents collected water from outdoor wells, springs, and watering holes. Residents had to collect and haul water to their dwellings and then heat the murky water over their open fire pit for cooking, cleaning, and bathing. Moreover, the residents shared community outhouses for bathroom facilities. At least once a week community members would empty the communal human waste from the outhouse. The lack of proper sewage made the community water sources dangerous because they were apt to be infected by the runoff of outhouse sewage. In addition to unsanitary water, the practice of placing the city's trash dumps in black neighborhoods made neighborhoods such as Summerhill reek from the stench of decomposing garbage. Most of the streets in the migrants' neighborhood were not paved and most thoroughfares lacked sidewalks. The combination of rain and the periodic emptying of outhouse refuse kept the ground saturated. With no sewage, the neighborhood was seemingly always drowned in muck and mud. One child recalled having to "wade through seas of mud whenever it rained" just to get to the neighborhood's black primary school. Furthermore, the soiled land made it difficult to traverse, let alone build and maintain solid home foundations. The majority of the homes were built on low and uneven foundations, which made them prone to flooding. The few streets in Summerhill that were paved were located in the white residential sections. The roads were covered in a patchwork of granite block and broken stone, known as macadam, and typically bound with tar or bitumen. James and Nellie left the farms of the black belt and landed in one of Atlanta's underserved black working-class neighborhoods.[61] Such accommodations were meager, unlikely to gain the respect of the black professional class. In fact, the black middle class often viewed such neighborhoods as dens of vice.

Gates left his impoverished residence on Martin Street soon after the success of his media ministry. He purchased a new modern home on Fraser Street, joining the 15 percent of black families in Atlanta who owned their own homes. His new home was valued at $3,000, more than twice the median value of black-owned homes, ranking approximately in the ninetieth percentile of national black home values.[62] Not only did home ownership reflect the preacher's new status, but so did the socioeconomic and racial composition of the neighborhood. The couple's Martin Street home was a solidly black working-class neighborhood consisting of laundresses and unskilled laborers. However, the demographics of Fraser Street were very different. The Gates's new neighborhood on Fraser Street was made up primarily of white professionals, including a white railroad/street car conductor, a white city policeman, and a white postal worker. Living next door to the migrant preacher at 422 Fraser Street was Joseph Silverman, a grocery store proprietor, and his family. They were Russian Jews who had migrated to America in 1916. They lived on the second floor of their home and used the bottom floor to operate a small independent grocery store.[63]

When the preacher gazed upon his new neighborhood, he did not see the dirt floors and muddy thoroughfares of Martin Street. Rather, this majority-white neighborhood was complete with stable cement housing foundations and paved roads for the ease of automobile travel. The homes included garages, a new amenity among the wealthy classes. His prized Hupmobile demanded this feature. Moreover, the homes were loaded with "all the modern conveniences such as gas, electric lights, bath room, hot and cold water." Although Gates's former and current homes were a few blocks from one another, in reality they were worlds apart.[64] Gates's new home showed that he had climbed the social ladder from migrant folk preacher to respected clergyman.

Gates's new home also featured the luxury of phone service. Phones grew at an unprecedented rate in America during the interwar period. In 1900 there were 1.3 million telephones in the country. By 1930, that number had grown to 20.2 million. Despite this growth, phone service was still a relative rarity. In the 1930s, there were only 163 phones per thousand persons, on average. Nationally less than half of all U.S. households had telephones. Less than 25 percent of the homes in Reverend Gates's neighborhood had a telephone during this era.[65] The master communicator and nouveau riche preacher had to have a phone in his home. It reflected his new social standing.

The modern amenities of James and Nellie's new home provided the space and means for new forms of classed socializing. Electric and gas cook stoves, for example, transformed home fireplaces from cooking spaces to modern spaces of "recreation, listening, and hosting social gatherings." To entertain such fireside "chats" was a classed practice, one that could only be properly accomplished if one had the latest appliances. The couple took advantage of the social trend. Around 1927, the same mail order catalogs that sold the preacher's sermons began selling fireplace screens as a safety measure for socializing around the fireplace. Black newspapers lauded how the preacher joyously entertained reporters, friends, black socialites and business elite, and parishioners around his fireplace during gatherings and birthday parties. Moreover, the new modern cooking stove freed Nellie from the laborious task of cooking over a fireplace, giving her slightly more time to socialize and host gatherings alongside her well-known and respected spouse. The ability to throw such parties in one's home was rare in black Atlanta. As late as 1940, only slightly more than 10 percent of the city's black households had gas or electric stoves. The Gateses thoroughly enjoyed displaying their new class and elite status.[66]

•   •   •

The installation and dedication of Reverend Gates's new church were telling. Speakers at the celebratory front-page affair included professionally trained clergy such as Morehouse and Garrett Theological Seminary grad Reverend William Holmes Borders. After several special music selections and a number of speeches, the black middle class congregation dedicated its new building and installed its new pastor. The minister charged with introducing and "presenting the pastor" was none other than Reverend Martin Luther King, Sr. Gates did not follow the path of black professionalization like Borders and Kings, but he nonetheless, became a New Preacher for the New Negro.[67]

As Reverend Gates's life experience shows, commercial celebrity was a pathway for black religious clerics to maintain a sense of relevance and authority for their profession and gospel. Selling the gospel in the marketplace provided an avenue for clergy to maintain a sense of social authority and upward mobility during the New Negro era. And for some religious producers and buyers alike, the sanction of the market was more meaningful and influential than the recognition and channels of the black literati. The financial payoff from the media ministry of the phonograph gave clergy the opportunity to spend, drive, live, socialize, and communicate like other members of black America's growing middle classes at a time when the ministry was increasingly slipping out of the professional ranks and losing its social authority and legitimacy. The marketplace and mass media were thus significant factors in the shaping of modern black religious authority.

Building ministerial authority on the foundation of commercial celebrity was a swift and conspicuous process. However, there were limits to using the "new measures" of spiritual commodities to establish such standing. Charles Finney, the nineteenth-century spokesman for "new measures" in Christianity, warned new measures ministers to be careful that their innovations exposed sin and vice "without forming new hiding places for them." The new measure of phonograph religion utilized consumer capitalism to combat the sinfulness and immorality of modern life. However, phonograph religion was also, then, stalked by a lurking truth: It was deeply subject to the dictates and whims of corporate culture.[68]

"Say Good-Bye to Chain Stores!"

Recorded Sermons and Protest

"I tell ya!" Reverend James Gates passionately sermonized to the congregation gathered for his April 25, 1930 Okeh sermon recording in Atlanta, "I hear and see so much evil that is being done through the chain store manner!" The preacher's two-part recorded sermon, *Goodbye to Chain Stores*, directed "both white and colored too" to stop shopping at chain stores.[1] America was being increasingly engulfed by chain stores during this period. From 1920 to 1932, chain stores increased 500 percent, from 30,000 stores dotting the country to an inescapable 159,638 stores, the highest number in American history. By the close of the 1920s, chain stores comprised 10 percent of all retail stores, but accounted for 22 percent of total retail sales. Approximately 20 cents of every dollar spent in American retail went to the country's growing assortment of chain stores. American retail was rapidly shifting from the hands of individual proprietors of small local businesses to the hands of chain corporations.[2] Like countless other Americans, Gates viewed the meteoric rise of retail chains such as Sears, Montgomery Ward, and J. C. Penney, and grocery giants such as the Great Atlantic and Pacific Tea Company, better known as A&P, as profoundly detrimental to local economies as well as to Protestant faith communities.

Many opponents of chain stores viewed their emergence as a corporate invasion into daily life. Chain stores were financially supported and operated by distant Wall Street speculators and financiers. For example, by 1914 the chairman of Chase National Bank sat on the board of directors for Woolworth's and Sears. Charles Merrill of Merrill Lynch bankrolled and exercised considerable control over several chains, including Kresge—the predecessor of Kmart—and grocery chain Safeway. According to Reverend Gates and others, such "absentee" ownership undermined local financial, civic, and moral infrastructure, particularly upward mobility, schools, and faith communities—the foundations of Protestant America.[3]

Gates advocated instead for the traditional credit and delivery system of local retailers. This system of commerce accounted for the vagaries of an agrarian economy and the scarcity of cash wages—a life he had grown accustomed to in Hogansville as well as his corner of Atlanta.[4] It was an existence that went beyond commerce; independent retail was part of an "all-encompassing worldview." Such modes of exchange were constitutive of "the prevailing concept of community and a key link in the opportunity structure that was seen as a foundation of American democracy."[5] Independent retail provided the means for social mobility and investment in local churches as well as moral and physical infrastructure, whereas chains threatened this possibility. As one newspaper editor put it, "Chain stores are a menace to the well-being of any community. . . . The whole chain movement is un-American"[6] (Figure 6.1). In this worldview, independent retail was a synecdoche for patriotic Americans and Christian piety. Accordingly, Gates concluded his sermon by asking his parishioners and listeners to exclusively patronize independent merchants and stores, like that of his neighbor Philip Shefferman, who owned and operated the small independent neighborhood store.[7]

When Gates decided to use phonograph religion to challenge chain stores, he took on one of the most controversial issues of the interwar period. In 1928, the *Magazine of Business* editorialized that the consternation about the rise of chains "is to be found almost daily in the newspapers, and the weekly and monthly magazines echo the noise of the battle. It is, in short, on the front page."[8] Indeed, the *New York Times* announced that the rise of corporate retail was "the most serious economic condition which confronts this country today."[9] *Fortune Magazine* noted that the dissolution of chain stores had become a "popular cause," reaching the level of a "political axiom."[10] Likewise, the *Progressive* declared that the rise of chain stores was the "question that is uppermost today in the minds of the people of the republic."[11] The concern across the country was so dire that the *New Republic* saw fit to publish a five-part series on the conflict entitled "Chain Stores: Menace or Promise?" The magazine noted, "The rise of the chain store, as *New*

Figure 6.1: Opposition to chain stores, as pictured here in this 1930 political cartoon, was largely based on the lack of credit commerce in chain stores as well as the perception that chains failed to invest in the religious, moral, financial, and structural support of local communities. Source: *Business Week*, March 5, 1930, 21.

Republic readers do not need to be told, is one of the most important developments of American business."[12] Similarly, the *Nation*, a leading liberal magazine, completed a four-part series simply titled, "Chains Versus Independents."[13]

The nation's schools and universities also took notice of the heated issue. Chain stores were the most popular debate topic for high school and college debate teams during the Hoover administration. More than twenty-five state debate leagues and associations adopted the proposition, "Resolved: That chain stores are detrimental to the best interests of the American public."[14] According to congressional records, from 1928 to 1931 there were eight thousand such debates across the country, drawing an estimated audience of 2 million anxious and divided citizens.[15]

The U.S. Congress responded to the heated cultural and social debate on May 3, 1928 by unanimously passing Resolution 224, directing the Department of Justice (DOJ) and the Federal Trade Commission (FTC) to conduct the first national investigation of the phenomenon. The resolution, introduced by Iowa senator Smith Brookhart, maintained that an inquiry into chain stores was needed because chain stores constituted "a matter of serious concern to the public." As William Donovan, an attorney in the DOJ and later coordinator of information (a precursor to the CIA) explained to a group of worried chain store executives, "the public is warranted in having a feeling of concern." Local independent business "has been looked upon as a distinctly American institution." From this perspective, the rise of chain stores meant the destruction of a foundational principle of American life. America had a "chain store problem." In their investigation, the DOJ and FTC compiled thirty-three reports and conducted approximately 1,800 interviews hoping to find a solution.[16]

Several national opinion polls conducted in the 1930s revealed that the nation was almost evenly divided over the issue. A 1937 Gallup Poll revealed that 59 percent of Americans were in favor of excessive taxation of chain stores as a way to limit the advantages corporate retail enjoyed over independent stores.[17] The following year, *Fortune Magazine* found that a total of 49 percent were in favor of passing tax legislation to level the economic playing field or plainly "taxing chain stores out of business."[18] The country was deeply divided over the issue.

Politicians and lawmakers courted such public opinion. In 1929, an unnamed chain store executive leaked to the press that "a prominent United States Senator" disclosed to him "that one of the main issues— perhaps *the* main issue—in the next presidential campaign would be the question of whether the chain store interests of the country would be permitted to develop and progress in an economic way or be arbitrarily hampered by enacted law in the interest of the independent retailer and the individual community."[19] A journalist writing for the *New Republic* likewise wrote that every lawmaker was forced "to announce where he stands—on the side of the independent merchants or on the side of the chains." He concluded: "Whenever a little band of lawmakers are gathered together in the sacred name of legislation, you may be sure they are putting their heads together and thinking up things they can do to the chain stores."[20] This was not an exaggeration. Approximately 967 antichain tax bills were introduced across the country during the decade of the 1930s alone. In all, twenty-seven of the nation's forty-eight states passed variations of statewide anti–chain store taxation and legislation during the interwar period.[21]

The passage of such tax laws was often viewed in religious terms. Chain store opponents deemed such laws redemptive legislation on behalf of independent trading, local autonomy, and democracy: a moral Christian society. When one attorney made a passionate defense of statewide antichain legislation, the public congregational hearing morphed into a scene reminiscent of a Protestant revival. The attorney's soliloquy quickly turned into an antiphonal homily as onlookers interjected thunderous shouts of "Glory!" and "Hallelujah!" in support of anti–chain store sentiment and legislation.[22]

Evangelical clergy simultaneously demonstrated and stoked such religious fervor against chains. In fact, clerical involvement in opposing chain stores reached such a pitch that even the *Harvard Business Review* noted in 1930, "Pastors and Priests have joined hands with the independents in an attempt to wipe out the chains."[23] Many Americans were convinced that God was on their side in their fight against corporate retail and chain stores. Reverend Gates spoke for them when he provocatively declared in his recorded sermon, "The word to this country today, should be Stay out of the Chain Store, or Goodbye Chain Store!"

However, the irony of Reverend Gates utilizing phonograph religion to launch an offensive against chain stores is striking. Gates was deeply committed to the American credo of past traditions, particularly conventional channels of religious expression, knowledge, commerce, and opportunity structure. He was convinced that traditional religious beliefs and commerce went hand and hand and that the growth of chain stores undermined traditional American society. Yet corporate retail was a constitutive element of phonograph religion. Chain stores and their mail order catalogs were the primary retail outlets for phonographs and recorded sermons. Chains made phonograph religion a national phenomenon. Without corporate retail, phonograph preachers like Reverend Gates could not have effectively revived black Protestantism as a popular commodity and reaffirmed the social authority of the ministry through the consumer marketplace. Reverend Gates promoted consumer culture through phonograph religion even as he used phonograph religion to critique it.

The paradox was not lost upon Okeh Records. Executives of the Columbia-owned company made sure the anti–chain store homily recorded that day in April 1930 never made it to the marketplace or into the hands of consumers. The label never officially released it. Okeh's studio log simply lists the record as "Unissued."[24]

Scholars have debated whether phonograph religion aided or hindered black struggles for equality. Some studies have analyzed the style of religious race records, concluding that they were indeed a form of protest. Phonograph sermons offered resistance to (black) middle-class hegemony by stylistically authenticating and voicing the experiences of the black working class. Others, however, have rightly challenged this claim. Through a perusal of popular recorded sermons and their advertisements, including Reverend Gates's "Manish Women" and "Dead Cat on the Line" (a comedic "chastisement" of a black congregation's penchant for loose sexual practices), they conclude that phonograph religion served to reinforce "raced, classed, and gendered hierarchies." Record executives had no interest in recording formally schooled clerics proclaiming a social gospel, but rather purposely signed clergy who agreed to avoid sermons that openly challenged "widely accepted cultural conceptions of race, class, and gender stratification."[25] Phonograph religion, according to these two differing assessments, was either an inherently oppositional religious expression or a religious practice that primarily served to reinscribe the inequality of prevalent social arrangements.

The substance of phonograph sermons, then, is too dynamic to classify as an either/or cultural practice. Like their blues counterparts, phonograph preachers addressed race, class, romance, gender, and consumption from various and sometimes contradictory perspectives. Phonograph preachers did attack various forms of inequality even as they at times affirmed it. Reverend Gates clearly addressed the "race problem" in several sermons. In "Straining at a Gnat and Swallowing a Camel," for example, Gates confronted "a mixed congregation" for their racist practices. Based on the words of Jesus as recorded in Matthew 23:24 ("You blind guides, who strain out a gnat and swallow a camel!"), he chastised whites for professing to be Christians profession but adhering to Jim Crow laws in their personal and public relationships, calling them "Negro Haters!" In "A Hero Closes a War," seminary-trained cleric Sutton Griggs used Micah 4:3, "They will hammer their swords into plowshares and their spears into pruning hooks," as a vision describing the end of racial antipathy. And Reverend J. C. Burnett's "The Downfall of Nebuchadnezzar," "Babylon Is Falling Down," and "The Matchless King," for example, presented the God of Christianity as a deity who preferred the oppressed, poor, and weak, not the rich and strong. Such subversive cultural work has never been antithetical to commercialization; in fact, "commercialization often subsumes even the resistance to it." In short, the phonograph industry was not opposed to trained clerics or counter-hegemonic rhetoric, as long as there was a sizeable buying public for them.[26]

Moreover, cultural studies scholars (and increasingly historians) have persuasively argued that audiences "decode" and reinterpret mass media messages in ways that are sometimes in line with and at other times incongruent with the messenger's intent. This process of meaning making can be counterhegemonic or serve to support inequitable societal structures. Acknowledging such variance serves as "solvent(s)" to the hierarchal and absolutist binaries of "good" and "bad." It also helps to open the door to a host of imaginative interpretative possibilities, while still leaving space for evaluative assessments of the far-reaching influences of consumer capitalism on phonograph religion.[27]

Examining Reverend Gates's personal experience of chain stores and its effect upon his media ministry accomplishes this feat. It allows us to look beyond the multifaceted nature of sermon content to develop a more focused and nuanced view of the relationship between phonograph religion, consumer culture, and social protest. Phonograph preachers were not essentially ambassadors of social resistance nor principally passive ministers at the complete mercy of the phonograph industry, disinterested in the social and economic welfare and equality of black people. And consumers of phonograph religion were not lemmings, simply absorbing the monologue of a sermon. Buyers engaged in a conversation with the sermons, continually reinterpreting them, sometimes in ways that were at odds with their intended meanings. The travailing ordeal with chain stores, then, reveals that the best way to understand the relationship between phonograph preachers and social protest is to recognize that preaching on wax, due to the social location of the preachers and their connection with the phonograph industry, was "simultaneously progressive and coopted."[28]

Chains on Main Street

On a vernal Friday morning on April 25, 1930, Reverend Gates departed his house to record another lucrative round of sermons. When the celebrity preacher walked to his garage, sat in the high luster seats of his luxury car, and prepared to drive to the studio, he gazed upon the long-standing independent grocery store located next door. Philip Shefferman and his family had taken over the store after the departure of the Silvermans. The newly arrived Jewish family from Poland lived on the top floor of the house and used the bottom floor to join the ranks of the city's approximately 1,200 independent grocery proprietors. Like the Gates family, they had uprooted themselves and moved to the urban metropolis of Atlanta in the hope of attaining the American dream, one based upon the foundation of the nation's traditional opportunity structures and entrepreneurial energies.[29]

As did the proprietors of most local groceries of the time, the Sheffermans greeted their customers as soon as they stepped over the small store's threshold of broad wood floorboards, usually adorned with sawdust. Low-hanging incandescent light bulbs illuminated the wooden countertops that usually ran the length of the store. These establishments were not self-serve. The Sheffermans served their neighborhood acquaintances from behind the counter by retrieving and packaging a host of canned goods and household wares upon request. Store owners and customers built quite a rapport through the process. The relationship lent itself to the system of procuring items through store credit and delivery service if consumers were unable to transport their own groceries—a common dilemma during an era when car ownership was a novelty.[30]

Typically positioned between the store length service counters were bins and crates filled with an assortment of nonperishable items. Polk Brockman's local warehouse of Columbia and Okeh Records made certain that popular records, such as Reverend Gates's sermons, were featured at small stores alongside candies, tobacco, cigarettes, bottles of the local Coca-Cola beverage, and various sorts of medicine. Toward the back of the store, near the requisite scale and coffee mill, outlets customarily situated bulk goods such as coffee, sugar, wheels of cheddar, kerosene, and, for the adventurous soul, whiskey. Mr. Shefferman's store, while tiny and limited in selection, offered the Summerhill neighborhood convenient shopping for many spiritual and physical wants.[31]

In addition to accessibility, such local stores were also icons of tradition and social mobility. Independent retail, particularly in the grocery business, was one of America's most popular careers in the early twentieth century. Urban immigrants and migrants, especially those with limited command of English and/or urban decorum, took to opening up their own shops where they could sell to their ethnic and class folk. This vocational path offered a decent living and respectful profession without the vagaries or physical dangers of industrial and manual labor. Minority grocery store managers made about $17 a week, a contemporary economic equivalent of about $80,000 a year, a solid middle-class income. A black economics study went so far as to conclude that black store owners occupied a social standing "which among whites would correspond perhaps to that of the owner of a chain store system." Socially, black proprietors were "expected to measure up relatively as high socially, with all that this implies." Owning a butcher shop, grocery, dry goods store, or bakery thus offered a respectable path to entrepreneurship, financial independence, and the resulting communal respectability.[32] For immigrants and migrants alike, Mr. Shefferman's ability to become a self-employed entrepreneur was nothing short of the embodiment of the American dream—a dream that Reverend Gates, an urban migrant preacher turned celebrity, knew all too well.

Chain stores, however, threatened this worldview. Reverend Gates witnessed this menace firsthand when he drove to the studio that day. Sears Roebuck and Co. had recently opened a store on the city's historic Ponce De Leon Boulevard. The nine-story department store and mail order warehouse totaled 750,000 square feet of floor space. The store dwarfed proprietors like Philip Shefferman. The corporate retail outlet, according to the *Atlanta Constitution,* was a "monument to progressive prosperity." The modern store was put in motion by its very own power plant and was built complete with a system of pneumatic tubes to move merchandise throughout the store for customer convenience and to assist the mail order functions that operated out of the basement of the colossal building. If customers grew weary or parched from their shopping excursion in the 65,000 square foot retail section of the store, the modern cafeteria and dining room offered plenty of nourishment, including a modern soda fountain and a wide selection of ready-made foods. In addition, a physician and an assortment of trained nurses were on site to assist with any first aid or medical needs. The building's third floor was level with the adjoining tracks of the southern railway, enabling the store to easily receive and ship merchandise from across the country and the world, such as diamonds from South Africa and clothing from Switzerland. Moreover, for the city's growing European immigrant population, the store boasted phonographs and records from Germany, Italy, and Mr. Shefferman's native Poland, as well as race records. The company's mail order catalog, if not the department store, even carried Reverend Gates's sermons. Neighborhood stores sold recorded sermons, but not in the volume or with the reach of chains and mail order catalogs.[33]

Any nonperishable commodity one could need or want was seemingly always available at the new Sears store. Consumers did not have to fret if small local shops like that of Mr. Shefferman did not have their desired attire, home wares, or spiritual commodities. If Sears did not have the desired item, a simple mail order request rendered almost any object only as far away as a consumer's mail box. One independent store owner spoke for many local proprietors when he conceded the convenience and superiority of chain stores like Sears. "The chain stores have complicated things," he declared. "Their specialization in cheap, flashy merchandise, attractively displayed, and carrying easy to read price tags gets the business. . . . [T]hey usually have more attractive stores, know how to dress their windows, makes shopping so easy." Indeed, the ease of chain store retail and mail order commerce and their wide selection made chains like Sears a favorite of phonograph enthusiasts during the 1920s. The record industry estimated that by 1927 chain stores accounted for 30 percent of all musical merchandise sales, and the number was rising.[34] Neighborhood stores like Mr. Shefferman's sold Reverend Gates's sermons and helped him become a local notoriety; but corporate retail like Sears had helped Reverend Gates became a national celebrity. The Sears building was a short distance from Mr. Shefferman's small store, but worlds apart in terms of selection, shopping, and cultural impact.

The preacher's journey to the studio that day, therefore, was marked in part by a stark contrast of worlds. A traditional worldview deeply intertwined with independent local retail was in conflict with a modern world of corporate commerce. Both independent and corporate retail sold wax sermons, but the rise of chain stores and their increasing dominance in phonograph merchandising signaled the passing of commerce, as Reverend Gates had known it. Gates's aim was to use his sermon and mass media ministry to help save local proprietors and the traditional way of life that he valued. But his very embeddedness in the commercial world attenuated his impact.

Say Good-Bye

Reverend Gates made his antagonism toward chain stores known when he arrived in the studio pulpit that Friday. Corporate retail had significantly facilitated his rise to prominence and it appeared that the future marketing and sale of spiritual commodities would be in the hands of chain stores. Nevertheless, Gates laid out several reasons for his anti–chain store bias in a prophetic manner. To contemporary ears the sermon may sound crude, but it was in line with the popular entertainment of the day. First, Gates used his sermon to express grave concern for the preservation of American individualism and social mobility through employment, entrepreneurship, and small businesses—all hallmarks of the traditional American ethos.[35] Appropriately, he warned his congregation that the proliferation of chain stores would, first and foremost, result in "No Jobs!"

Gates's proclamation reflects the socioeconomic divide in the practices of chain stores in America during the interwar period. One chain store survey revealed that 94 percent of chain employees were men, roughly twenty-eight years old, with at least a high school education.[36] Gates, like the majority of his urban migrant parishioners, did not have a high school education. Moreover, the professionalization of chains threatened to drive independent merchants out of business. Such prospects did not favor the preacher's predominantly working- and migrant-class listeners, neighbors, and proponents of small businesses. Simply put, chains were crushing the opportunity of the (black) working class to share in the American dream.

Gates's sermon insightfully utilized staged testimonies by serial characters Deacon Davis and Sister Jordan to illustrate the experiences of countless Americans who were not store owners but were nonetheless affected by chain stores. Deacon Davis testified that he was unemployed because his local employers went out of business because "the chain store ruined them." Likewise, Sister Jordan testified that she was no longer serving as a domestic servant nor living "in the big house" of a local proprietor because the family could no longer afford her services. Instead, the family was "cooking for themselves," leaving Sister Jordan unemployed. Deacon Davis and Sister Jordan epitomized the concerns of both the majority of black workers in Atlanta and of countless individuals who were not directly connected with the retail business but who nonetheless bore the burden of the economic shift to chain stores. Gates's homily demonstrated that corporate retail had a domino effect upon working-class employment.[37]

Moreover, Reverend Gates's diatribe against chains articulated how the rise of chain stores affected the financial support of religious organizations, especially local congregations. Gates's recording uses Deacon Davis's unemployment at the hands of chain stores and subsequent lack of monetary support for the church to exemplify how chains were a menace to churches and to the moral fabric of communities (Figure 6.1). And this dire financial situation, Reverend Gates declared to his affirming congregation, "will never change as long as you stay in the chain store!"

The 1934 publication of the FTC investigation into chain stores confirmed the preacher's insightful sermon. A Methodist pastor lamented to federal investigators that "the merchants of my church who are conducting independent stores complain that they can not contribute largely to the church support, basing their plea on the reduction of business caused by the coming of the chain store."[38] Ministers found chain stores hesitant about such charitable giving. One minister told federal researchers: "Any effort to secure contributions from chains has nearly always proven unsatisfactory, as such requests were usually submitted to district managers, or to the head office, and by the time a reply had been received, the need had often passed, or the request was denied."[39] Reverend Gates foresaw that the economic tentacles of chain stores would reach far and wide, even into the church offering plate.

Finally, Gates's sermon drew attention to the lack of support chain stores gave to the physical infrastructure of communities. Gates intoned that he knew a man who "boasted" about being a truck driver but had lost his job because of the efficiency of the national distribution networks of chain stores. (Gates was perhaps referring to his next-door neighbor James B. who, according to census notes, was employed as a truck driver for a local bakery in 1930.) The preacher proclaimed that the man was unemployed due to the chain stores' modern distribution networks. To make matters worse, Gates declared, chain store delivery trucks traveled over local roads, but "[t]hey don't help to pay to pave these highways nor streets, or pay for nothing in town!" Gates saw chain stores as destructive to local infrastructure.[40]

Federal investigators shared similar sentiments in their 1934 conclusions. They discovered that "the opinion most frequently voiced" by consumers was that they chose to shop with locally owned stores in part because independent owners were "the mainstays of community activities" and continually expressed "loyalty" to community building. One pastor, a longtime customer of a grocery chain, told the DOJ that he had asked local proprietors to financially support his church remodeling project. A number of independent business owners responded with donations. However, the chain store declined his request. The disgruntled clergyman in turn boycotted the store.[41] Likewise, one clergyman complained that chain organizations refused to "support the civic and charitable activities of the town" and therefore "do not serve to benefit the community."[42]

A Presbyterian pastor who federal investigators noted was "one of the wealthiest citizens of the town," was disgusted at the high turnover rate among chain store managers. He lamented the damage transient store managers did to the local tapestry of civic life. The revolving system of personnel, he argued, cultivated a lack of concern for "the civic, political, religious, and social life of the community." This lackluster attitude toward the communal well-being was not "the custom of owners and managers of independent owned stores." Likewise, a Lutheran pastor stated that chain store managers were only concerned with promotion, and therefore "[h]ave no interest in the community. They are mere cogs in big machines that are operated for the purpose of filling the coffers of corporations that do not have a personal interest in the town."[43] According to these clerics, chains were utterly destructive for community formation.

An angry churchgoer from New Jersey summed up the aforementioned concerns in a letter to President Franklin Roosevelt. In poetic form she denounced chain stores, writing: "Oh yes their stores are pretty, and their windows have a flash. But they never know a person, if they haven't got the cash. For their bosses live on Wall Street and we're a bunch of fools; if we think these fellows give a damn about our *church* and schools."[44] According to religious opponents, chains undermined all that was right with America.

Part 2 of Reverend Gates's progressive sermon was a song that put the issue even more plainly. The aesthetics of the a cappella male chorus may sound outdated or comical to the contemporary ear. However, their polyphonic style was in vogue in many churches at the time, especially in faith communities that frowned upon church music that incorporated percussion, wind instruments, or anything that sounded too much like blues or jazz.

Reverend Gates introduced the quartet in concert style, informing his audience that the group was going to sing a song titled "Stay Out of the Chain Stores." He told his audience, "I want you to listen and then put it into action! Stay out of the chain store!"

After Gates's introduction, the quartet bellowed in four-part harmony, "Just let me tell you people, both white and colored too, its time for you to wake up and see how they're treating you." Followed by the chorus, "You betta stay out, outta these chain stores, you betta stay out, outta these stores, you betta stay out, outta these chain stores, they'll ruin you sure as your born!" The remaining song lyrics echoed Reverend Gates's sermon, and those of a vast constituency:

> "They'll send their advertisements, in order to draw you to their store
> > Lord as soon as you get your payroll to the chain store you will go.
> Chorus
> "When you get your money, you better be for sure, that when you
> > give it to your wife, that she stays out these chain stores,
> Chorus
> You can walk up to the chain store, and they you'll find a key, and as
> > soon as you get your money spent they ship it to another city.
> Chorus
> There are two things about these chain stores, Lord you'll find it to be
> > true, they do not give you work to do and they will not credit
> > you. Now let me tell you people, the best thing for this land, you
> > betta stay out of these chain stores and visit your credit man.
> Chorus

For all these reasons—concerns about employment, upward mobility, church support, and local moral and structural infrastructure—the preacher concluded the sermon series by shouting to his listeners, "Stay out of these chain stores!

Wall Street

As Okeh was preparing to press Reverend Gates's sermon, Albert Morrill—the head of Kroger's—wrote to the heads of the nations leading chain stores: "The chain store industry is going through a period of unwarranted attacks. . . . Never in the past and probably never in the future will the call for cooperation . . . among the chains be as urgent as it is today." Morrill's warning shot came with an invitation to join the National Chain Store Association (NCSA). The NCSA was established as the first cooperative effort to unite department, grocery, restaurant, clothing, automotive, and other specialty chain stores for the stated purpose of promoting corporate retail. The modus operandi, however, was to squelch the kind of antichain sentiment voiced by Reverend Gates. The lobbying group was made up of representatives from more than five hundred retail corporations, controlling more than 16,000 stores throughout the nation. The NCSA included executives from signature companies such as J. C. Penney, Sears, Kresge, Montgomery Ward, and Kress—a now defunct 5 and 10 cent store. Collectively, the organization represented a total of $750 million in annual business, the contemporary equivalent of $116 billion. The powerful group was headquartered at the towering Woolworth Building on Broadway in Manhattan, not too far from Columbia's Okeh studios.[45]

Under Morrill's leadership, the NCSA created several committees to systematically address anti–chain store rhetoric and legislation. The community relations committee addressed the view proffered by Reverend Gates and other critics that chain stores were community parasites. The committee's job was to make chains appear to be local. Chain stores aimed to use charity and community immersion to convince communities that they were not draining the local moral and physical infrastructure, as Reverend Gates and others claimed. Rather, they were just as committed and invested in local flourishing as the locally owned neighborhood store.

The public relations efforts of chain stores matched the proselytization efforts of chain store opponents during the decade, and they also methodically squelched anti–chain store oratory. The NCSA was not only successful in silencing the opposition of notable organizations representing labor, agriculture, real estate, and journalism; they also maneuvered to have such groups issue resolutions against anti–chain store legislation. The American Federation of Labor (AFL), once fierce critics of chain stores, agreed to a series of collective bargaining deals with the country's largest chain, A&P. Subsequently, at their 1938 convention the AFL adopted resolutions against excessive chain store taxation. According to the AFL, organized labor efforts were easier to accomplish with chain stores than with independents. Agriculture, once a vibrant source of chain store opposition, altered its stance against chains. Chain stores staged special campaigns to help sell surplus crops, particularly during the Great Depression. Farmers increasingly relied on chain organizations and their agricultural relief programs to purchase and distribute large quantities of crops. The American Farm Bureau Federation, the umbrella organization for agriculture, issued a resolution opposing all antichain tax proposals in 1938. Real estate agents followed suit as their firms were increasingly being consulted and compensated for assisting chain organizations in plotting and forecasting new store locations. The National Association of Real Estate Boards issued a resolution against anti–chain store legislation. Similarly, the National Editorial Association, which represented over 5,000 "nonmetropolitan" weekly and daily newspapers, also repudiated anti–chain store sentiment. Despite their mostly rural readership, the editors of such papers could not resist the sizable advertising revenues they received from chain stores.[46] At one time, all these organizations had opposed and vilified chains. However, as the decade proceeded they became increasingly dependent on their former foe.

In a similar manner, Reverend Gates's sermon also fell prey to the NCSA. His chain store homily was recorded along with several other titles, including "The Woman and the Snake," "Clean the Corners of Your Mind," and "David and Uriah," all of which addressed aspects of morality. Okeh sound engineers remastered all the titles before issuing them. During the Depression, recordings, studio time, and labor hours were rarely wasted. Money was short and the profit margin of record purchases was shrinking. Therefore, every sermon had to be maximized. The recording engineer had Reverend Gates record multiple takes of both parts of the sermon to be certain he was able to capture the perfect pitch and tone. Nevertheless, Okeh released all the sermons from the session, except the chain store diatribe. Customers would never get the opportunity to purchase or hear the sermon.[47]

The protest sermon never had a chance. Appointed label executives periodically visited the regional "head buyers" of chain stores to inform "them what was coming up." These top level and high-salaried chain store employees decided what and how many records would be placed in their stores. Even if the label had promoted the sermon, head buyers would never have allowed it to hit their shelves. And labels could not afford to lose the bulk buying of chain stores. NCSA companies such as Montgomery Ward, J.C. Penney, Sears, and Woolworth's all sold Columbia phonographs as well as race records and sermons. In fact, Woolworth's was the exclusive retailer of Reverend Gates's sermons on Bluebird Records. Kress, the 5 and 10 cent chain retailer, followed suit on Romeo Records. Corporate retail was too closely allied and vital to the phonograph industry, and to Columbia in particular, for the label to consider harboring or promoting any opposition to corporate retail. The chain store collective silenced Gates's oppositional rhetoric, as it did to so many other chain store opponents.[48]

After preaching his chain store sermon in 1930, Gates was relegated to recording exclusively for chain store labels. When he began his career in 1926, he recorded for a host of local and nation labels. However, by 1934 corporate retail brands had taken over record distribution. No one else would—or for that matter could—afford to sign him during the Depression. Gates did not back down from sermons that engaged social criticism and protest. His sermons continued to engage the Great Depression, praise the New Deal and President Roosevelt, and critique the color line; no easy feat in the south. Homilies such as "President Roosevelt Is Everybody's Friend" and "No Bread Line in Heaven," appeared on Victor/RCA's Woolworth's chain store label Bluebird. Moreover, from 1939 to 1940 the preacher recorded ten sermons for the Montgomery Ward label, including "Baptist World Alliance in Atlanta," which praised the meeting for shunning racial segregation and enforcing integrated worship. These sermons were sold through Montgomery Ward's national mail order catalog as well as in the company's retail stores across urban America, including stores in Albany, New York, and Baltimore, Maryland, on the east coast; Chicago, Kansas City, the Twin Cities, and Fort Worth, Texas, in middle America; and Denver, Oakland, and Portland, Oregon, out west. Gates still had a nationwide ministry, but one that never returned to the issue of chain stores again. The labels, mail order catalogs, and retail stores left him little room to explicitly critique consumer culture or the practices of corporate America.

Gates's last phonograph sermon was recorded on Thursday, October 2, 1941. America's involvement in World War II placed a government restriction of the use of shellac. To close out his mass media ministry, Gates preached "Getting Ready for Christmas Day," a reminder that Jesus and salvation, not conspicuous consumption, were the real reason for the season. The sermon was recorded on the Bluebird label and, ironically, was sold exclusively through Woolworth's retail chain.[49]

•   •   •

Phonograph sermons provided the aural sound track for black rural diaspora life and worship. They offered spiritual sustenance to all those who found themselves morally and religiously shipwrecked, as one study put it, by the refusal of established urban churches to reconceptualize their church work according to the needs and desires of the black rural diaspora. Phonograph religion proclaimed faith in a manner that was outside the purview and preference of the black literati and the educated New Negro clergy, but thoroughly embraced by urban migrants across the country. More than just relying on aesthetics, phonograph preachers aligned their sermons with those most affected by structural ills by engaging topics such as racial and economic inequality from a black working-class perspective. The means to achieving equality, according to phonograph religion, was not based upon black performances or the aspirations of bourgeois culture; but rather solely on the insistence of black humanity. The phonograph industry boosted and popularized this brand of religion and its evangelists across the country in black life.

However, the prophetic utterances and influences of phonograph religion were also limited due to the relationship between phonograph religion and corporate retail. Sermon topics were subject to the dictates of corporate America. Nowhere is this more visible than in the dynamics surrounding the rise of chain stores. Phonograph preachers like Reverend Gates labored to exploit the commercial marketplace and the emergent medium of the day to establish urban ministries that could address the vicissitudes of modern life and bolster the social authority of the ministry in the process. However, the vitality of their national mass media ministry and fame depended upon the very resources and structures, namely corporate retail, which they aimed to critique. The phonograph industry was keen on profit margins, but not on challenging certain structural arrangements. To be sure, there was a growing market for protest music, art, and poetry, particularly along racial lines, during the New Negro era. However, there was little room in the phonograph industry specifically, and the commercial entertainment business more broadly, for aggressive critiques of the trends and ills of modern consumer culture. Reverend Gates's sermon pulled on the heartstrings and evangelical populist sensibilities of his listeners to convince them to boycott chain stores, even as his profitable and popular utilization of corporate retail further enamored his listeners to the market. Phonograph religion constantly existed in this paradox of manifesting progressive impulses while simultaneously being coopted by the powers that be. In the end, corporate retail significantly amplified the voices of phonograph preachers, but it also attenuated their tone.[50]

Conclusion

Let the Record Play!
Communication and Continuity in African
American Religion and Culture

In the early part of 1945, Reverend Gates suffered an acute cerebral hemorrhage. The prolific sermon recorder, once described by reporters as "jovial," was left incapacitated for months. His physician, Dr. P. J. Yancey, last saw him on June 17, 1945. Two months later, on Saturday, August 18, 1945, James M. Gates died at his home on Fraser Street. He was sixty-one years old.[1]

On Tuesday, August 21, the preacher's remains were displayed in the sanctuary of his church. Parishioners, friends, and admirers who had formerly visited their preacher during one of his fireside soirées, came to the church to visit with him one last time. When the doors of the sanctuary opened for the funeral on Wednesday morning at 11.00, thousands reportedly came to say good-bye to the charismatic icon who was "a master in his own way that could bring his sermon to a climax that could touch all men" and who "always had some witty saying to say after greeting you" that would surely "drive your blues away."[2] When the four-hour memorial concluded, clergymen from the Baptist Ministers Union carried their fallen colleague to a hearse driven by the respected Auburn Avenue Haugabrooks and Company funeral home. The processional passed through the city on its way to Gates's rural place of birth. Polk Brockman, his one-time agent, recalled that an exceptionally large crowd lined the cortege to obtain a final glimpse of the celebrity preacher. According to the businessman, the funeral was the largest black funeral in Atlanta until the city laid to rest native son and religious icon Martin Luther King, Jr.[3] Gates was buried where he was born, Hogansville, Georgia. His life had come full circle, but so much had changed in the interval.

When Gates was born in 1884, African Americans had yet to even be recorded on the phonograph. The entire industry was focused on white consumer desires. However, by the time of his death, Gates had been instrumental in the rise of the talking machine to shape African American religious experience in four fundamental ways: commodification, popular broadcasting, commercial celebrity, and the prevailing nature of black religious authority.

Black consumers began to flock to the record player once the phonograph industry began to record race records. African Americans, with newfound discretionary income in urban America, fervently purchased these popular musical recordings. The voices of Bessie Smith, Ma Rainey, and Blind Lemon Jefferson bellowing their sometimes explicit folk tunes were heard in countless black neighborhoods.

Black faith communities largely opposed the race record phenomenon. The musical sagas and suggestive advertisements of sexuality, alcohol consumption, and black working-class life challenged established notions of black decorum and propriety. Pouring salt into the proverbial wound, black faith communities witnessed black consumers splurging on phonographs and race records even as their churches experienced a proportional decrease in religious giving. Moreover, race records became a significant aspect of a black entertainment market that was decentering the church as the primary amusement venue. As a result, black ministers, women's clubs, and the black literati deemed the records to be dangerous hindrances to racial progress. This ruling class agreed that race records were as intoxicating and perilous as liquor. However, they disagreed on how to respond. Some mainline black churches addressed the challenge by using church resources and facilities to produce bourgeois-styled amusements. Others viewed such efforts as a waste, preferring to keep the church focused on spiritual matters and relying on trained black professionals outside the church to produce wholesome amusements. Both efforts were fundamentally unsuccessful.

Some evangelical black clergy chose a third way. They joined the phonograph industry to have their sermons recorded and sold in an effort to steer black amusement and black consumer culture back toward the church. The most recognizable companies in the phonograph industry recorded these wax homilies and used their resources to advertise and market the sermonic wares ubiquitously. Black preachers desperately sought the exposure and reach afforded by mass media religion while the industry welcomed the market share.

Phonograph religion became exceedingly popular when black evangelical preachers brought black folk religion to the studio pulpit. Phonograph sermons transmitted the good news to listeners in a familiar and mostly male manner as the black rural diaspora attempted to adjust to a new urban world with larger churches, an air of urbanity, and a host of leisure and religious options. As that world attempted to impose its refined values upon migrants, the faithful simply put on the phonograph and experienced "church" in a style to which they were accustomed.

The popularity of these records made some phonograph preachers into commercial celebrities. Their esteem in the market, as opposed to the world of letters, bestowed them with clout at a time when old forms of ministerial authority were being severely challenged by the emergence of black professionals. Phonograph religion placed black ministers on an equal plane with leading black entertainment celebrities. Whether observers loved them or hated them, black celebrity preachers were difficult to ignore. Their names, images, and products were seemingly everywhere and they appeared to be living the high life. The black professional classes distinguished their own leading clergy, while the consuming public chose its own leading preachers. Reverend Gates, in particular, used such status as a means to maintain his societal influence as well as the socioeconomic status of a black professional.

However, the market circumscribed these preachers' authority even as it gave it to them. Teaming up with the phonograph industry gave black evangelical preachers extraordinary influence and reach. Recorded sermons were a constant in the marketplace. Consumers could rarely avoid seeing religion. Yet this fame came at a price. The content of the preachers' sermons was curtailed by the principles of corporate America.

In all, the placement of these black Protestant preachers and their phonograph sermons on the market shelf significantly changed the face of African American religion and culture during the first half of twentieth century. The innovators of phonograph religion established the practice of commodifying sermons in accordance with black popular entertainment forms. This practice drafted the blueprint for trendy black religious broadcasting, commercial celebrity preachers, and the prevailing nature of religious authority in black Christian experience.

After Reverend James Gates was laid to rest, a journalist for the *Atlanta Daily World* praised the phonograph preacher and memorialized him, concluding, "His memory will linger long."[4] Reverend Gates is not well remembered or chronicled compared to other celebrity preachers in American history. However, the ethos of the religious culture he helped to popularize endures to this day.

Evangelical expressions of African American religion have been a conspicuous aspect of every popular medium. These media preachers package their sermons, ministries, authority, and lifestyles according to the popular trends and personas of the black entertainment industry. For example, the increase in black radio ownership during and after World War II witnessed the rise of celebrity radio preachers such as Elder Solomon Michaux, C. L. Franklin, and Elder Lucy Smith.[5] Beginning in the 1970s, the growth of black television ownership contributed to the emergence of iconic televangelists such as Reverend Frederick "Ike" Eikerenkoetter II, and later Bishop Carlton Pearson, Creflo Dollar, Juanita Bynum, and T. D. Jakes. These media icons follow in the footsteps of black phonograph preachers who blazed the trail.[6]

Like their phonograph forbears, today's black religious broadcasters seek to find new and persuasive ways to preach an old message to a changing society as a means to bring revival to the church. Instead of teaming up with Columbia Records and RCA-Victor (both now owned by Sony Entertainment), today's "phonograph preachers" team up with Sony, Viacom (parent of BET), Trinity Broadcast Networks, and other media conglomerates to transmit their brand of Christianity to televisions, computers, and movie screens across the nation and globe. Their religious messages, like popular sermons on wax, avoid scholarly discourse. Instead they rely on plain "folk" speech to impart "biblical" instruction for life, and are constricted by the dictates of the market. All of this is encapsulated in an expressive worship service modeled after whatever happens to be the latest trend(s) in popular entertainment (music genre, movies, daytime talk show, or reality television format). Many meet with resounding success, demonstrated through the purchase of ultra expensive cars and other modern luxuries for all to see. Their publicly demonstrated wealth is used as a means to authenticate their social influence and celebrity, as well as the status and legitimacy of their ministries in an increasingly professionalized black culture.

Technology today is more advanced, offering seemingly boundless opportunities, and black consumer culture is larger, yielding appearance fees and royalties that easily surpass the status achieved by Reverends Gates and McGee. Yet the ideology remains the same. Black (mostly male) evangelicals today, as in the 1920s, firmly believe that mass media and entertainment, commercial viability, and the life of celebrity—not the elite and/or professional channels of education, elected office, or leadership in black civic organizations—are the best means to bring about the revival of the church and to reestablish ministerial authority. And the record plays on. . . .

NOTES

INTRODUCTION

1. U.S. Department of Commerce, National Oceanic Atmosphere Administration National Climatic Data Center, *Climate at a Glance,* http://www.ncdc.noaa.gov/cag/, accessed November 9, 2013.

2. U.S. Bureau of the Census, *Twelfth Census of the United States, Population Schedule, Mountville, Troup, Georgia, Roll: 225, Page: 11a, Enumeration District: 66, Fhl Microfilm: 12402251900;* U.S. Bureau of the Census, *Thirteenth Census of the United States, Population Schedule, Odessadale, Meriwether, Georgia, Roll: T624_203, Page: 12a, Enumeration District: 0083, Image: 817, Fhl Microfilm: 13742161910;* U.S. Bureau of the Census and Enumerator 5778, *Fourteenth Census of the United States:1920–Population Schedule of Atlanta, Georgia, Fulton County 3rd Ward Supervisor's District 5, Roll: T625_251 Page: 21a, Enumeration District 72, Image: 1051.* Sheet No. 21; *Atlanta City Directory,* 1914. Gates first appears in the city directory in 1914. However, the directory was issued on December 15, 1913. Hence it appears that Gates would have arrived in Atlanta in the latter part of 1913.

3. Robert M. W. Dixon, John Godrich, and Howard Rye, *Blues & Gospel Records, 1890–1943,* 4th ed. (Oxford, U.K.: Clarendon Press, 1997), 287–294.

4. *Talking Machine World,* August 15, 1926, 80, 86. Order figures for Columbia may be found in Dan Mahony, *The Columbia 13/14000–D Series: A Numerical Listing,* 2nd ed. (Highland Park, N.J.: Walter C. Allen, 1973), 34; U.S. Bureau of Labor Statistics, *100 Years of U.S. Consumer Spending: Data for the Nation, New York City, and Boston,* May 2006. Report 991; U.S. Department of Labor, Bureau of Labor Statistics, *National Occupational Employment and Wage Estimates* (May 2012).

5. Dixon et al., *Blues & Gospel Records,* 287–294. On record labels, see Allan Sutton and Kurt Nauck, *American Record Labels & Companies: An Encyclopedia, 1891–1943* (Denver, Colo.: Mainspring Press, 2000). By the early twentieth century, phonograph records were almost universally made with a hardened beeswax material known as shellac resin. During and after World War II, records were increasingly pressed with a synthetic wax material known as vinyl. For ease and brevity, I use the terms wax and vinyl interchangeably.

6. *Atlanta Daily World*, May 22, 1937, 2.

7. *Chicago Defender*, December 18, 1920, 3, 10; January 29, 1921, 3; December 8, 1926, 6; David L. Lewis, *When Harlem Was in Vogue* (New York: Alfred K. Knopf, 1981; reprint, Penguin Books, 1997), 150, 217; David Freeland, *Automats, Taxi Dances, and Vaudeville: Excavating Manhattan's Lost Places of Leisure* (New York: NYU Press, 2009), 228–229; *Comprehensive Historic Preservation Plan, Prepared by Michael Sandler, New York City Community Planning Fellows* (City of New York: Manhattan Community Board 10 Land Use and Landmarks Committee, April 2012).

8. Paul Oliver, *Songsters and Saints: Vocal Traditions on Race Records* (Cambridge: Cambridge University Press, 1984), 145; Davarian L. Baldwin, *Chicago's New Negroes: Modernity, the Great Migration, & Black Urban Life* (Chapel Hill: University of North Carolina Press, 2007), 5. For an example of such work, see Jon Michael Spencer, "The Black Church and the Harlem Renaissance," *African American Review* 30, no. 3 (Autumn 1996).

9. Data calculated from U.S. Bureau of the Census, *Negro Population in the United States, 1790–1915*, ed. Department of Commerce, reprint of 1918 ed. (New York: Arno Press, 1968); U.S. Bureau of the Census, *Negroes in the United States, 1920–32*, ed. U.S. Department of Commerce, reprint of original 1935 ed. (New York: Kraus Reprint Company, 1969).

10. On defining revivals see, William Gerald McLoughlin, *Revivals, Awakenings, and Reform: An Essay on Religion and Social Change in America, 1607–1977* (Chicago: University of Chicago Press, 1978), xiii–2; Benjamin E. Mays and Joseph William Nicholson, *The Negro's Church* (New York: Institute of Social and Religious Research, 1933), 102–103.

11. John Michael Giggie, "Preachers and Peddlers of God: Ex-Slaves and the Selling of African American Religion in the American South," in *Commodifying Everything: Relationships of the Market*, ed. Susan Strasser (New York: Routledge, 2003). Low literacy rates among African Americans prevented black published sermons from the eighteenth and nineteenth centuries from being popular commodities.

12. While black net worth remained low, cash income did help to shift the black social and consumer world of black Americans. See James R. Grossman, *Land of Hope: Chicago, Black Southerners, and the Great Migration* (Chicago: University of Chicago Press, 1989), 261–262; U.S. Bureau of Labor Statistics, *100 Years of U.S. Consumer Spending: Data for the Nation, New York City, and Boston*, May 2006. Report 991; Stanley Lebergott, *Pursuing Happiness: American Consumers in the Twentieth Century* (Princeton, N.J.: Princeton University Press, 1993), 142–143; F. Scott Fitzgerald, "Echoes of the Jazz Age," *Scribner's Magazine* XC, no. 5 (November 1931), 459–465; F. Scott Fitzgerald, "Early Success," *American Cavalcade* 1, no. 6 (October 1937), 74–79.

13. Jonathan L. Walton, *Watch This! The Ethics and Aesthetics of Black Televangelism* (New York: NYU Press, 2009), 2.

14. The earliest documented national radio broadcast of a black preacher occurred in 1933. See Norman W. Spauling, "History of Black Oriented Radio in Chicago, 1929–1963" (Ph.D. dissertation, University of Illinois at Urbana-Champaign, 1981); Gilbert Anthony Williams, *Legendary Pioneers of Black Radio* (Westport, Conn.: Praeger, 1998); Hal Erickson, *Religious Radio and Television in the United States, 1921–1991: The Programs and Personalities* (Jefferson, N.C.: McFarland, 1992).

15. Emily Ann Thompson, *The Soundscape of Modernity: Architectural Acoustics and the Culture of Listening in America, 1900–1933* (Cambridge, Mass.: MIT Press, 2002), 3–4.

16. Walton, *Watch This!* 10, 33–41.

17. See, for example, Walton, *Watch This!*; Scott Billingsley, *It's a New Day: Race and Gender in the Modern Charismatic Movement* (Tuscaloosa, Ala.: University of Alabama Press, 2008); Shayne Lee, *T. D. Jakes: America's New Preacher* (New York: NYU Press, 2005); Heather Hendershot, *Shaking the World for Jesus: Media and Conservative Evangelical Culture* (Chicago: University of Chicago Press, 2004).

18. To be sure, Word of Faith churches are indeed a postwar phenomenon in black Christian practices. On defining "Black Protestant Establishment" or "the black church," see David Wills, "An Enduring Distance: Black Americans and the Establishment," in William R. Hutchison, ed., *Between the Times: The Travail of the Protestant Establishment in America, 1900–1960* (Cambridge, U.K.: Cambridge University Press, 1990); C. Eric Lincoln and Lawrence H. Mamiya, *The Black Church in the African American Experience* (Durham: Duke University Press, 1990).

19. Thomas A. Edison, "The Phonograph and Its Future," *North American Review* 126, no. May–June (1878), 527–538. Edison's aim to see a phonograph in every home is from "The New Thomas A. Edison's Final Achievement," undated Amberola advertisement, quoted in Allan R. Sutton, *A Phonograph in Every Home: The Evolution of the American Recording Industry, 1900–1919* (Denver, Colo.: Mainspring Press, 2010), xi.

CHAPTER 1. "THE MACHINE WHICH TALKS!"

1. "The Talking Phonograph," *Scientific American* XXXVII, no. 25 (December 1877), 384–385; *Washington Post*, April 19, 1878, 4; Erika Brady, *A Spiral Way: How the Phonograph Changed Ethnography* (Jackson, Miss.: University Press of Mississippi, 1999), 11; Leigh Eric Schmidt, *Hearing Things: Religion, Illusion, and the American Enlightenment* (Cambridge, Mass.: Harvard University Press, 2000), 113; Eric W. Rothenbuhler and John Durham Peters, "Defining Phonography: An Experiment in Theory," *Musical Quarterly* 81, no. 2 (Summer 1997), 245–253.

2. *Washington Post*, April 19, 1878, 1; Robert E. Conot, *A Streak of Luck: The Life and Legend of Thomas Alva Edison*, 1st ed. (New York: Seaview Books, 1979), 109.

3. See Georges Duhamel, *In Defense of Letters* (New York: Greystone Press, 1939); Donald Bean, "Books vs. Movies, Phonographs, and Radios," *Peabody Journal of Education* 17, no. 4 (1940).

4. Conot, *A Streak of Luck*, 110.

5. Ibid.,104.

6. *Washington Post*, April 19, 1878, 1.

7. *Chicago Daily Tribune*, May 1, 1878, 4.

8. Quoted in David Suisman, *Selling Sounds: The Commercial Revolution in American Music* (Cambridge, Mass.: Harvard University Press, 2009), 101.

9. Emile Berliner, "The Gramophone: Etching the Human Voice," *Journal of the Franklin Institute of the State of Pennsylvania for the Promotion of the Mechanic Arts* CXXV, no. 6 (June 1988): 446; Richard Lacayo et al., "Time Inc. Specials: Thomas Edison: His Electrifying Life," *Time* (2013), 47.

10. Dane Yorke, "The Rise and Fall of the Phonograph," *American Mercury* XXVII, no. 105 (1932); *Atlanta Constitution*, August 25, 1889, 2; July 23, 1890, 7; August 29, 1920, 7D; Andre J. Millard, *America on Record: A History of Recorded Sound*, 2nd ed. (Cambridge, U.K.: Cambridge University Press, 2005),1, 43.

11. Yorke, "The Rise and Fall of the Phonograph"; Millard, *America on Record*, 49.

12. *Atlanta Constitution,* August 25, 1889, 2; Thomas Edison National Historical Park, "Quantity of Disc Phonographs and Disc Records Sold," Radio-Phonograph Division Accounting Department Report to W. H. Meadowcroft, April 9, 1929. The Mainspring: Resources for Collectors of Historic Recordings, http://www.mainspringpress.com/edison_disc-sales.html, retrieved March 22, 2013; *America on Record*, 49; Victor Record Sales Statistics, 1901–1941, *U.S. District Court, S.D. of N.Y., January 26 1943*, "Victor Sales by Class of Record and Total Sales of Records by Units, Years 1901 and 1941 Inclusive," The Mainspring: Resources for Collectors of Historic Recordings, http://www.mainspringpress.com/victorsales.html#anchor178841, retrieved March 22, 2013; Yorke, "The Rise and Fall of the Phonograph," 1–12; William Howland Kenney, *Recorded Music in American Life: The Phonograph and Popular Memory, 1890–1945* (New York: Oxford University Press, 1999), 59; Alex van der Tuuk, *Paramount's Rise and Fall: A History of the Wisconsin Chair Company and Its Recording Activities* (Denver: Mainspring Press, 2003), 20; Roland Gelatt, *The Fabulous Phonograph, from Tin Foil to High Fidelity* [1st ed. (Philadelphia: Lippincott, 1955),142; Suisman, *Selling Sounds*, 101; Tim Brooks, "High Drama in the Record Industry: Columbia Records, 1901–1934," *ARSC Journal* 33, no. 1 (Spring 2002). On advertising expenditure, see *New York Times*, July 9, 1922, 40. Columbia ranked seventeenth.

13. A 1977 national poll of two thousand adults found that 35 percent still readily recognized the slogan "His Master's Voice" and the accompanying Victor/RCA products. See *Roper Report, 77–3,* February 1977 The Roper Center for Public Opinion Research, University of Connecticut in the iPOLL Databank http://www.ropercenter.uconn.edu, accessed October 12, 2012.

14. Yorke, "The Rise and Fall of the Phonograph," 1.

15. *Talking Machine World* , December 15, 1918, 94.

16. Ibid., 95.

17. Robert Staughton Lynd and Helen Merrell Lynd, *Middletown: A Study in American Culture*, 1956 ed. (New York: Harcourt, Brace, Jovanovich, 1929; reprint, 1956), 244, fn35. The authors noted, "With the exception of a few wealthy families, people do not have collections of unframed prints as they do of books and Victrola records," 249; "Nation-Wide Survey of Phonographs and Radios in Homes," *Talking Machine World* XXIII (April 1927).

18. Letter from Mrs. Mary Kelly, Providence, Rhode Island, to Thomas Edison, Inc., January 12, 1921 in Thomas A Edison, Inc., "A Special Request to a Selected List of Edison Owners: Thomas A. Edison Phonograph Surveys," *Special Collections: Music Library, University of Michigan, Ann Arbor*. Ann Arbor: University of Michigan.

19. Tuuk, *Paramount's Rise and Fall*, 21; Yorke, "The Rise and Fall of the Phonograph," 8; Kenney, *Recorded Music in American Life*, 14, 54; Gelatt, *The Fabulous Phonograph*, 208–212; David Suisman, "Co-Workers in the Kingdom of Culture: Black Swan Records and the Political Economy of African American Music," *Journal of American History* 90, no. 4 (2004), 1300; Tim Brooks, "'Might Take One Disc of This Trash as a Novelty': Early Recordings by the Fisk Jubilee Singers and the Popularization of 'Negro Folk Music,'" *American Music* 18, no. 3 (2000), 298; "Nation-Wide Survey of Phonographs and Radios in Homes"; Millard, *America on Record*, 49. Phonograph prices in *Atlanta Constitution*, December 24, 1918, 7.

20. Mr. George Rhulen to Thomas Edison, Inc., dated February 18, 1921.

21. Garvin Bushell and Mark Tucker, *Jazz from the Beginning*, ed. Richard Crawford, Michigan American Music Series (Ann Arbor: University of Michigan Press, 1988),1.

22. "Nation-Wide Survey of Phonographs and Radios in Homes"; *Talking Machine World,* August 15, 1923, 116; May 15, 1926, 11; January 15,1926; David L. Cohn and Sinclair Lewis, *The Good Old Days: A History of American Morals and Manners as Seen through the Sears Roebuck Catalogs, 1905 to the Present* (New York: Simon and Schuster, 1940), 37; Stephen Calt and Gayle Dean Wardlow, "The Buying and Selling of Paramount—Part 3," *78 Quarterly* 1, no. 5 (1990), 21.

23. H. L. Mencken and George Jean Nathan, *The American Credo: A Contribution toward the Interpretation of the National Mind* (New York: A. A. Knopf, 1920), 28.

24. Lynd and Lynd, *Middletown*, 244.

25. "Nation-Wide Survey of Phonographs and Radios in Homes," *Talking Machine World*, August 15, 1923, 116. On car radios, see "Radio News and Programs: Radio Equipped Cars," *New York Amsterdam News,* January 15, 1930, 11.

26. Letter from W. E. Slocum, Saginaw Michigan to Thomas Edison, Inc., dated March 16,1921.

27.Letter from Lawrence Dreger of Pittsburgh, January 23,1921, and from Frank M. Burns of Pitcairn, Pa., January 24,1921, to Thomas Edison, Inc.

28. Adolph Lonk, Chicago, to Thomas Edison, Inc., dated March 9, 1921.

29. Letter from Ira K. Harris of Pittsburgh, Pa., and from Mrs. Frank A Eaton Lima, Ohio, January 23, 1921 to Thomas Edison, Inc.

30. Mrs. Marie A Piest to Thomas Edison, Inc., dated March 10, 1921.

31. Letter from Phillip S. Gibbons, Milton, Oreg., to Thomas Edison, Inc., dated February 21, 1921.

32. Ira De A. Reid, "Race Records," *Ira De A. Reid Papers, Schomburg Center for Research in Black Culture*, Box 1, Folder 17; Nathaniel Shilkret, *Nathaniel Shilkret: Sixty Years in the Music Business*, ed. Niel Shell and Barbara Shilkret (Lanham, Md.: Scarecrow Press, 2005), 37.

33. Cohn and Lewis, *The Good Old Days*, 34.

34. Kenney, *Recorded Music in American Life*, xvii–xviii, 5–8.

35. Letter from Mrs. George F. Utz of New Washington, Ohio, to Thomas Edison, Inc., dated February 2, 1921.

36. Letter from Thomas Edison, Inc., to Lawrence Dreger of Pittsburgh, Pa., February 10, 1921.

37. Brooks, "'Might Take One Disc of This Trash as a Novelty': Early Recordings by the Fisk Jubilee Singers and the Popularization of 'Negro Folk Music,'" 297; "Fisk Jubilee Singers," in Dixon et al., *Blues & Gospel Records*; Robert M.W. Dixon and John Godrich, *Recording the Blues* (New York: Stein and Day Publishers, 1970), 60.

38. Letter from Mrs. Harry Mangan to Thomas Edison, Inc., no month or day, 1921; Mrs. Frank A. Eaton Lima, Ohio, to Thomas Edison, Inc., dated January 23, 1921.

39. Letter dated January 1921.

40. Letter dated January 1921.

41. Letter dated January 30,1921.

42. Letter, dated February 2, 1921.

43. Letter dated March 27, 1921.

44. For Bryan quotes, see Michael Kazin, *A Godly Hero: The Life of William Jennings Bryan*, 1st ed. (New York: Knopf, 2006), 157–158, 272.

45. *Chicago Defender*, August 8, 1925, 3; Starr-Gennett Foundation, Inc., "Gennett Records," http://www.starrgennett.org, retrieved May 3, 2013. Bryan's speech is reprinted in *The Annals of America*, Vol. 12, *1895–1904: Populism, Imperialism, and Reform* (Chicago: Encyclopedia Britannica, 1968), 100–105.

46. *Atlanta Constitution*, "Advertising Club Hears Interesting Talks at Luncheon," September 24, 1920, 4; on presidential recordings, see Cohn and Lewis, *The Good Old Days*, 27; Allan Sutton, *Recording the 'Twenties* (Denver, Colo.; Wilmington, Del.: Mainspring Press, 2008), 56, 61; Suisman, *Selling Sounds*, 5; Booker T. Washington recorded the historic speech on December 5, 1908. In 1920, black label owner George W. Broome purchased copies of Washington's record and pasted his own record label's name, Broome Special Phonograph label, over Columbia's label. Broome's "version" of Washington's speech was, somewhat ironically, advertised in the NAACP's organ *Crisis* (November 1920, 37; and

December 1920, 92), which was edited by W. E. B. Du Bois. See Tim Brooks, *Lost Sounds: Blacks and the Birth of the Recording Industry, 1890-1919* (Urbana: University of Illinois Press, 2004), 503–504.

47. On Amos and Andy, see Elizabeth McLeod, *The Original Amos 'n' Andy: Freeman Gosden, Charles Correll, and the 1928-1943 Radio Serial* (Jefferson, N.C.: McFarland & Co., 2005); Elizabeth McLeod, *Amos 'n' Andy—In Person: An Overview of a Radio Landmark*, http://www.midcoast.com/~lizmcl/aa.html, retrieved November 11, 2010; also see Spauling, "History of Black Oriented Radio in Chicago," 30; Robin R. Means Coleman, *African American Viewers and the Black Situation Comedy: Situating Racial Humor* (New York: Garland, 1998); Barbara Dianne Savage, *Broadcasting Freedom: Radio, War, and the Politics of Race, 1938-1948* (Chapel Hill: University of North Carolina Press, 1999).

48. Tim Brooks, "High Drama in the Record Industry: Columbia Records, 1901–1934," *ARSC Journal* 33, no. 1 (Spring 2002), 44.

49. Sears advertised such records in their mail order catalog. See Cohn and Lewis, *The Good Old Days*, 38.

50. *Atlanta Constitution*, September 24, 1920, 4; Albert T. Martin, "The Oral Interpreter and the Phonograph," *Quarterly Journal of Speech* 38, no. 2 (1952).

51. *Talking Machine World*, July 22, 1911, 56.

52. Letter from Annie Pike Greenwood to the Educational Department of the Victor Talking Machine Company, January 1914, in "The Victrola in Rural Schools" (Camden, N.J.: Educational Department of the Victor Talking Machine Co., 1919); Victor advertisement for Kiddie records in *Atlanta Constitution*, December 15, 1918, 4.

53. Jacob Henry Landman, "Phonograph Records as an Aid in the Teaching of American History," *School Review* 35, no. 9 (1927); letter from C. E. Barrett from Entiat, Wash., to Thomas Edison, Inc.

54. *Atlanta Constitution*, September 24, 1920, 4.

55. On Taft and Bryan, see the 1908 entries of Raymond Sooy, *Memoirs of My Recording and Traveling Experiences for the Victor Talking Machine Company, 1898-1925*, entries for June 15, 1905 (*sic*) and August 5, 1908 in the David Sarnoff Library, Princeton, New Jersey. http://www.davidsarnoff.org/soo-maintext.html, retrieved March 27, 2013; *Talking Machine World*, August 15, 1908, 36–37. On Wilson and Roosevelt, see Harry O. Sooy, *Memoir of My Career at Victor Talking Machine Company*, entries Friday, September 20 and September 24, 1912, in ibid., retrieved March 27, 2013.

56. *Atlanta Constitution*, September 24, 1920, 4. Harding continued to make recordings after the election. Victor recording engineer recorded the president for Victor on April 23, 1922, as well as May 24, 1922. See Harry O. Sooy, *Memoir of My Career at Victor Talking Machine Company*, entry March 12, 1922; Raymond Sooy, *Memoirs of My Recording and Traveling Experiences for the Victor Talking Machine Company, 1898-1925*, entries for May 24, 1922.

57. *Moving Picture World,* "Mr. Johnson Talks," August 13, 1910, 394; *New York Age,* July 14,1910; November 10, 1910; *Talking Machine News,* "More Edison Bell Enterprise—Jack Johnson Makes Records," July 1914. On the first radio broadcast of the professional sports of boxing and baseball in 1921 as well as other radio firsts, see *New York Times,* September 11, 1927, p. XX17. The recording of professional sporting events continued throughout the 1920s. As late as 1927, Paramount recorded the Dempsey-Tunney "Long Count" boxing match held at Chicago's Soldier Field on September 22, 1927. The label made approximately five thousand copies of the legendary event. The match was the highest grossing sporting event of its day. The recordings of the fight were, however, a commercial failure. The recordings could not compete with the visual footage of the fight, which cost about a quarter. One Paramount executive recalled that "One dealer in Cleveland took ten." See Max E. Vreede, *Paramount 12/13000 Series* (London: Storyville Publications, 1971), 12531; Stephan Calt and Gayle Dean Wardlow, "Paramount's Decline and Fall—Part 5," *78 Quarterly* 1, no. 7 (1992), 25 fn14.

58. Cohn and Lewis, *The Good Old Days,* 34. For reports on the Scopes phonograph record, see Mike Seeger, "'Who Chose These Records': Interview with Frank Walker on June 19,1962," in *Anthology of American Folk Music,* ed. Josh Dunson et al. (New York: Oak Publications, 1973),8. Radio ownership is reported in Craig, "How America Adopted Radio: Demographic Differences in Set Ownership Reported in the 1930–1950 U.S. Censuses."

59. Berliner, "The Gramophone: Etching the Human Voice," 446.

60. "The Pope and the Phonograph," *Scientific American,* April 15, 1893, 229; "The Pope's Phonographic Message to America," *Scientific American,* May 20, 1893, 308; Brooks, "High Drama in the Record Industry," 51.

61. *Chicago Defender,* August 8, 1925, 3.

62. *Talking Machine World,* January 15, 1925, 68.

63. Tony Russell, Bob Pinson, and Country Music Hall of Fame & Museum (Nashville, Tenn.), *Country Music Records: A Discography, 1921-1942* (New York: Oxford University Press, 2004); Tony Russell, "Recorded Sermons" (electronic personal communication with author, May 24, 2013); Calt and Wardlow, "The Buying and Selling of Paramount—Part 3,"19; David Evans, "Interview with H. C. Speir," *John Edwards Memorial Foundation Quarterly* 8, no. 8 (1972), 118–119.

64. McPherson recordings listed at the Flower Pentecostal Heritage Center, Item Numbers: 10380248, 10405721. For more on McPherson's recorded sermons, see Matthew Avery Sutton, *Aimee Semple Mcpherson and the Resurrection of Christian America* (Cambridge, Mass.: Harvard University Press, 2007), 78. For Fuller, see Tona J. Hangen, *Redeeming the Dial: Radio, Religion, & Popular Culture in America* (Chapel Hill: University of North Carolina Press, 2002), 63, 86.

65. Geospatial and Statistical Data Center, *Historical Census Browser,* http://mapserver.lib.virginia.edu (2004); Craig, "How America Adopted Radio."

66. U.S. Bureau of the Census, *Negroes in the United States, 1920–32*, 254; University of Virginia, Geospatial and Statistical Data Center, *Historical Census Browser*; Craig, "How America Adopted Radio"; Stephen Calt and Gayle Dean Wardlow, "The Buying and Selling of Paramount—Part 3," *78 Quarterly* 1, no. 5 (1990); Stephen Calt and Gayle Dean Wardlow, "Paramount—Part 4: The Advent of Arthur Laibly," *78 Quarterly* 1, no. 6 (1991); Stephen Calt and Gayle Dean Wardlow, "Paramount's Decline and Fall—Part 5, *78 Quarterly* 1, no. 7 (1992) ."

CHAPTER 2. "RAGTIME MUSIC, RAGTIME MORALS"

1. Quoted in Robert E. Hemenway, *Zora Neale Hurston: A Literary Biography* (Urbana: University of Illinois Press, 1977), 92; Lawrence W. Levine, *Black Culture and Black Consciousness: Afro-American Folk Thought from Slavery to Freedom* (New York: Oxford University Press, 1977), 227.
2. W. E. Burghardt Du Bois, "Phonograph Records," *Crisis* (February 1921),152.
3. Dixon et al., *Blues & Gospel Records,* xxiii; Dixon and Godrich, *Recording the Blues,* 20, 41; Lebergott, *Pursuing Happiness,* 142–143.
4. Evelyn Brooks Higginbotham, "Rethinking Vernacular Culture," in *African American Religious Thought: An Anthology,* ed. Cornel West and Eddie S. Glaude, Jr.(Louisville: Westminster John Knox Press, 2003). My definition of hegemony draws upon T. J. Jackson Lears, "From Salvation to Self-Realization: Advertising and the Therapeutic Roots of the Consumer Culture, 1880–1930," in *The Culture of Consumption in America: Critical Essays in American History, 1880–1980,* ed. Richard Wightman Fox and T. J. Jackson Lears (New York: Pantheon Books, 1983). My argument draws upon the excellent and related discussion on the contested relationship of black religion and film in Judith Weisenfeld, *Hollywood Be Thy Name: African American Religion in American Film, 1929-1949* (Berkeley: University of California Press, 2007).
5. Suisman, *Selling Sounds,* 207.
6. For a complete listing of the twenty-nine languages, see Reid, "Race Records," 1.
7. Perry Bradford, *Born with the Blues* (New York: Oak Publications, 1964), 29–128; Kyle Crichton, "Thar's Gold in Them Hillbillies," *Collier's* (April 30, 1938).
8. Quote found in Ronald C. Foreman, Jr., "Jazz and Race Records, 1920–1932: Their Origins and Their Significance for the Record Industry and Society" (Ph.D. dissertation, University of Illinois, 1968), 129.
9. Letter from Victor Recording Laboratory to African American classical Violinist Clarence Cameron White, September 25, 1915, quoted in Brooks, *Lost Sounds,* 494.
10. Ibid.
11. Census, *Negro Population in the United States, 1790–1915,* 509–530; Census, *Negroes in the United States, 1920–32,* 303.

12. "Period of Unparalleled Popularity for Phonograph," *Talking Machine World*, December 15, 1918, 94.

13. Bradford, *Born with the Blues*,117.

14. Sutton, *Recording the 'Twenties*, 46; Bradford, *Born with the Blues*, 29–128; Crichton, "Thar's Gold in Them Hillbillies."

15. Sutton, *Recording the 'Twenties*, 46–47; *Encyclopedia of Recorded Sound in the United States* (New York: Garland, 1993), s.v., "Mamie Smith," 629; Bradford, *Born with the Blues*, 29–128; Crichton, "Thar's Gold in Them Hillbillies"; *Chicago Defender*, March 13, 1920, 6. The same article was printed again in the *Defender* several months later. "The Golden Age of Blues—Recording," *Record Research* 2, no. 11 (1957), 3.

16. Polk Brockman, interview with Ed Kahn and Archie Green Atlanta, Ga., August 11, 1961. (Audiotapes FT-12660, 12661, and 12662 in the Ed Kahn Collection #20360, Southern Folklife Collection, Wilson Library, University of North Carolina at Chapel Hill), Audio; *Encyclopedia of Recorded Sound in the United States.*

17. U.S. Department of Labor, *Statistics, Problems, and Policies relating to the Greater Inclusion of Negro Wage Earners in American Industry and Agriculture* (Washington, D.C.: Government Printing Office, 1921), Table 9, 17.

18. Du Bois, "Phonograph Records; Calt and Wardlow, "The Buying and Selling of Paramounts—Part 3," 8; Polk Brockman, interview with Ed Kahn and Archie Green Atlanta, Ga., August 11, 1961.

19. *Norfolk Journal and Guide*, January 22, 1921, 8; U.S. Department of Labor, *Statistics, Problems, and Policies relating to the Greater Inclusion of Negro Wage Earners in American Industry and Agriculture*, 9; Bradford, *Born with the Blues*, 29–128; W. C. Handy, Arna Wendell Bontemps, and Abbe Niles, *Father of the Blues, an Autobiography* (New York: Macmillan Company, 1941), 200–201; Foreman, "Jazz and Race Records, 1920–1932," 61; Kenney, *Recorded Music in American Life*, 114; *Chicago Defender*, July 21, 1923, 6. Record sales cannot be confirmed with Okeh files. The company's files from this period were destroyed. See Sutton, *Recording the 'Twenties*, 49.

20. *Talking Machine World*, July 15, 1926; Anita Sheer, "Blues Galore: The Story of Victoria Spivey," *Record Research* 2, no. 8 (May/June 1956).

21. Seeger, "'Who Chose These Records'"; Chris Albertson, *Bessie* (New Haven: Yale University Press, 2003), 37, 49, 59, 65–66, 90; Kenney, *Recorded Music in American Life*, 110, 119–121; Paul Oliver, *Bessie Smith, Kings of Jazz* (London: Cassel, 1959), 8–17; Tuuk, *Paramount's Rise and Fall*, 64–68.

22. "Dealers Expect Big Sale of Blues Records by Bessie Smith, Who Has Joined Columbia Artists," *Music Trades* (February 16, 1924).

23. On recording totals, see Foreman, "Jazz and Race Records, 1920–1932," 92, 95, 99,134; "The Golden Age of Blues—Recording," 8; Kenney, *Recorded Music in American Life*, 110–129.

24. Mahalia Jackson and Evan McLeod Wylie, *Movin' on Up*, 3rd ed. (New York: Hawthorn Books, 1967), 29–30.

25. Charles Hiroshi Garrett, *Struggling to Define a Nation: American Music and the Twentieth Century* (Berkeley: University of California Press, 2008), 90.

26. Quoted in Phyl Garland, *The Sound of Soul* (Chicago: H. Regnery Co., 1969), 90.

27. Paul V. Murphy, *The New Era: American Thought and Culture in the 1920s* (Lanham, Md.: Rowman & Littlefield, 2012), 55.

28. Calt and Wardlow, "The Buying and Selling of Paramount—Part 3," 18; Evans, "Interview with H.C. Speir," 118. In 1942 Speir's store burned to the ground. He left the business.

29. Art Satherly, taped interview by Norm Cohen and G. Earle with Ken Griffis and Bill Ward, June 12, 1971, Audio Tapes FT1647-1648 in the Southern Folklife Collection, Wilson Library, University of North Carolina at Chapel Hill; Lizabeth A. Cohen, *Making a New Deal: Industrial Workers in Chicago, 1919–1939* (Cambridge, U.K.: Cambridge University Press, 1990), 155; LeRoi Jones, *Blues People* (New York: Morrow Quill Paperbacks, 1963), 101.

30. Calt and Wardlow, "The Buying and Selling of Paramount—Part 3," 22.

31. *Talking Machine World*, June 15,1926, 6, 18.

32. Ibid.; *Chicago Defender*, June 12, 1926, A5.

33. Ibid..

34. Ibid., A5, A8, 6.

35. Ibid.

36. Ibid.

37. Langston Hughes, "The Negro Artist and the Racial Mountain," *Nation* 122, no. 3181 (June 23, 1926), 693–694; Erin D. Chapman, *Prove It on Me: New Negroes, Sex, and Popular Culture in the 1920s* (New York: Oxford University Press, 2012), 7.

38. *New York Times*, October 7, 1928, SM19.

39. Kevin Kelly Gaines, *Uplifting the Race: Black Leadership, Politics, and Culture in the Twentieth Century* (Chapel Hill: University of North Carolina Press, 1996), xiv–4, 62.

40. Ibid., xiv–4; *Atlanta Constitution*, "Bars Ragtime Music," June 30, 1913, 5; "Music and Morals Related, Declares Colored Pastor in Opposing 'Ragtime,'" July 6, 1914, p. 3.

41. Evelyn Brooks Higginbotham, *Righteous Discontent: The Women's Movement in the Black Baptist Church, 1880–1920* (Cambridge, Mass.: Harvard University Press, 1993), 14-15, 182.

42. Deborah G. White, *Too Heavy a Load: Black Women in Defense of Themselves, 1894–1994* (New York: W. W. Norton, 1999), 24; Higginbotham, *Righteous Discontent*, 182–183.

43. Angela Y. Davis, *Blues Legacies and Black Feminism: Gertrude "Ma" Rainey, Bessie Smith, and Billie Holiday* (New York: Pantheon Books, 1998), 120; Higginbotham, *Righteous Discontent*, 15.

44. White, *Too Heavy a Load*, 126–129.

45. Chapman, *Prove It on Me*, 1–2; Fitzgerald, "Echoes of the Jazz Age," 462. On "Flappers," see for example, Kenneth A Yellis, "Prosperity's Child: Some Thoughts on the Flapper," *American Quarterly* 21, no. 1 (1969).

46. Hughes, "The Negro Artist and the Racial Mountain," 693.

47. *Talking Machine World*, January 15, 1922, 48.

48. *Chicago Defender*, May 31, 1924, 12; July 19, 1924, 5. Not all race record ads were caricatures. Even the industry recognized as much. See "Okeh Race Records Featured," *Talking Machine World*, May 15, 1925, 116.

49. "Dramatic Action in Window Nets Big Sale in Records—Jail House Blues Advertised by Live Boy in Striped Uniform in Window of Kaplan Furniture Co. Alexandria, La," *Music Trades* (January 26, 1924).

50. *Pittsburgh Courier*, February 25, 1928, A1;William P. Jones, *The March on Washington: Jobs, Freedom, and the Forgotten History of Civil Rights* (New York: W. W. Norton, 2013), 4–6.

51. *Pittsburgh Courier*, August 1, 1925, 16.

52. Ibid.; *Pittsburgh Courier*, February 25, 1928, A1.

53. "Widening the Gap," *Half-Century Magazine* 18, no. 1 (January–February 1925), 3, 21. On *Half Century Magazine,* see Noliwe M. Rooks, *Ladies' Pages: African American Women's Magazines and the Culture That Made Them* (New Brunswick, N.J.: Rutgers University Press, 2004), 4. Also see Albert Kreiling, "The Rise of Black Consumer Magazines: The Case of the 'Half-Century,'" in *63rd Annual Meeting of the Association for Education in Journalism* (Boston, Mass.: 1980).

54. "The People's Forum," *Half-Century Magazine* 18, no. 1 (January–February 1925), 21.

55. Nannie Helen Burroughs, *Philadelphia Tribune*, November 27, 1930, 14.

56. *New York Amsterdam News*, April 11, 1923, 12; *Baltimore Afro-American*, April 20, 1923, 6.

57. Albertson, *Bessie*, 47.

58. *New York Amsterdam News*, April 11, 1923, 12; *Baltimore Afro-American*, April 20, 1923, 6.

59. Census, *Negro Population in the United States, 1790–1915*, 87; Census, *Negroes in the United States, 1920–32*, xv, 530–538.

60. Curtis J. Evans, *The Burden of Black Religion* (Oxford: Oxford University Press, 2008), 153.

61. W. E. B. Du Bois, "The Problem of Amusement," in *W.E.B. Du Bois on Sociology and the Black Community*, ed. Dan S. Green and Edwin D. Driver (Chicago: University of Chicago Press, 1980), 228–229; see also W. E. B. Du Bois, *The Philadelphia Negro: A Social Study*, reprint of 1899: Publications of the University of Pennsylvania Series in Political Economy and Public Law, ed., *The Oxford W. E. B. Du Bois* (New York: Oxford University Press, 2007).

62. Ibid., 229–234; Mark Hulsether, *Religion, Culture, and Politics in the Twentieth-Century United States* (New York: Columbia University Press, 2007)., 118.

63. George E. Haynes, "The Church and Negro Progress," *Annals of the American Academy of Political and Social Science* 140, no. *The American Negro* (November 1928), 266–267.

64. *Afro-American*, August 15, 1925, A11.

65. Lacy Kirk Williams, "Urbanization of Negroes: Effect on Their Religious Life," *Chicago Sunday Tribune*, January 13, 1929, in Milton C. Sernett, *African American Religious History: A Documentary Witness*, 2nd ed. (Durham, N.C.: Duke University Press, 1999), 372ff. For an excellent look at Williams and black urban Protestantism in Chicago, see Best, *Passionately Human, No Less Divine*.

66. Jane Edna Hunter, *A Nickel and a Prayer: The Autobiography of Jane Edna Hunter* (Nashville: Parthenon Press-Elli Kani Publishing Co., 1941). Reprint, edited by Rhondda Robinson Thomas (Morgantown: West Virginia University Press, 2011), 104, 106, 112.

67. Henry Hugh Proctor, *Between Black and White: Autobiographical Sketches* (Freeport, N.Y.: Books for Libraries Press, 1971, reprint of the 1925 ed.), 99.

68. *Atlanta Constitution*, "Proctor Makes Statement," August 17, 1902, 12; "Bars Ragtime Music," June 30, 1913, 5; "Music and Morals Related, Declares Colored Pastor in Opposing 'Ragtime,'" July 6, 1914, 3; "Last Concert Proves the Best of Colored Musical Festival," July 11, 1914, 7. On wholesome amusement in Atlanta, see Tera W. Hunter, *To 'Joy My Freedom: Southern Black Women's Lives and Labors after the Civil War* (Cambridge, Mass.: Harvard University Press, 1997).

69. Zechariah Johnson, "The People's Forum," *Half Century Magazine* (November–December 1922).

70. Langston L. Davis, "Is the Church Fulfilling Its Primary Objective," *Half Century Magazine*, (September–October 1922), 9, 15.

71. W. E. B. Du Bois, *Darkwater: Voices from within the Veil*, ed. Julie Nord (New York: Harcourt, Brace and Company, 1920; reprint, Dover Thrift edition,1999), 49.

72. W. E. B. Du Bois, "The Problem of Amusement," 234.

73. Here I am using William Gerald McLoughlin's description of awakenings and revivals. See McLoughlin, *Revivals, Awakenings, and Reform*.

74. *Chicago Defender*, October 1, 1927, A1.

75. Richard R. Wright, Jr., "Social Work and Influence of the Negro Church," *Annals of the American Academy of Political and Social Science* 30, Social Work of the Church (1907), 92. For an insightful analysis of Richard R. Wright, Jr., and his views on urban black Protestantism and social work, see Best, *Passionately Human, No Less Divine*.

76. "The People's Forum," *Half-Century Magazine* (November–December 1922).

77. *Chicago Defender*, October 1, 1927, A1.

78. Record Research, Black Swan Part 1 & 2, September and October 1955; Stephen Calt, "The Anatomy of a 'Race' Label—Part 2," *78 Quarterly*, no. 1 (1989),13; Suisman, "Co-Workers in the Kingdom of Culture"; Du Bois, "Phonograph Records"; W. E. Burghardt Du Bois, "The Black Swan," *Crisis* (March 1921).

79. Quoted in Suisman, "Co-Workers in the Kingdom of Culture,"1304; Suisman, *Selling Sounds*, 215.

80. Record Research, Black Swan Part 1 & 2, September and October 1955; Calt, "The Anatomy of a 'Race' Label—Part 2," 13; Suisman, "Co-Workers in the Kingdom of Culture"; Du Bois, "Phonograph Records"; Du Bois, "The Black Swan."

81. Ibid.

82. Record Research, "Black Swan Part 1 & 2," September and October 1955; Suisman, "Co-Workers in the Kingdom of Culture." On Smith and Black Swan, see ibid., 1310; Angela Y. Davis, *Blues Legacies and Black Feminism: Gertrude "Ma" Rainey, Bessie Smith, and Billie Holiday* (New York: Pantheon Books, 1998), 123, 379 n7. On the recording plan and pseudonyms of Black Swan, see "White Performers on Black Swan," *Mainspring* http://www.mainspringpress.com/BSpseudo.html, retrieved March 22, 2013; Allan Sutton, *A Guide to Pseudonyms on American Records, 1892–1942* (Westport, Conn.: Greenwood Press, 1993).

83. Art Satherly, taped interview by Norm Cohen and G. Earle with Ken Griffis and Bill Ward, June 12, 1971; Calt, "The Anatomy of a 'Race' Label—Part 2," 13–16; Dixon and Godrich, Recording the Blues, 22-23; Suisman, "Co-Workers in the Kingdom of Culture," 1297.

84. Rainey performed this show for several years in the north and south. See, for example, *Chicago Defender*, April 12, 1924, 6; February 13, 1926, 6. Thomas Dorsey's account is printed in Albertson, *Bessie*, 114–115.

85. Calt and Wardlow, "The Buying and Selling of Paramount—Part 3," 10.

86. Higginbotham, *Righteous Discontent*, 14, 200.

87. Robert Earl Hayden, *Collected Prose*, ed. Frederick Glaysher (Ann Arbor: University of Michigan Press, 1984), 144.

88. John Michael Giggie and Diane H. Winston, eds., *Faith in the Market: Religion and the Rise of Urban Commercial Culture* (New Brunswick, N.J.: Rutgers University Press, 2002), 1–5.

89. R. Laurence Moore, *Selling God: American Religion in the Marketplace of Culture* (New York: Oxford University Press, 1994), 9.

90. See Harry S. Stout, "Religion, Communications, and the Career of George Whitefield," in *Communication and Change in American Religious History*, ed. Leonard I. Sweet (Grand Rapids, Mich.: Eerdmans, 1993); Harry S. Stout, *The Divine Dramatist: George Whitefield and the Rise of Modern Evangelicalism* (Grand Rapids, Mich.: W. B. Eerdmans, 1991).

91. Charles G. Finney, *Lectures on Revivals of Religion*, 6th ed. (New York: Leavitt, Lord & Co., 1835), 167, 251.

92. See Philip Goff, "'We Have Heard the Joyful Sound': Charles E. Fuller's Radio Broadcast and the Rise of Modern Evangelicalism," in *Embodying the Spirit: New Perspectives on North American Revivalism*, ed. Michael James McClymond (Baltimore: Johns Hopkins University Press, 2004); Sutton, *Aimee Semple McPherson and the Resurrection of Christian America*; Joel A. Carpenter, *Revive Us Again:*

The Reawakening of American Fundamentalism (New York: Oxford University Press, 1997); Hangen, *Redeeming the Dial.*

93. Giggie and Winston, eds., *Faith in the Market*, 5.

94. *Afro-American*, May 19, 1928, 7.

CHAPTER 3. SELLING TO THE SOULS OF BLACK FOLK

1. *Chicago Defender*, March 07, 1925, 2; *Chicago Defender*, January 30, 1926, 7.

2. Ibid., September 26, 1925. Low rates of black literacy hindered published black sermons from being popular commodities.

3. Dixon et al., *Blues & Gospel Records*, 219; Sutton and Nauck, *American Record Labels & Companies*, 262; "The Gotham Banks Buys on Broadway," *New York Times*, June 28, 1922.

4. *Afro-American*, February 25, 1928, 4; William Gerald McLoughlin, *Modern Revivalism: Charles Grandison Finney to Billy Graham* (New York: Ronald Press, 1959). Several black evangelists prior to and concurrent with Dixon also took the name Black Billy Sunday. See *Norfolk Journal and Guide*, April 28, 1917, 4–5; May 5, 1917, 1. On wax, Reverend Dr. J. Gordon McPherson also took the name Black Billy Sunday. He recorded six sermons with Paramount records circa January 1931. See Dixon et al., 74. He was reportedly the inspiration for "De Lawd" in *The Green Pastures*. See *Norfolk Journal and Guide*, January 21, 1933, 8.

5. *Talking Machine World*, March 15, 1925, 102.

6. Sut Jhally, "Image-Based Culture: Advertising and Popular Culture," in *Gender, Race and Class in Media: A Text-Reader*, ed. Gail Dines and Jean M. Humez (Thousand Oaks, Calif.: Sage, 2003), 249–251; Lears, "From Salvation to Self-Realization."

7. Calt and Wardlow, "The Buying and Selling of Paramount—Part 3," 22; Calt and Wardlow, "Paramount—Part 4: The Advent of Arthur Laibly," 20–21.

8. Kyle Crichton, "Thar's Gold in Them Hillbillies," *Collier's* (April 30, 1938), 24, 27.

9. Evans, "Interview with H. C. Speir," 119; Gayle Dean Wardlow Interviews H.C. Speir in Jackson, Mississippi, on May 18, 1968. Audio. Inventory Number: tta 0182w; and Gayle Dean Wardlow Interviews H.C. Speir in Jackson, Mississippi, February 8, 1970. Audio. Inventory Number: tta 0182i, both in Gayle Dean Wardlow Audio Field Recorded Interviews, Center for Popular Music Archives Collection, Middle Tennessee State University, Murfreesboro, Tenn.

10. Calt and Wardlow, "Paramount—Part 4: The Advent of Arthur Laibly," 20–21.

11. *Norfolk Journal and Guide*, September 24, 1927, 12; July 21, 1923, 5.

12. *Newport News City Directory*, 1923, 153; *Norfolk Journal and Guide*, July 15, 1922, 1.

13. *Norfolk Journal and Guide*, July 16, 1921, 4; October 15, 1921, 1; July 21, 1923, 5; April 25, 1936, 17; September 9, 1939, 10.

14. Mike Seeger, "'Who Chose These Records': Interview with Frank Walker on June 19, 1962," in *Anthology of American Folk Music*, ed. Josh Dunson et al. (New York: Oak Publications, 1973).

15. *Norfolk Journal and Guide*, January 10, 1925, 2; February 7, 1925, 2; *Talking Machine World*, March 15, 1925, 102.

16. *The Online Discographical Project*, ed. Steve Abrams and Tyrone Settlemier, http://www.78discography.com, retrieved August 3, 2013; Albertson, *Bessie*, 193–196.

17. Dixon et al., *Blues & Gospel Records*, 219; Sermon catalogue number Co 14057-D; Albertson, *Bessie*, 35ff.

18. Dixon et al., *Blues & Gospel Records*, 219; Sermon catalogue number Co 14057-D. For another interpretation of the sermon, see Paul Oliver, *Songsters and Saints: Vocal Traditions on Race Records* (Cambridge, U.K.: Cambridge University Press, 1984), 156–157.

19. King James Version; Sermon from Co 14057-D; *Afro-American*, August 11, 1928, 19.

20. Several scholars have studied the debate between evangelicals and fundamentalists and liberal Protestants in the early twentieth century. See, for example, George M. Marsden, *Understanding Fundamentalism and Evangelicalism* (Grand Rapids, Mich.: W. B. Eerdmans, 1991); George M. Marsden, *Fundamentalism and American Culture*, 2nd ed. (New York: Oxford University Press, 2006). For a look at evangelical fundamentalists and media in early America, see Joel Carpenter, "Fundamentalist Institutions and the Rise of Evangelical Protestantism, 1929–1942," *Church History* 49, no. 1 (1980); Carpenter, *Revive Us Again*. For an insightful overview of the relationship of the trial to fundamentalism, see Michael Lienesch, *In the Beginning: Fundamentalism, the Scopes Trial, and the Making of the Antievolution Movement*, H. Eugene and Lillian Youngs (Chapel Hill: University of North Carolina Press, 2007).

21. *Afro-American*, August 1, 1925, A11; *Pittsburgh Courier*, June 6, 1925, 16.

22. *Afro-American*, July 25, 1925, A17.

23. Seeger, "'Who Chose These Records.'"

24. Dixon et al., *Blues & Gospel Records*, 1024; Sutton and Nauck, *American Record Labels & Companies*, 298; Vreede, 12301; Alex van der Tuuk, *Paramount's Rise and Fall: A History of the Wisconsin Chair Company and Its Recording Activities* (Denver: Mainspring Press, 2003), 57.

25. Gayle Dean Wardlow Interviews Alfred Schultz, August 2, 1968. Audio; David Luhrssen, "Blues in Wisconsin: The Paramount Records Story," *Wisconsin Academy Review*, no. (Winter 1998–1999), 18–19; Lynn Dumenil, *The Modern Temper: American Culture and Society in the 1920s* (New York: Hill and Wang, 1995), 58–61.

26. Gayle Dean Wardlow Interviews Alfred Schultz, August 2, 1968; "Plant in Which the Paramount Records Are Made," *Talking Machine World*, November 15, 1918, 62, 64; Norm Cohen, "I'm a Record Man, Uncle Art Reminisces," *John Edwards Memorial Foundation Quarterly* 8, no. 25 (1972), 20–21; Calt and Wardlow, "The Buying and Selling of Paramount—Part 3," 8–10.

27. Ibid.

28. Ibid. John Hammond, "Sights and Sounds," *New Masses* (May 25, 1937), 35–38; John Hammond and Irving Townsend, *John Hammond on Record: An Autobiography* (New York: Ridge Press, 1977),189–190.

29. Hammond, "Sights and Sounds"; Henry Johnson, "Phonograph Music," *New Masses* (April 20, 1937), 27; Hammond and Townsend, *John Hammond on Record*, 189–190. Following Hammonds's tour the factory was cleaned up and unionized, signing a closed shop contract with the United Electrical and Radio Workers, a Congress of Industrial Workers affiliate.

30. Gayle Dean Wardlow Interviews Alfred Schultz, August 2, 1968; Calt and Wardlow, "The Buying and Selling of Paramount—Part 3," 10; Crichton, "Thar's Gold in Them Hillbillies."

31. "Persistent Advertising Necessary To-Day," *Talking Machine World*, March 15, 1922, 8.

32. Robert Updegraff, "Tomorrow's Business and the Stream of Life," *Advertising and Selling*, April 20, 1927, 44, 52; President Calvin Coolidge, "President Coolidge Pays Advertising Its Highest Tribute," *Printers' Ink* 137, no. 5, November 4, 1926.

33. *Recent Social Trends in the United States: Report of the President's Research Committee on Social Trends with a Foreword by President Herbert Hoover*, ed. Wesley C. Mitchell-Chairman, vol. 1 (New York and London: McGraw-Hill Book Company, 1933), 207; Marchand, *Advertising the American Dream*, 7; Daniel Pope, *The Making of Modern Advertising* (New York: Basic Books, 1983), 22–29; *Printer's Ink,* May 27, 1915.

34. Paul K. Edwards, *The Southern Urban Negro as a Consumer* (New York: Prentice-Hall, 1932; reprint, Negro Universities Press, 1969),168, 185–196.

35. St. Clair Drake and Horace R. Cayton, *Black Metropolis: A Study of Negro Life in a Northern City* (New York: Harcourt, Brace, 1945), 399; Frederick German Detweiler, *The Negro Press in the United States* (Chicago, Ill.: University of Chicago Press, 1922), 9.

36. Edwards, *The Southern Urban Negro as a Consumer*, 171–175; Detweiler, *The Negro Press in the United States*, 6–8; Gene Roberts and Hank Klibanoff, *The Race Beat: The Press, the Civil Rights Struggle, and the Awakening of a Nation* (New York: Alfred A. Knopf, 2006), 12–16; *Pittsburgh Courier*, October 3, 1931, 6; *Atlanta City Director,* 1932. The Baltimore *Afro-American* was officially founded in 1892. Edwin Harleton, an aspiring writer, founded the *Pittsburgh Courier* in 1907. For more on the historical outlines of such black newspapers, see Henry Lewis Suggs, *P. B. Young, Newspaperman: Race, Politics, and Journalism in the New South, 1910–62* (Charlottesville: University Press of Virginia, 1988); Henry Lewis Suggs, *The Black Press in the Middle West, 1865–1985* (Westport, Conn.: Greenwood Press, 1996); Henry Lewis Suggs, *The Black Press in the South, 1865–1979* (Westport, Conn.: Greenwood Press, 1983); Hayward Farrar, *The Baltimore Afro-American, 1892–1950* (Westport, Conn.: Greenwood Press, 1998); Calt and

Wardlow, "The Buying and Selling of Paramount—Part 3," 10; quote by Horace M. Bond, "Negro Leadership since Washington," *South Atlantic Quarterly* XXIV, no. 2 (April 1925), 123–124.

37. Guy B. Johnson, "Newspaper Advertisements and Negro Culture," *Journal of Social Forces* 3, no. 4 (May 1925), 706–709; Edwards, *The Southern Urban Negro as a Consumer*, 169, 194–196.

38. Calt and Wardlow, "The Buying and Selling of Paramount—Part 3"; Edwards, *The Southern Urban Negro as a Consumer*, 185.

39. Edwards, *The Southern Urban Negro as a Consumer*, 172–173, 185–186; *Pittsburgh Courier*, February 25, 1928, 1.

40. See, for example, Calt and Wardlow, "The Buying and Selling of Paramount—Part 3." *Talking Machine World*, January 15, 1922; Sheer, "Blues Galore."

41. Marchand, *Advertising the American Dream*, 4–12; see also Dumenil, *The Modern Temper*, 6.

42. "Chains Will Now Court Public Opinion in Earnest," *Printers' Ink*, October 3, 1929, 168; President Calvin Coolidge, "President Coolidge Pays Adverting Its Highest Tribute, " *Printers' Ink* 137, no. 5 (November 4, 1926).

43. Jhally, "Image-Based Culture," 249–253. For examples of the effectiveness of such advertising in black life in the 1920s, see Edwards, *The Southern Urban Negro as a Consumer*, 197–214.

44. *Talking Machine World*, January 15, 1922, 48; *Pittsburgh Courier*, February 25, 1928, A1.

45. C. Luther Fry, *The U. S. Looks at Its Churches* (New York: Institute of Social and Religious Research, 1930), 62–63; Census, *Negroes in the United States, 1920–32*, xvi.

46. Calt and Wardlow, "The Buying and Selling of Paramount—Part 3," 10; Gayle Dean Wardlow Interviews Harry Charles in Birmingham, Alabama, 1968; Reverend W. A. White, "Divine Relationship of God to Man," *Preachers and Congregations Volume 7, 1925–1928,* Document Records, 2005, Audio; Advertisement in *Chicago Defender,* September 26, 1925, 7. Emphasis in the original.

47. In their initial study of chain stores, the Federal Trade Commission defined chain stores as "Organizations owning a controlling interest in two or more establishments which sell substantially similar merchandise at retail." This is inclusive of stores that operated mail order commerce as well. See U.S. Federal Trade Commission, *Chain Store Inquiry*, vol. 1: *Character and Extent of Chain and Cooperative Chain Store Business*, 72nd Congress, First Session, Senate Government Document No. 31 (Washington, D.C.: U.S. Government Printing Office, 1932), ix–32. On the estimated number of chain stores and retail sales, see U.S. Federal Trade Commission, *Chain Stores: Growth and Development of Chain Stores*, vol. 1: *Character and Extent of Chain and Cooperative Chain Store Business*, 72nd Congress, First Session, Senate Government Document No.100 (Washington, D.C.: U.S. Government Printing Office, 1932), 67; U.S. Federal

Trade Commission, *Chain Stores: State Distribution of Chain Stores, 1913–1928*, 72nd Congress, Second Session, Senate. Government Document No. 130 (Washington, D.C.: U.S. Government Printing Office, 1934), xi–xii.

48. Calt and Wardlow, "The Buying and Selling of Paramount—Part 3,"18–20; Gayle Dean Wardlow Interviews Harry Charles in Birmingham, Alabama, 1968, Audio, Inventory Number: tta 0182j and 0182K, Gayle Dean Wardlow Audio Field-Recorded Interviews, Center for Popular Music Archives Collection, Middle Tennessee State University, Murfreesboro, Tenn.

49. *Recent Social Trends in the United States: Report of the President's Research Committee on Social Trends with a Foreword by President Herbert Hoover*, 192–193, 870; U.S. Department of Commerce and the Bureau of Foreign and Domestic Commerce, *Statistical Abstract of the United States:1926*, ed. Department of Commerce: Bureau of Foreign and Domestic Commerce, vol. No. 49 (Washington, D.C.: Government Printing Office, 1927), 342; *Talking Machine World*, January 15, 1922, 48; Thomas J. Schlereth, "Country Stores, County Fairs, and Mail-Order Catalogues: Consumption in Rural America," in *Consuming Visions: Accumulation and Display of Goods in America, 1880–1920*, ed. Simon J. Bronner (New York: Norton, 1989), 349, 364–370; Cohn and Lewis, *The Good Old Days*, xxi.

50. "Rural Mail Service," *Half-Century Magazine* 18, no. 1 (January–February 1925).

51. *Chicago Defender*, September 26, 1925, 7; Calt and Wardlow, "The Buying and Selling of Paramount—Part 3," 11. Gayle Dean Wardlow Interviews Alfred Schultz, August 2, 1968.

52. *Chicago Defender*, October 31, 1925, 7; *Norfolk Journal and Guide*, March 20, 1926, 11.

53. *Pittsburgh Courier*, May 16, 1925, 9; September 19, 1925, 9; October 3, 1925, 11.

54. Calt and Wardlow, "The Buying and Selling of Paramount—Part 3," 22–24; Luhrssen, "Blues in Wisconsin: The Paramount Records Story," 19.

55. *Pittsburgh Courier*, February 19, 1927, 15. Emphasis in original.

56. *Afro-American*, March 21, 1925, A6; *Chicago Defender*, October 31, 1925, 7; *Pittsburgh Courier*, October 3, 1925, 11.

57. Calt and Wardlow, "The Buying and Selling of Paramounts—Part 3," 18.

58. Polk Brockman, Interview with Ed Kahn and Archie Green, Atlanta, Georgia, August 11, 1961; Polk Brockman, Interview with Helen Sewell, Ed Kahn, and Archie Green, Atlanta, Georgia, August 27, 1963. Transcript in "The Archie Green Papers #20002, Folder 44: Polk Brockman, Southern Folklife Collection, Wilson Library, University of North Carolina at Chapel Hill"; Gayle Dean Wardlow Interviews P.C. "Polk" Brockman, March 20, 1970 in Atlanta, Georgia, Inventory Number tta 0182j2, Gayle Dean Wardlow, Audio Field-Recorded Interviews, Center for Popular Music Archives Collection, Middle Tennessee State University, Murfreesboro, Tenn.; "Atlanta," *Talking Machine World*, June 15, 1922, 155; Roger S. Brown, "Interview with Polk Brockman, Recording Pioneer," *Living Blues*, no. 23 (1975).

59. *Talking Machine World*, February 15, 1921, 118–119; Calt and Wardlow, "The Buying and Selling of Paramount—Part 3," 19–24.

60. Ibid.

61. Art Satherly, Taped Interview by Norm Cohen and G. Earle with Ken Griffis and Bill Ward, June 12, 1971.

62. Ibid.; Cohen, "I'm a Record Man, Uncle Art Reminisces"; *Chicago Defender*, August 19, 1922, 6, emphasis in original; Calt and Wardlow, "The Buying and Selling of Paramount—Part 3," 11.

63. Calt and Wardlow, "The Buying and Selling of Paramount—Part 3," 11,18; Tuuk, *Paramount's Rise and Fall*, 96.

64. Crichton, "Thar's Gold in Them Hillbillies," 24.

65. Quoted in Roland Marchand, *Advertising the American Dream: Making Way for Modernity, 1920–1940* (Berkeley: University of California Press, 1985), xv. For a listing of the top hundred advertising campaigns, including those of N. W. Ayer and Son, see Bob Garfield, "Ad Age Advertising Century: Top 100 Campaigns," *Advertising Age*, March 29, 1999, http://adage.com/article/special-report-the-advertising-century/ad-age-advertising-century-top-100-advertising-campaigns/140150/, retrieved September 19, 2013; Percy Waxman, "Are We as Mean as All That?" *Printers' Ink*, June 23, 1927, 41–44.

66. *Afro-American*, July 27, 1929, 1; Dixon and Godrich, *Recording the Blues*, 64. Black Billy Sunday eventually established a radio ministry. See *Norfolk Journal and Guide*, December 28, 1929, 3; March 1, 1930, 2.

67. Dixon et al., *Blues & Gospel Records*, 1024; Calt, "The Anatomy of a 'Race' Label—-Part 2," 16; Calt and Wardlow, "The Buying and Selling of Paramount—Part 3;" Gayle Dean Wardlow Interviews H. C. Speir in Jackson, Mississippi, N.D. 1969; Art Satherly, Taped Interview by Norm Cohen and G. Earle with Ken Griffis and Bill Ward, June 12, 1971.

CHAPTER 4. APOSTLES OF MODERNITY

1. *Talking Machine World,* August 15, 1926, 80, 86.

2. Ibid., 80; *Afro-American,* August 21, 1926, 5. Emphasis in the original.

3. "Columbia Atlanta Branch Manager Visits New York," *Talking Machine World*, September 15, 1926, 124; "Atlanta," *Talking Machine World*, June 15, 1922, 155.

4. "Sells Thousand Records a Week of One Number," *Talking Machine World*, September 15, 1926, 70.

5. *Talking Machine World,* August 15, 1926, 80. I have provided prices for both 1918 and 1935 as a way to accommodate and control for the inflation of World War I and the decrease in prices and wages during the Great Depression. See Statistics, Table 9, 17.

6. See Zora Neale Hurston, *The Sanctified Church* (Berkeley: Turtle Island, 1981), 49–68,79–84,103–107; Albert Raboteau, "The Chanted Sermon," in Albert J. Raboteau, *A Fire in the Bones: Reflections on African American Religious History* (Boston: Beacon Press, 1995), 141–151. Michael W. Harris, *The Rise of Gospel*

Blues: The Music of Thomas Andrew Dorsey in the Urban Church (New York: Oxford University Press, 1992), 155–163. Harris credits Reverend Nix with many of the innovations in recorded sermons, especially preaching on the quotidian. I argue that Reverend Gates, as the first popular phonograph preacher, deserves much of the credit.

7. Hurston, 107; Mays and Nicholson, *The Negro's Church*, 97–99; Peter David Goldsmith, *When I Rise Cryin' Holy: African American Denominationalism on the Georgia Coast* (New York: AMS Press, 1989), 50, 65.

8. *Atlanta Daily World,* July 14, 1937, 6; *Afro-American*, May 19, 1928, 7; Harris, *The Rise of Gospel Blues,* 155–163.

9. Groundbreaking work on African Americans and televangelism has yielded several rubrics for describing black religious broadcasting. In her analysis of black women and televangelism, Marla F. Frederick characterized televangelism as being focused on individuals, prosperity, and "simplistic multiculturalism." Marla Faye Frederick, *Between Sundays: Black Women and Everyday Struggles of Faith* (Berkeley: University of California Press, 2003), 131–159. Jonathan L. Walton identifies the overarching characteristics of the phenomenon as "personality driven, crowd dependent, and entertainment orientation." Walton, *Watch This!* 5–8.

10. Census, *Twelfth Census of the United States, Population Schedule, Mountville, Troup, Georgia, Roll: 225, Page: 11a, Enumeration District: 66, Fhl Microfilm: 1240225.* Here the family lists him as Jim. Gates first appears in the city directory in 1914. However, the directory was issued on December 15, 1913. See *Atlanta City Directory, 1914.* The census enumerator reported that Gates was born in February. However, at some point Gates began to celebrate his birthday in July. Either the census enumerator was wrong or like many African Americans born during the era, Gates, lacking a birth certificate, chose July as his birth month. See *Atlanta Daily World,* July 16, 1934, 6. Scholars have tended to follow suit. See, for. example, Guido Van Rijn, "Praying for the Pastor: The Life of Rev. Jim Gates," *Living Blues*, no. 152 (2000). Auburn Avenue Research Library on African American Culture and History, "Summerhill Community Oral History Interviews," Archives Division (Atlanta-Fulton Public Library System). Neighborhood information and housing configurations may be found in U.S. Bureau of the Census and Enumerator Mrs. Edward S. Wellons, *Fifteenth Census of the United States: 1930—Population Schedule of Atlanta Ward 3 Roll: 361 Page: 31a, Enumeration District: 50, Supervisor's Distrct 4, Image: 138.0, Fhl Microfilm: 2340096.* Sheet No. 3A; Sanborn Map Company, "Digital Sanborn Maps, 1867–1970 Georgia" (Ann Arbor, Mich.: ProQuest Information and Learning Company, 2001), Vol. 1, 1931, Sheet #26. Summerhill is also described in Benjamin J. Davis, *Communist Councilman from Harlem: Autobiographical Notes Written in a Federal Penitentiary,* 1st ed. (New York: International Publishers, 1969); Karen Ferguson, *Black Politics in New Deal Atlanta* (Chapel Hill: University of North Carolina Press, 2002), 27. Domestic life in turn-of-the-century Atlanta is also thoroughly described in Hunter, *To 'Joy My Freedom.*

11. Martin Luther King, Sr., and Clayton Riley, *Daddy King: An Autobiography* (Boston: G. K. Hall, 1981), 15, 100–102. In his autobiography King reports that his parents never agreed on his name. His father maintained that his name was "Martin Luther," the respective names of the younger King's paternal uncles. His mother, however, maintained that his name was "Michael." King, not having a birth certificate, had gone by the name Michael for most of his life. However, upon his father's death in 1933, King stated that he legally changed his name to "Martin Luther" in honor of his father. See Martin Luther King and Clayton Riley, *Daddy King: An Autobiography* (New York: Morrow, 1980), 87–88; United States of America Bureau of the Census, *Fifteenth Census of the United States, 1930 Atlanta, Fulton, Georgia Roll 361 Page 20a Enumeration District 63 Image 831.0 Fhl Microfilm: 2340096*; United States of America Bureau of the Census, *Sixteenth Census of the United States, 1940 Atlanta, Fulton, Georgia Roll T627_733 Page 13b Enumeration District 160-241.*

12. King, Sr., and Riley, *Daddy King*, 101–102, 140–144, 166–169, 178, 187, 213.

13. Mount Calvary Baptist Church Journal Committee, "100th Anniversary," ed. Mount Calvary Baptist Church (Atlanta: 2000), 12. On black migration clubs and congregations established along regional networks, see Best, *Passionately Human, No Less Divine.*

14. Earl Lewis, *In Their Own Interests: Race, Class, and Power in Twentieth-Century Norfolk, Virginia* (Berkeley: University of California Press, 1991), 95.

15. Mount Calvary Baptist Church Journal Committee, 12; *Atlanta Daily World*, June 11, 1934, 6. After a long pause, Reverend Gates announced in one of his sermons in 1940 that he had been pastor at Mount Calvary for twenty-six years, which would have placed him at the church in 1914. However, the aforementioned church records and newspaper reports differ with this calculation, placing Gates at the church in late 1915 or early 1916. It is very possible that Reverend Gates's calculation during the live on-location recording is simply a mathematical error. See the front page of the *Atlanta Daily World* on November 24, 1934. Also see "Men and Women Talk Too Much," Bluebird BB8382. All sermons accessed from Reverend J. M. Gates, *Rev. J. M. Gates: Complete Recorded Works in Chronological Order* (Newton Stewart, U.K.: Document Records, 2005), Audio.

16. Polk Brockman, Interview with Ed Kahn and Archie Green Atlanta, Georgia August 11, 1961 (Audiotapes FT-12660, 12661, and 12662 in the Ed Kahn Collection #20360, Southern Folklife Collection, Wilson Library, University of North Carolina at Chapel Hill), Audio; Polk C. Brockman to Archie Green, September 3, 1957, in the Archie Green Papers #20002, Folder 44: Polk Brockman, Southern Folklife Collection, Wilson Library, University of North Carolina at Chapel Hill; Brown, "Interview with Polk Brockman, Recording Pioneer"; Gayle Dean Wardlow Interviews P. C. "Polk" Brockman, March 20, 1970, in Atlanta, Georgia.

17. Polk Brockman, Interview with Ed Kahn and Archie Green Atlanta, Georgia, August 11, 1961; Calt and Wardlow, "Paramount's Decline and Fall—Part 5," 3; Dixon et al., *Blues & Gospel Records*, 287.

18. On acoustic recording, see Frank Hoffman, *Encyclopedia of Recorded Sound*, 2nd ed., 2 vols., vol. 1 (New York: Routledge, 2005), 364–365; Thompson, *The Soundscape of Modernity*, 264; James Lastra, "Fidelity Versus Intelligibility," in Jonathan Sterne, ed., *The Sound Studies Reader* (New York: Routledge, 2012), 248; Sutton and Nauck, *American Record Labels & Companies*, xvii.

19. Thompson, *The Soundscape of Modernity*, 264; Albertson, *Bessie*, 97–98; *Talking Machine World*, February 15, 1925, 118; Gary Marmorstein, *The Label: The Story of Columbia Records* (New York: Thunder's Mouth Press, 2007), 54–55. Columbia released the first electronically recorded record in March 1925. Seven other labels followed by the end of the year. Labels such as Paramount that did not quickly adapt their recording methods suffered. One local dealer complained about Paramount, "They wasn't putting out good records . . . just wouldn't track [play] right. It just wasn't a quality record." Eventually, he recalled, "Dealers cut 'em off . . . quit handling their products." See Calt and Wardlow, "Paramount's Decline and Fall—Part 5," 9; Hoffman, *Encyclopedia of Recorded Sound*, 364–365.

20. On Finney and revivalism, see Finney, *Lectures on Revivals of Religion*; Charles E. Hambrick-Stowe, *Charles G. Finney and the Spirit of American Evangelicalism* (Grand Rapids, Mich.: W. B. Eerdmans, 1996); McLoughlin, *Modern Revivalism*. For a look at a contemporary who opposed the practice, see Reverend J. W. Nevin, *The Anxious Bench* (Chambersburg, Pa.: Weekly Messenger, 1843).

21. The popularity of Death's Black Train kept the tune in circulation. Hillbilly artist Emry and Henry Arthur, for example, performed the song for the Brunswick Company in January 1928 and it was recorded May 7, 1935 by the American Record Corporation. See Norm Cohen and David Cohen, *Long Steel Rail: The Railroad in American Folksong*, 2nd ed. (Urbana: University of Illinois Press, 2000), 625–628.

22. Giggie, *After Redemption*, 51; Giggie, "'When Jesus Handed Me a Ticket': Images of Railroad Travel and Spiritual Transformation among African Americans, 1865–1917," in David Morgan and Sally M. Promey, eds., *The Visual Culture of American Religions* (Berkeley: University of California Press, 2001), 250; Milton C. Sernett, *Bound for the Promised Land: African American Religion and the Great Migration* (Durham: Duke University Press, 1997), 59; *Atlanta Daily World*, June 11, 1934, 6.

23. *Chicago Defender*, August 21, 1926, 8.

24. *Talking Machine World*, August 15, 1926, 86.

25. "Sells Thousand Records a Week of One Number," *Talking Machine World*, September 15, 1926, 70; *Atlanta Daily World*, August 24, 1945, 6.

26. *Atlanta Daily World*, August 24, 1945, 6. For firsthand accounts of common phonograph listening practices in black neighborhoods during the 1920s, see,

for example, Jackson and Wylie, *Movin' on Up*; Bushell and Tucker, *Jazz from the Beginning*; Garland; Levine, *Black Culture and Black Consciousness*.

27. Order figures for Columbia found in Mahony, *The Columbia 13/14000-D Series*, 34; Albertson, *Bessie*, 130–131. A few sales numbers are available through the archives of Columbia, Edison, and Victor. See Sutton, *A Phonograph in Every Home*, 307–310.

28. Mahony, *The Columbia 13/14000-D Series*; Albertson, *Bessie*, 130–131.

29. Gates was the copyright owner, but probably agreed to a publishing arrangement with Brockman. See Library of Congress Copyright Office, *Catalogue of Copyright Entries, Part 3: Musical Compositions for the Year 1926*. Vol. 21, Nos. 1–12 (Washington, D.C.: Government Printing Office, 1927), ii, 1174; Transcriptions of John K. Mackenzie Interviews of J. Mayo Williams, July 28 and August 5, 1970. The John K. MacKenzie Collection, Part 1, Box 2, Folder 13, Manuscripts and Archives, Department of the Indiana Historical Society; William Sachs, "Land o' Melody: Melody Mart Notes," *Billboard*, September 18, 1926, 21; Bruce Bastin, *Never Sell a Copyright: Joe Davis and His Role in the New York Music Scene 1916–1978* (Chigwell, Essex, U.K.: Storyville Publications Ltd., 1990); Bruce Bastin, with Kip Lornell, *The Melody Man: Joe Davis and the New York Music Scene, 1916–1978* (Jackson: University Press of Mississippi, 2012); Cohen and Cohen, *Long Steel Rail*, 625–628.

30. Polk Brockman, Interview with Ed Kahn and Archie Green, Atlanta, Georgia, August 11, 1961; Polk Brockman to Archie Green, May 31, 1963, in The Archie Green Papers #20002, Folder 44: Polk Brockman, Southern Folklife Collection, Wilson Library, University of North Carolina at Chapel Hill. U.S. Dept of Labor, Bureau of Labor Statistics, "Family Income and Expenditure in the Southeastern Region; 1935–1936 Prepared by A.D.H. Kaplan," 116.

31. Polk Brockman, Interview with Ed Kahn and Archie Green Atlanta, Georgia August 11, 1961; Calt and Wardlow, "The Buying and Selling of Paramount—Part 3." H. C. Speir claimed he and the artists he discovered received $100 each. Gayle Dean Wardlow Interviews H. C. Speir in Jackson, Mississippi, February 8, 1970. Audio.

32. Dixon et al., *Blues & Gospel Records*, 287–294.

33. Abrams and Settlemier, "The Online Discographical Project," http://www.78discography.com, accessed December 13, 2013; Dixon et al., *Blues & Gospel Records*, 287–294; Dixon and Godrich, *Recording the Blues*, 42; Polk Brockman, Interview with Helen Sewell, Ed Kahn, and Archie Green Atlanta Georgia, August 27, 1963. Transcript in the Archie Green Papers, #20002, Folder 44: Polk Brockman, Southern Folklife Collection, Wilson Library, University of North Carolina at Chapel Hill; Brown, "Interview with Polk Brockman, Recording Pioneer." On record label descriptions, see Sutton and Nauck, *American Record Labels & Companies*.

34. Dixon et al., *Blues & Gospel Records*, 287–294; Sutton and Nauck, *American Record Labels & Companies*; Dixon and Godrich, *Recording the Blues*, 70.

35. Brown, "Interview with Polk Brockman, Recording Pioneer." Dixon et al., *Blues & Gospel Records*, 287–294.

36. Thomas A. Edison, "Trial Books," ed. Edison National Historic Site (West Orange, N.J.), September 10, 1926, quoted in Mark A. Humphrey, "Holy Blues: The Gospel Tradition," in *Nothing but the Blues: The Music and the Musicians*, ed. Lawrence Cohn (New York: Abbeville Press, 1993); Lacayo et al., "Time Inc. Specials: Thomas Edison: His Electrifying Life," 48. Edison tried his hand in the race record genre between 1923 and 1925. Although he recorded race record artists who were previously successful on other labels, Edison's weak marketing and self-imposed limited distribution produced poor sales and provided the company with sufficient justification to exit the race record genre.

37. Dixon et al., *Blues & Gospel Records*, 287–294.

38. Polk Brockman, Interview with Ed Kahn and Archie Green, Atlanta, Georgia, August 11, 1961; Dixon and Godrich, *Recording the Blues*, 64–65, 74–77, 83, 95; Dixon et al., *Blues & Gospel Records*, xxiii, 287–294.

39. Gayle D. Wardlow, "Rev. D. C. Rice: Gospel Singer," *Storyville*, no. 23 (1969).

40. *Pittsburgh Courier*, November 13, 1943, 8.

41. On black holiness groups and their orientation to the market, see Giggie, "Preachers and Peedlers of God"; Giggie, *After Redemption: Jim Crow and the Transformation of African American Religion in the Delta, 1875–1915*; James Earl Massey, *African Americans and the Church of God, Anderson, Indiana: Aspects of a Social History* (Anderson, Ind.: Anderson University Press, 2005); David Douglass Daniels, III, "The Cultural Renewal of Slave Religion: Charles Price Jones and the Emergence of the Holiness Movement in Mississippi, " Ph.D. dissertation, Union Theological Seminary, New York City, 1992; Cheryl Jeanne Sanders, *Saints in Exile: The Holiness-Pentecostal Experience in African American Religion and Culture* (New York: Oxford University Press, 1996), 89; Wardlow, "Rev. D. C. Rice: Gospel Singer," 167.

42. Oliver, *Songsters and Saints*, 170; Dixon et al., *Blues & Gospel Records*, 576–577; Dixon and Godrich, *Recording the Blues*, 95.

43. In 1910 slightly more than 20 percent of the country's black population was labeled "Mulatto," meaning that they appeared to have "a perceptible trace of white blood." Census enumerators were directed to use the designation of Mulatto when they perceived, using their own judgment, that someone was "not evidently a full-blooded Negro," but had "some proportion or perceptible trace of Negro blood." See Census, *Negro Population in the United States, 1790–1915*, 22–23, 207, 479; *Thirteenth Census of the United States*, 1910, Hillsboro Ward 3, Hill, Texas, Roll: T624_1564, Page: 15B, Enumeration District: 0156, FHL microfilm: 1375577; *Fourteenth Census of the United States*, 1920: Little River, Cleveland, Oklahoma, Roll: T625_1456, Page: 3A, Enumeration District: 10, Image: 857; Don Kent, "An Interview with Reverend F. W. Mcgee," in *The American Folk Music Occasional: The Voice of Authentic American Folk Music*, ed. Chris Strachwitz and Pete Welding (New York: Oak Publications, 1970), 49–52.

44. Kent, "An Interview with Reverend F. W. Mcgee," 49–52; Census, *Negro Population in the United States, 1790–1915*, 22–23, 207, 479; *Thirteenth Census of the United States*, 1910, Hillsboro Ward 3, Hill, Texas; Roll: T624_1564, Page: 15B, Enumeration District: 0156, FHL microfilm: 1375577; *Fourteenth Census of the United States*, 1920: Little River, Cleveland, Oklahoma, Roll: T625_1456, Page: 3A, Enumeration District: 10, Image: 857. Ford recounts his conversion and call experience on "My Wife's a Holy Roller," Victor V38596 Tuesday, April 15, 1930.

45. Kent, "An Interview with Reverend F. W. Mcgee," 49–52.

46. Ibid., 49–52; United States of America, Bureau of the Census. *Fifteenth Census of the United States*, 1930: Chicago, Cook, Illinois; Roll: 421 Page: 1B Enumeration District: 155, Image: 408.0, FHL microfilm: 2340156; *Chicago Defender*, May 27, 1922, 4; *Chicago Defender*, July 24, 1926, 5; Harris, *The Rise of Gospel Blues,*108–111; Randall K. Burkett, "The Baptist Church in the Years of Crisis: J. C. Austin and Pilgrim Baptist Church, 1926–1950," in *African-American Christianity: Essays in History*, ed. Paul E. Johnson (Berkeley: University of California Press, 1994), 137–138. James Mundy resigned from Pilgrim in 1926. In an interview with Michael Harris he recalled resigning from several churches on account of being offered more money and more musical control at another church. Famed pastor J. C. Austin became pastor of Pilgrim in 1926 and continued this classical form of worship by hiring classically trained chorus director Edward Boatner. However, in 1932 he invited Thomas Dorsey to the church, gaining Pilgrim the reputation as the mainline Black Baptist church that catapulted Dorsey and Gospel music to fame.

47. Kent, "An Interview with Reverend F. W. Mcgee."

48. Ibid.; Wardlow, "Rev. D. C. Rice: Gospel Singer."

49. Anthea D. Butler, *Women in the Church of God in Christ: Making a Sanctified World* (Chapel Hill: University of North Carolina Press, 2007), 14–15.

50. Dixon et al., *Blues & Gospel Records*, 576–577; Kent, "An Interview with Reverend F. W. Mcgee," 51; Oliver, *Songsters and Saints*, 176. Studio location listed in Sutton and Nauck, *American Record Labels & Companies*, 335.

51. Abrams and Settlemier, "The Online Discographical Project," accessed December 13, 2013; Dixon et al., *Blues & Gospel Records*, 576–577.

52. Dixon et al., *Blues & Gospel Records*, 576–577; Kent, "An Interview with Reverend F. W. Mcgee," 51; Harris, *The Rise of Gospel Blues*, 228; Oliver, *Songsters and Saints,*176. Reverend F. W. McGee, *Three Ways–Parts 1&2*, Victor 21581, Saturday, June 16, 1928.

53. *Chicago Defender*, October 1, 1927, 8.

54. Kent, "An Interview with Reverend F. W. Mcgee"; Malcolm Shaw, "Arizona Dranes and Okeh," *Storyville* 27 (February 1970); Duke Ellington, *Music Is My Mistress* (Garden City, N.Y.: Doubleday, 1973); Albertson, *Bessie*.

55. Kent, "An Interview with Reverend F. W. McGee," 51–52; Dixon et al., *Blues & Gospel Records*, 576–577. For a different historical assessment of black

Pentecostalism and contemporary black religious broadcasting, see Walton, *Watch This!* 79–86.

56. Calculated from Census, *Negro Population in the United States, 1790–1915,* 509–530; Census, *Negroes in the United States, 1920–32,* xvi, 303; Best, *Passionately Human, No Less Divine,* 1–3.

57. See Hopson's sermon ad in *Afro-American,* August 21, 1926, August 28, 1926. On the recording date, see Abrams and Settlemier, "The Online Discographical Project." Previously the date was believed to be April 1926. See Dixon et al., *Blues & Gospel Records.* Paul Oliver omits Hopson from his otherwise detailed discussion of black women phonograph preachers. Oliver, *Songsters and Saints,* 183–188.

58. Evangelist R. H. Harris recorded for Gennett on March 16, 1927. Evangelist R. H. Harris, "Jesus Is Coming Soon," Wednesday, March 16, 1927, Gennett 6148; Sister Ernia Mae Cunningham, "Sign of Judgment," circa April 1927, Paramount 12473; Missionary Josephine Miles, "God's Warning to the Church," Gennett 6676 and "Holiness" Gennett 6571, Wednesday, May 16, 1928. Sermon dates and names found in Dixon et al., *Blues & Gospel Records*; Oliver, *Songsters and Saints,* 183–188.

59. Ibid.

60. U.S. Census, 1930, Cincinnati, Hamilton, Ohio. Roll: 1813, Page 12A, Enumeration District: 201. Image: 332.0. FHL microfilm: 2341547. Leora is listed as unemployed in the 1930 Census report. However, in 1940 she is listed as a "worker at the church." See U.S. Census, 1940, Cincinnati, Hamilton, Ohio Roll: T627_3197. Page 3B, Enumeration District: 91–276A. The 1940 Census incorrectly identifies the family as "Muscleus" and "Leola" Ross. However, the house number, duration of residence, and Virgil Faulkner are identified correctly.

61. Dixon et al., *Blues & Gospel Records,* 773; Abrams and Settlemier, "The Online Discographical Project," accessed December 13, 2013; Sutton and Nauck, *American Record Labels & Companies,* 306.

62. *Chicago Defender,* August 27, 1927, 3; Yellis, "Prosperity's Child: Some Thoughts on the Flapper," 47–48.

63. On Victor, see Raymond Sooy, *Memoirs of My Recording and Traveling Experiences for the Victor Talking Machine Company, 1898–1925,* entry July 11, 1927. Dixon et al., *Blues & Gospel Records,* 773; Paul Oliver, *Songsters and Saints,* 183–185; New American Standard Bible.

64. White, *Too Heavy a Load,* 114.

65. E. Franklin Frazier, "Three Scourges of the Negro Family," *Opportunity* 4, no. 7 (July 1926); *Negro World,* June 9, 1923, quoted in White, 121; *New York Times,* February 25, 1930, 26.

66. "Manish Women," Okeh 9779, December 16, 1929.

67. Gallup Poll, May 1947. Retrieved May 20, 2013 from the iPOLL Databank, Roper Center for Public Opinion Research, University of Connecticut. http://www.ropercenter.uconn.edu/data_access/ipoll/ipoll.html.

68. "Dealers Expect Big Sale of Blues Records by Bessie Smith, Who Has Joined Columbia Artists," *Music Trades*, February 16, 1924.

69. *Chicago Defender*, October 9, 1926, 6; April 2, 1927, 4. Unfortunately, the Circuit Court records of the suit have been lost. *Afro-American*, May 19, 1928, 7; *Atlanta Daily World*, December 8, 1938, 5; Dixon et al., *Blues & Gospel Records*, 123–125; Mahony, *The Columbia 13/14000-D Series*; Frank Driggs and Chuck Haddix, *Kansas City Jazz: From Ragtime to Bebop—a History* (New York: Oxford University Press, 2005), 50–51; Dixon and Godrich, *Recording the Blues*, 32; Bastin, *Never Sell a Copyright*.

70. Wardlow, "Rev. D. C. Rice: Gospel Singer"; Dixon et al., *Blues & Gospel Records*, 753, 845.

71. Dixon et. al., *Blues & Gospel Records*, 680–682; Oliver, *Songsters and Saints*, 150–153; Harris, *The Rise of Gospel Blues,*156–163. On the map, see Dixon and Godrich, *Recording the Blues*, 57; *Chicago Defender*, June 11, 1927, 3.

72. Oliver, *Songsters and Saints*, 145.

CHAPTER 5. A NEW PREACHER FOR A NEW NEGRO

1. *Atlanta Daily World*, August 19, 1945, 3; *Atlanta City Directory*, 1932. The Atlanta Baptist Institute was also known as the Atlanta Baptist Preparatory Institute as well as the Sylvia Bryant Preparatory School. The school boasted an annual expenditure of $1,400. Sylvia Bryant died on January 11, 1920. Robert G. Gardner, "Baptist Educational Institutions in Georgia," in *Georgia Baptist History Depository, Special Collections, Jack Tarver Library* (Macon, Ga.: Mercer University, September 12, 2007); Martin Luther King, Sr., and Clayton Riley, *Daddy King: An Autobiography* (Boston: G. K. Hall, 1981), 20–21, 110; Higginbotham, *Righteous Discontent*, 157, 272 n20.

2. King, Sr., and Riley, *Daddy King*, 20–21, 110, 150; W. A. Daniel, *The Education of Negro Ministers: Based upon a Survey of Theological Schools for Negroes in the United States Made by Robert L. Kelly and W. A. Daniel*, ed. Galen M. Fisher, Committee on Social and Religious Surveys, the Institute of Social and Religious Research (New York: George H. Doran Company, 1925; reprint, Negro University Press, 1969), 27, 53–55; Davis, *Communist Councilman from Harlem*, 34. Emphasis added.

3. King, Sr., and Riley, *Daddy King*, 101–102, 140–144, 166–167, 178, 187, 213.

4. United States of America, Bureau of the Census, *Sixteenth Census of the United States, 1940 Atlanta, Fulton, Georgia Roll T627_733 Page 13b Enumeration District 160-241*; Census, *Negroes in the United States, 1920–32*, 253; Mays and Nicholson, *The Negro's Church*, 186–189, 206, 216, 263–264; New Negro Clergyman Reverend Adam Clayton Powell, Jr., of Harlem's Abyssinian Baptist Church reported the same income in 1939. See United States of America, Bureau of the Census, *Sixteenth Census of the United States, 1940 New York, New York Roll: T627_2667 Page 5b Enumeration District: 31-1811*.

5. King, Sr., and Riley, *Daddy King*, 6. *Atlanta City Directory*, 1926–1932; *Atlanta Independent*; "Biographical/Historical Note," Yates and Milton Drugstore

Records, Archives Division, Auburn Avenue Research Library on African American Culture and History, Atlanta-Fulton Public Library System.

6. *Atlanta Daily World*, March 21, 1937, 3.

7. *Atlanta Daily World*, July 14, 1932, 6; October 20, 1935, 1; August 2, 1936, 4; March 21, 1937, 3. In an interview with Michael Harris, Thomas Dorsey detailed his friendship with Reverend Gates. Harris, *The Rise of Gospel Blues*.

8. *Atlanta Daily World*, July 14, 1932, 6.

9. E. Brooks Holifield, *God's Ambassadors: A History of the Christian Clergy in America* (Grand Rapids, Mich.: W. B. Eerdmans, 2007), 1–3; W. E. B. Du Bois, "The Religion of the American Negro," *New World: A Quarterly Review of Religion* 9 (December 1900), 615.

10. *Recent Social Trends in the United States: Report of the President's Research Committee on Social Trends with a Foreword by President Herbert Hoover*, 309.

11. Gerald Early, "The New Negro Era and the Great African American Transformation," *American Studies* 491/2 (Spring/Summer 2008), 15–16; Edward Franklin Frazier, *Black Bourgeoisie* (Glencoe, Ill.: Free Press, 1957; reprint, New York: Free Press, 1997), 124–129.

12. W. E. B. Du Bois, *The College-Bred Negro: Report of a Social Study Made under the Direction of Atlanta University; Together with the Proceedings of the Fifth Conference for the Study of the Negro Problems, Held at Atlanta University, May 29–30, 1900*, ed. Corresponding Secretary of the Conference W. E. Burghardt Du Bois, 2nd abridged edition, Atlanta University Publications (Atlanta, Ga.: Atlanta University Press, 1900; reprint, 1902), 13; W. E. B. Du Bois, *The College-Bred Negro American: Report of a Social Study Made by Atlanta University under the Patronage of the Trustees of the John F. Slater Fund: With the Proceedings of the 15th Annual Conference for the Study of the Negro Problems, Held at Atlanta University, on Tuesday, May 24th, 1910*, Atlanta University Publications (Atlanta, Ga.: Atlanta University Press, 1910); Mays and Nicholson, *The Negro's Church*, 41–57, 301–304.

13. I have chosen to use the 1931 to 1932 educational statistics of black urban ministers as opposed to the published data from the 1926 Government Census of religious bodies, because the 1926 survey is heavily slanted toward rural black ministers. Only 26 percent of the twenty thousand black ministers studied were urban clergy. However, the findings reported in 1931 to 1932 are slightly slanted toward the urban south, which is apropos for this book. The study was made up of 609 urban churches and 591 urban ministers. Of the 609 churches studied, 358 were in the urban south, including Atlanta, Birmingham, Charleston, Houston, Memphis, New Orleans, and Richmond. The remaining 251 were in the urban north, and included Baltimore, Chicago, Cincinnati, Detroit, and Philadelphia. See Mays and Nicholson, *The Negro's Church*, 4–57, 301–304. For 1926 data, see Fry, *The U.S. Looks at Its Churches*.

14. Bond, "Negro Leadership since Washington," 126.

15. For number of black professionals, see Census, *Negro Population in the United States, 1790–1915*, 509–530; Census, *Negroes in the United States, 1920–32*, 290.

According to the census, black professionals consisted of actors, architects, artists, author, professors and college presidents, teachers, dentists, designers, lawyers, judges, justices, musicians and music teachers, photographers, physicians and surgeons, trained nurses, and veterinarians.

16. *Chicago Defender*, October 1, 1927, A1.

17. Mays and Nicholson, *The Negro's Church*, 50–51, 193–194.

18. Davarian L. Baldwin, *Chicago's New Negroes: Modernity, the Great Migration, & Black Urban Life* (Chapel Hill: University of North Carolina Press, 2007), 5.

19. *New York Amsterdam News*, January 8, 1930, 1; *New York Times*, January 6, 1930, 20; Adam Clayton Powell, *Against the Tide: An Autobiography* (New York: R. R. Smith, 1938; reprint, New York: Arno Press, 1980), 59.

20. Edward M. Brawley, ed., *The Negro Baptist Pulpit: A Collection of Sermons and Papers on Baptist Doctrine and Missionary and Educational Work by Colored Baptist Ministers* (Philadelphia: American Baptist Publication Society, 1890). Reprinted from a copy in the Fisk University Library Negro Collection, Freeport (New York: Books for Libraries Press, 1971), 7; Sutton E. Griggs, *Life's Demands or According to Law* (Memphis, Tenn.: National Public Welfare League, 1916), 51–52; Reverdy Ransom, "The New Negro," *New York Amsterdam News*, January 3, 1923, 10.

21. Oliver, *Songsters and Saints*, 146–147.

22. *Pittsburgh Courier*, December 24, 1927, 15; February 25, 1928, A1; *Victor Race Record Catalogue, 1929*, Radio Corporation of America, RCA Victor Division, Camden, N.J. RCA Victor Company,1929. Library of Congress, American Memory Collection, *Prosperity and Thrift: The Coolidge Era and the Consumer Economy, 1921–1929*, ML156 .R249 1929, 44 pp. A picture of Reverend Gates is featured prominently on page 13, as is Duke Ellington on page 10. Gates's sermons are also listed on page 10 along with Ellington's records.

23. *Atlanta Daily World*, December 30, 1932, 6A. A special thank you to Lance Ledbetter for bringing the *Defender* calculations to my attention. While some have argued that black newspapers tended to exaggerate the accomplishments of black Americans. The *Chicago Defender*, for example, has been criticized as a leader in "yellow journalism." See Thomas Sancton, "The Negro Press," *New Republic*, April 26, 1943. See also Frazier, *Black Bourgeoisie*, 180–181. However, in the case of Reverend Gates, his success and notoriety are also supported by a host of other sources, including phonograph trade journals, record order numbers, repeated returns to the studio, as well as primary sources detailing the preacher's life in Atlanta.

24. *Pittsburgh Courier*, July 28, 1923, 11.

25. *Chicago Defender*, August 30, 1930, 13 and February 3, 1940, 10; *Atlanta Daily World*, February 18, 1940, 5.

26. *Atlanta Daily World*, September 25, 1932, 4A; May 11, 1935, 2.

27. *Pittsburgh Courier*, February 25, 1928, A1.

28. Ibid.; Mark Arthur May, *The Education of American Ministers*, trans. William Adams in collaboration with Brown et al., vol. 2: *The Profession of the Ministry: Its Status and Problems* (New York: Institute of Social and Religious Research, 1934), 103–108.

29. Congregationalist and Methodist ministers, on average, made slightly more, annually netting $1,901; ibid., 103–107; "Honest Pay for the Preacher," *Homiletical Review*, December 1923, 437; Mays and Nicholson, *The Negro's Church*, 188–189, 206, 216, 263–264; Arthur Franklin Raper, *Preface to Peasantry; a Tale of Two Black Belt Counties* (Chapel Hill: University of North Carolina Press, 1936), 366–368. See H. N. Morse, Edmund de S. Brunner, and Institute of Social and Religious Research., *The Town and Country Church in the United States: As Illustrated by Data from One Hundred Seventy-Nine Counties and by Intensive Studies of Twenty-Five*, Institute of Social and Religious Research, Town and Country Studies, 11 (New York: George H. Doran Company, 1923), 43. "Georgia Department of Education Fifty-Fourth and Fifty-Fifth Annual Reports of the Department of Education to the General Assembly of the State of Georgia," ed. State Superintendent of Schools Fort E. Land (Atlanta, Ga.: Department of Education, 1927), 153, 190–193.

30. May, *The Education of American Ministers*, vol. 2, 103–107; "Honest Pay for the Preacher," *Homiletical Review*, December 1923, 437; Mays and Nicholson, *The Negro's Church*, 186–189, 206, 216, 263–264; Census, *Negro Population in the United States, 1790–1915*, 509–530; Census, *Negroes in the United States, 1920–32*, 303. According to the 1929 Handbook of Labor Statistics of the Bureau of Labor Statistics, the weekly entrance wages of white laborers (brick, foundry, iron, leather, lumber, paper, petroleum, meat packing, public utilities, and general contracting) in the southern Atlantic states ranged from $16 to $26. In these fields African American wage laborers were consistent with their white counterparts. See Edwards, *The Southern Urban Negro as a Consumer*, 30–31.

31. "Honest Pay for the Preacher," *Homiletical Review*, December 1923, 437–441.

32. W. E. B. Du Bois, *The Souls of Black Folk* (Chicago: A. C. McClurg and Co., 1903; reprint, Dover Publications, 1994), 50.

33. Karen Sternheimer, *Celebrity Culture and the American Dream: Stardom and Social Mobility* (New York: Routledge, 2011), 9–13. Frazier, "Black Bourgeoisie, 127."

34. Polk Brockman, Interview with Ed Kahn and Archie Green Atlanta, Georgia, August 11, 1961; U.S. Department of Labor, Bureau of Labor Statistics, *Family Income and Expenditure in the Southeastern Region, 1935–36, Prepared by A. D. H. Kaplan Faith M. Williams, Jessie S. Bernard, Assisted by Lenore A. Epstein*, ed. U.S. Bureau of Labor Statistics, Study of Consumer Purchases: Urban Series, no. 4 (Washington, D.C.: U.S. Government Printing Office, 1939), 116.

35. "Spivey's Records Biggest Seller," *Pittsburgh Courier*, February 25, 1928, A1; Sheer, "Blues Galore," 3; Kenney, *Recorded Music in American Life*, 136; "As Music Streaming Grows, Royalties Slow to a Trickle," *New York Times*, January

28, 2013. Some labels cheated artists out of their royalties. See discussion about Alice Hunt and Bessie Smith in Tuuk, *Paramount's Rise and Fall*, 62–68.

36. United States of America, Bureau of the Census, *Sixteenth Census of the United States, 1940 Atlanta, Fulton, Georgia Roll T627_733 Page 13b Enumeration District 160–241*; Mays and Nicholson, *The Negro's Church*, 186–189, 206, 216, 263–264; "Georgia Department of Education Fifty-Fourth and Fifty-Fifth Annual Reports of the Department of Education to the General Assembly of the State of Georgia," 153, 190–193. Teachers' salaries may be found in ibid., 190.

37. When Mays was appointed acting dean of Morehouse College, his annual salary increased to $1,800. See Benjamin E. Mays, *Born to Rebel: An Autobiography* (New York: Scribner, 1971), 66, 92, 97. By 1925 faculty salaries at Howard University, according to the President's Report, were higher than they were at Morehouse, ranging from $2,500 to over $3,000. Salaries reprinted in Zora Neale Hurston, "The Hue and Cry about Howard University," *Messenger* 7 (September 1925).

38. "Spivey's Records Biggest Seller," *Pittsburgh Courier*, February 25, 1928, A1; Kenney, *Recorded Music in American Life*, 136. During the 1930s, Paramount race record executive J. Mayo Williams recalled that he paid his race record artist $25 to $50 in cash per title. See Tuuk, *Paramount's Rise and Fall*, 62–68; Calt and Wardlow, "The Buying and Selling of Paramount—Part 3."

39. Mays, *Born to Rebel*, 66, 92, 97.

40. Flat payment figures based on the number of recorded, not released, titles found in Dixon et al., *Blues & Gospel Records*, 287–290.

41. Quoted in the *Atlanta Constitution*, April 4, 1922, 10; Automobile Numbers found in U.S. Bureau of Labor Statistics, *Bulletin Number 648*, Vol. VI, Tabular Summary, Table 3; National Automobile Chamber of Commerce, *Facts and Figures of the Automobile Industry*1930, 15; *Recent Social Trends in the United States: Report of the President's Research Committee on Social Trends with a Foreword by President Herbert Hoover*, 172–173. Motor vehicle registration was required by all states in 1913. Between 1913 and 1931, motor vehicle registration increased twentyfold. See ibid., 172–173. See also David E. Kyvig, *Daily Life in the United States, 1920–1940: How Americans Lived through the "Roaring Twenties" and the Great Depression* (Chicago: Ivan R. Dee, 2004), 27.

42. Atlanta's streetcar segregation was passed in 1891 and was particularly strictly enforced after the 1906 riot. The law remained intact until 1959. George S. Schuyler, "Traveling Jim Crow," *American Mercury* (1930), 423–432; Hunter, *To 'Joy My Freedom*, 99; Ronald H. Bayor, *Race and the Shaping of Twentieth-Century Atlanta* (Chapel Hill: University of North Carolina Press, 1996), 188; Mays, *Born to Rebel*, 79.

43. "Automobile and the Jim Crow Regulations," *Negro World*, October 11, 1924, 6.

44. Alfred Edgar Smith, "Through the Windshield," *Opportunity*, May 1933.

45. Schuyler, "Traveling Jim Crow," 423, 432; Paul Gilroy, "Driving While Black," in *Car Cultures*, ed. Daniel Miller (Oxford: Berg Publishers, 2001), 94.

46. Gilroy, "Driving While Black," 84–87, 94–97; Albertson, *Bessie*, 53.

47. See, for example, *Chicago Defender*, March 31, 1934, 9; *Pittsburgh Courier*, February 25, 1928, A1.

48. Ellington, *Music Is My Mistress*, 35; Beverly Rae Kimes and Henry Austin Clark, *Standard Catalog of American Cars, 1805–1942* (Iola, Wis.: Krause, 1985), 254–256, 662–685. In his biography of Ellington, Harvey G. Cohen states that Ellington bought the car in 1919. It was worth about $2,000. See Harvey G. Cohen, *Duke Ellington's America* (Chicago: University of Chicago Press, 2010), 22.

49. Ethel Waters and Charles Samuels, *His Eye Is on the Sparrow: An Autobiography* (Garden City, N.Y.: Doubleday, 1951), 189–192; Marmorstein, *The Label*, 59; Calt, "The Anatomy of a 'Race' Label—Part 2," 19; Kimes and Clark, *Standard Catalog of American Cars*, 819–826.

50. On Bessie and cars, see Albertson, *Bessie*, 67, 125–126, 248; Auto Editors of Consumer Guide, *Encyclopedia of American Cars: A Comprehensive History of the Automakers and the Cars They Built* (Lincolnwood, Ill.: Publications International Ltd., 2002), 691–704; Kimes and Clark, *Standard Catalog of American Cars*, 939–956.

51. *Atlanta Daily World*, July 14, 1932, 6.

52. The Hupmobile was produced from 1908 through the summer of 1940. On Hupmobile, Ford, and Chevrolet, see Beverly Rae Kimes and Henry Austin Clark, *Standard Catalog of American Cars, 1805–1942*, 2nd ed. (Iola, Wis.: Krause Publications, 1989); James H. Moloney and George H. Dammann, *Encyclopedia of American Cars, 1930–1942*, Crestline Auto Books (Sarasota, Fla: Crestline Publishing Company, 1977); Guide. On the national average net price of cars, see U.S. Department of Labor, *Statistics*, 16.

53. Kimes and Clark, *Standard Catalog of American Cars*, 723–725; Moloney and Dammann, *Encyclopedia of American Cars, 1930–1942*, 187–196; Auto Editors of Consumer Guide, 573–577. On ads, see *MacLean's Magazine*, October 1, 1928, 41; *MacLean's Magazine*, May 15, 1929.

54. United States Work Projects Administration. Georgia, *A Statistical Study of Certain Aspects of the Social and Economic Pattern of the City of Atlanta, Georgia, Official Project 465-34-3-4. 1939* ([Atlanta]: 1939), 92; *Atlanta Daily World*, April 16, 1937, 6; December 12, 1937, 4; January 10, 1941, 6.

55. Albertson, *Bessie*, 47, 205.

56. United States of America, Bureau of the Census, *Fifteenth Census of the United States, 1930 Philadelphia, Pennsylvania Roll 2094 Page 13b Enumeration District: 50 Image: 341.0 Fhl Microfilm: 2341828*; Census, *Negroes in the United States, 1920–32*, 253.

57. United States of America, Bureau of the Census, *Fifteenth Census of the United States, 1930 Manhattan, New York, New York Roll 1577 Page 8a Enumeration District 1020 Image 342.0 Fhl Microfilm 2341312*; Lewis, *When Harlem Was in Vogue*, 217.

58. Edwards, *The Southern Urban Negro as a Consumer*, 12; Frazier, *Black Bourgeoisie*, 126–128.

59. Charles S. Johnson, *Negro Housing: Report of the Committee on Negro Housing*, ed. Chairman Nannie H. Burroughs, John M. Gries, and James Ford, The President's Conference on Home Buidling and Home Ownership Called by President Hoover, vol. 6 (Washington, D.C.: President's Conference on Home Building and Home Ownership, 1932), 32–33, 36–39. On the shifting laws of residential segregation in Atlanta, see "Segregation Law Passes Council," *Atlanta Constitution*, June 17,1913, 1; Christopher Silver, "The Racial Origins of Zoning in American Cities," in *Urban Planning and the African American Community: In the Shadows*, ed. June Manning Thomas and Marsha Ritzdorf (Thousand Oaks, Calif.: Sage, 1997), 7–9.

60. W. E. B. Du Bois, *The Negro American Family; Report of a Social Study Made Principally by the College Classes of 1909 and 1910 of Atlanta University, under the Patronage of the Trustees of the John F. Slater Fund; Together with the Proceedings of the 13th Annual Conference for the Study of the Negro Problems, Held at Atlanta University on Tuesday, May the 26th, 1908*, Atlanta University Publications (Atlanta, Ga.: Atlanta University Press, 1908), 58–60.

61. On the location of his residence, see Sanborn Map Company, Vol. 1, 1931 Sheet #325, Vol. 3, 1932 Sheet #314. Firsthand accounts of the conditions of Summerhill are described in the *Atlanta Independent*, February 14, 1914, 4; Davis, *Communist Councilman from Harlem*, 28–30; Clifford M. Kuhn, Harlon E. Joye, and E. Bernard Wes, *Living Atlanta: An Oral History of the City, 1914–1948* (Athens, Ga.: University of Georgia Press, 2005), 3–4. Black housing in Atlanta is also described in Du Bois, *The Negro American Family; Report of a Social Study Made Principally by the College Classes of 1909 and 1910 of Atlanta University*, 58–60. Summerhill is also described in Hunter, *To 'Joy My Freedom*, 45; Allison Dorsey, *To Build Our Lives Together: Community Formation in Black Atlanta, 1875–1906* (Athens, Ga.: University of Georgia Press, 2004), 35–36. Daily household life is also described in Kyvig, *Daily Life in the United States, 1920–1940*, 53–70.

62. See Census and Mrs. Edward S. Wellons; U.S. Bureau of the Census and Enumerator Robert H. Hart, *Sixteenth Census of the United States: 1940 Population Schedule Atlanta, Fulton, Georgia Ward 1 Block Number 24 Sheet No. 4a.*; Census, *Negroes in the United States, 1920–32*, 253; *Fifteenth Census of the United States: 1930*, Population Volume VI, State Tables 4 and 21; Bureau of Foreign and Domestic Commerce, *Consumer Use of Selected Goods and Services, by Income Classes*,1935–1937, pt. Numbers 5–12, Table 5; U.S. Department of Labor, *Statistics*, 95, Table 67; *Atlanta Daily World*, December 30, 1932, 6A.

63. *Atlanta City Directory*, Home construction found in Sanborn Map Company, Vol. 1, 1931, Sheet #26.

64. *Atlanta Independent*, May 3,1923, 8. Home construction found in Sanborn Map Company, Vol. 1, 1931, Sheet #26.

65. Home construction information found in ibid., 1932, Vol. 3, Sheet #351.On telephone and service statistics, see *Recent Social Trends in the United States: Report of the President's Research Committee on Social Trends with a Foreword by President Herbert Hoover*, 198; *Atlanta City Directory*, 1939; United States, Work Projects Administration, Georgia, *A Statistical Study of Certain Aspects of the Social and Economic Pattern of the City of Atlanta, Georgia*, , 82–83; Kyvig, *Daily Life in the United States, 1920–1940*, 69–70.

66. *Atlanta Daily World*, December 30, 1932, 6A; July 16, 1934, 6; *U.S. Bureau of the Census. Sixteenth Census of the United States: 1940: Housing, 1943*. Vol. 2. pt. 2, 561; United States, Work Projects Administration, Georgia, *A Statistical Study of Certain Aspects of the Social and Economic Pattern of the City of Atlanta, Georgia*, 82–83; Susan Atherton Hanson, "Home Sweet Home: Industrialization's Impact on Rural Households, 1865–1925" (Ph.D. dissertation, University of Maryland, 1986), 170, 172–190; Kyvig, *Daily Life in the United States, 1920–1940*, 66.

67. *Atlanta Daily World*, April 20, 1940, 1

68. Finney, *Lectures on Revivals of Religion*, 165–166; Gilroy, "Driving While Black," 91; Moore, *Selling God*, 268.

CHAPTER 6. "SAY GOOD-BYE TO CHAIN STORES!"

1. On Gates's sermon, see Dixon et al., *Blues & Gospel Records*, 292; "Goodbye to Chain Stores," Atlanta, Friday, April 25, 1930, Okeh Records in Gates. For a full transcription of Part 1 of Reverend Gates's sermon, see Martha J. Simmons and Frank A. Thomas, *Preaching with Sacred Fire: An Anthology of African American Sermons, 1750 to the Present* (New York: W. W. Norton, 2010).

2. The Federal Trade Commission defined chain stores as "Organizations owning a controlling interest in two or more establishments which sell substantially similar merchandise at retail." This is inclusive of stores that operated mail order commerce as well. See U.S. Federal Trade Commission, *Chain Store Inquiry* , ix–32. On the estimated number of chain stores and retail sales, see U.S. Federal Trade Commission, *Chain Stores: Growth and Development of Chain Stores*, 67; U.S. Federal Trade Commission, *Chain Stores: State Distribution of Chain Stores, 1913–1928*, xi–xii.

3. Daniel Scroop, "Where Does the Local Have an End and the Nonlocal a Beginning? The Anti-Chain Store Movement, Localism, and National Identity," in *Consuming Visions: New Essays on the Politics of Consumption in Modern America*, ed. Daniel Scroop (Newcastle: Cambridge Scholars, 2007), 8; Merryle Stanley Rukeyser, "Chain Stores: The Revolution in Retailing," *Nation*, November 28, 1928, 568; Joseph Nocera, *A Piece of the Action: How the Middle Class Joined the Money Class* (New York: Simon & Schuster, 1994), 37; Charles W. Calhoun, *The Gilded Age: Perspectives on the Origins of Modern America*, 2nd ed. (Lanham, Md.: Rowman & Littlefield, 2007), 18–19; Comparatively, while chains had corporate Wall Street financing, black independent stores, for example, were only netting an average of $3,000 a year. Small independents, particularly

independent African American proprietors, were dwarfed in size as well as capital. See Census, *Negroes in the United States, 1920–32*, xvi, 494–529; The Man on the Street, "What It's All About," *Progressive*, March 29, 1930, 3.

4. Scroop, "Where Does the Local Have an End and the Nonlocal a Beginning?" 8; Merryle Stanley Rukeyser, "Chain Stores: The Revolution in Retailing," *Nation*, November 28,1928, 568; Nocera, 37; Calhoun, *The Gilded Age*, 18–19.

5. Darren Dochuk, *From Bible Belt to Sunbelt: Plain-Folk Religion, Grassroots Politics, and the Rise of Evangelical Conservatism* (New York: W. W. Norton, 2011), xx; Paul Ingram and Hayagreeva Rao, "Store Wars: The Enactment and Repeal of Anti Chain Store Legislation in America," *American Journal of Sociology* 110, no. 2 (2004), 447.

6. Merryle Stanley Rukeyser, "Chain Stores: The Revolution in Retailing," *Nation*, November 28, 1928, 568.

7. Neighborhood information and housing configurations found in Census and Mrs. Edward S. Wellons; Company, Vol.1, 1931, Sheet No. 26.

8. M. H. Karker, "The Battle of the Chains," *Magazine of Business*, June 1928, 735.

9. *New York Times*, July 21, 1928, 6.

10. "Fortune Survey," *Fortune*, January 1938, 88.

11. The Man on the Street, "What It's All About," *Progressive*, March 29, 1930, 3.

12. John T. Flynn, "Chain Stores: Menace or Promise?" *New Republic*, April 15, 1931, 223. For the series, see John T. Flynn, "Chain Stores: Menace or Promise?" Parts I–V: April 15, 22, 29, and May 6, 13, 1931.

13. For the *Nation* series, see Edward G. Ernst and Emil M. Hartl, "Chains versus Independents," *Nation*, November 12, 19, 26, and December 3, 1930.

14. On chain store debate manuals, see John Somerville, *Chain Store Debate Manual: A Digest of Material for Debate on the Chain Store Question* (New York: National Chain Store Association, 1930); E. C. Buehler, *Chain Store Debate Manual: A Digest of Material on the Chain Store Question* (New York: National Chain Store Association, 1931).

15. "Chains Will Now Court Public Opinion in Earnest," 36. Congressional reports derive from the Congressional Committee of Investigation of Trade Practices of Big-Scale Buying and Selling, House of Representatives, Seventy-Fourth Congress, 1935–1937. Findings reprinted in Charles G. Daughters, *Wells of Discontent: A Study of the Economic, Social, and Political Aspects of the Chain Store* (New York: C. G. Daughters, 1937), 43.

16. U.S. Congress, *The Congressional Digest: Congress and the Chain Stores*, vol. 9: August–September, nos. 8–9 (Washington, D.C.: U.S. Government Printing Office, 1930),193–224; William J. Donovan, "How Anti-Trust Laws Affect Chain Stores: An Address Delivered before the National Chain Store Association in Chicago, September 24, 1929," *Printers' Ink*, October 3, 1929, 133–134.

17. Gallup Poll (AIPO), June 1937, Roper Center for Public Opinion Research, University of Connecticut in the iPOLL Databank, http://www.ropercenter.uconn.edu, accessed October 12, 2012.

18. Roper/Fortune Survey, November 1938, Roper Center for Public Opinion Research, University of Connecticut in the iPOLL Databank, http://www.roper-center.uconn.edu (accessed October 12, 2012).

19. "Chains Will Now Court Public Opinion in Earnest," 34. Emphasis in the original.

20. John T. Flynn, "Chain Stores: Menace or Promise?" *New Republic,* April 15, 1931, 223.

21. On state antichain legislation, see U.S. Federal Trade Commission, *Chain Stores: Final Report on the Chain-Store Investigation,* 74th Congress, First Session, Senate Document No.4 (Washington, D.C.: U.S. Government Printing Office, 1935); U.S. Congress, *The Congressional Digest: Congress and the Chain Stores.* For a listing of such laws, see *Business Week,* July 8, 1939, 28; T. Eugene Beatie, "Public Relations and the Chains," *Journal of Marketing,* January 1943, 254; Ingram and Rao, "Store Wars," 447.

22. Harry W. Schacter, "War on the Chain Store," *Nation,* May 7, 1930, 545.

23. Boyce F. Martin, "Independents et al., versus the Chains," *Harvard Business Review,* October 1930, 47.

24. Dixon et al., *Blues & Gospel Records,* 292.

25. See Higginbotham, "Rethinking Vernacular Culture," and Jonathan L. Walton, "The Preachers' Blues: Religious Race Records and Claims of Authority on Wax," *Religion and American Culture: A Journal of Interpretation* 20, no. 2 (2010).

26. Walton, "The Preachers' Blues: Religious Race Records and Claims of Authority on Wax"; Oliver, *Songsters and Saints,* 146. Oliver wrongly concludes that Sutton Griggs's sermon "A Hero Closes a War" was "almost alone among recorded sermons in making any specific reference to racial tension." Leigh Eric Schmidt, *Consumer Rites: The Buying & Selling of American Holidays* (Princeton, N.J.: Princeton University Press, 1995), 5.

27. Stuart Hall, "Encoding/Decoding," in *Culture, Media, Language,* ed. Stuart Hall et al. (London: Hutchinson, 1980); Schmidt, *Consumer Rites,* 15; See also Lawrence W. Levine, "The Folklore of Industrial Society: Popular Culture and Its Audiences," and Robin D. G. Kelley, "Notes on Deconstructing 'the Folk,'" in *American Historical Review* 97, no. 5 (1992).

28. Hall, "Encoding/Decoding"; Kelley, "Notes on Deconstructing 'the Folk'"; Cornel West, "The New Cultural Politics of Difference," *October* 53, The Humanities as Social Technology (Summer 1990), 94.

29. Neighborhood information and housing configurations may be found in the census and 5778; Census and Mrs. Edward S. Wellons; Company, vol. 1, 1931, Sheet No. 26. Specifically on Summerhill, see Summerhill Community Oral History Interviews, Archives Division, Auburn Avenue Research Library on African American Culture and History, Atlanta-Fulton Public Library System. Atlanta's independent retailers and small businesses found in *Fifteenth Census of the United State –1930–Volume 1: Retail Distribution,* Part II: Reports by States

Alabama-New Hampshire, 538; U.S. Federal Trade Commission, *Chain Stores: Growth and Development of Chain Stores*, xii–xiii.

30. Detailed description of the customary independent grocery store found in, Marc Levinson, *The Great A & P and the Struggle for Small Business in America* (New York: Hill and Wang, 2011), 76.

31. Ibid., 76; Schlereth, "Country Stores, County Fairs, and Mail-Order Catalogues."

32. Levinson, *The Great A&P and the Struggle for Small Business in America*, 75–79; Joseph A. Pierce and Marion M. Hamilton, *The Atlanta Negro: A Collection of Data on the Negro Population of Atlanta Georgia*, ed. Robert L. Sutherland, American Youth Commission Negro Studies (Washington, D.C.: American Youth Commission of the American Council on Education in Cooperation with the National Youth Administration of Georgia, 1940), 74; Edwards, *The Southern Urban Negro as a Consumer*, 11.

33. "Sears, Roebuck Throw Open Magnificent New Atlanta Store to Public Monday," *Atlanta Constitution,* August 1, 1926, 13.

34. Calt and Wardlow, "The Buying and Selling of Paramount—Part 3," 19–20, 23 fn13.

35. Ingram and Rao, "Store Wars," 447.

36. R. W. Lyons, "Social Aspects of Chains Are Sound," *Chain Store Progress,* April 1931, 1, 6.

37. Gates, "Goodbye to Chain Stores," in *Rev. J. M. Gates: Complete Recorded Works.*

38. U.S. Federal Trade Commission, *Chain Stores: The Chain Store in the Small Town*, 72nd Congress Second Session. Senate. Government Document No. 93, vol. 1: Character and Extent of Chain and Cooperative Chain Store Business (Washington, D.C.: U.S. Government Printing Office, 1934), 70–71.

39. Ibid., 110.

40. Sermon quotes found in Reverend Gates, Atlanta, Friday, April 25, 1930; Census and Mrs. Edward S. Wellons.

41. Corporate headquarters did, however, send the preacher a donation of $30 sometime later. See Commission, *Chain Stores: The Chain Store in the Small Town*, 107.

42. Ibid., xii–xiii, 110.

43. Ibid., 70–71.

44. Poem quoted in David A. Horowitz, *Beyond Left & Right: Insurgency and the Establishment* (Urbana: University of Illinois Press, 1997), 117. Emphasis added.

45. *Atlanta Constitution*, September 29, 1930, 3; "Chains Will Now Court Public Opinion in Earnest," 36; *New York Times,* October 21, 1928, 39; "Chain Stores Organize to Build Good-Will, Fight Tax," *Business Week*, October 15, 1930, 10–11.

46. Harry W. Schacter, "War on the Chain Store," *Nation*, May 7, 1930, 544–545; Harper, "A New Battle on Evolution: The Anti-Chain Store Trade-at-Home Agitation of 1929–1930," 412; Raymond Moley, "The War against Efficiency,"

Newsweek, September 5, 1938, 40; "Plan New Anti-Chain Drive," *Business Week,* July 8, 1939, 28–30. On farmers, see "Unliked Taxes: Help the Farmer Sell His Surplus Crop," *Time,* January 31,1938, 61. For one farmer's opposition to the chain store system, see David Stevenson, "The Farmer Is Enchained," *Christian Century,* March 23, 1938, 365–367; Haas, "Social and Economic Aspects of the Chain Store Movement," 44–47, 232–247; Ryant, "The South and the Movement against Chain Stores"; Rao, "Store Wars: The Enactment and Repeal of Anti–Chain-Store Legislation in America," 459–460.
47. Dixon et al., *Blues & Gospel Records,* 292.
48. Ibid., 287–294; Art Satherly, Taped Interview by Norm Cohen and G. Earle with Ken Griffis and Bill Ward, June 12, 1971; Sutton and Nauck, *American Record Labels & Companies*; Suisman, *Selling Sounds,* 296; Ron Chernow, *The House of Morgan: An American Banking Dynasty and the Rise of Modern Finance* (New York: Atlantic Monthly Press, 1990), 257.
49. The preacher returned to Okeh's studio one more time in December 1930. He recorded sermons about the Depression, such as "These Hard Times Are Tight Like That" and "He'll Feed You When You're Hungry." The Depression hindered his return to the studio until 1934. Dixon et al., 287–294. See Bluebird and Montgomery Ward in Sutton and Nauck, *American Record Labels & Companies.*
50. West, "The New Cultural Politics of Difference."

CONCLUSION
1. *Atlanta Daily World,* December 14, 1935, 2; March 14, 1945, 2; August 19, 1945, 3; State of Georgia, *Indexes of Vital Records for Georgia: Deaths, 1919–1998.* Georgia, U.S.A.: Georgia Health Department, Office of Vital Records, Certificate No. 16131. Health care expenditures may be found in Richard Mauritz, Edvard Sterner, Lenore A. Epstein, and Ellen Winston, *The Negro's Share: A Study of Income, Consumption, Housing and Public Assistance* (New York: Harper & Brothers, 1943),149. Lydia doesn't appear as Mrs. Gates in the city directory until 1933; the couple probably married in 1932 as the proceeding directory was being prepared. See *Atlanta City Directory, 1933; Atlanta Daily World,* August 24, 1945, 6; Guido Van Rijn, "Praying for the Pastor: The Life of Rev. Jim Gates," *Living Blues,* no. 152 (2000): 48–51.
2. *Atlanta Daily World,* January 10, 1941, 6; August 19, 1945, 3; August 22, 1945, 3; August 24, 1945, 6; March 31, 1949, 1; April 5, 1949, 3; *Atlanta Constitution,* August 21, 1945, 15; Brown, "Interview with Polk Brockman, Recording Pioneer," 31; Pete Lowry, "Atlanta Black Sound: A Survey of Black Music from Atlanta during the 20th Century," *Atlanta Historical Bulletin* 21, no. 2 (1977); Rijn, "Praying for the Pastor: The Life of Rev. Jim Gates"; Oliver, *Songsters and Saints,* 280.
3. *Atlanta Daily World,* August 19, 1945, 3; August 22, 1945, 3; August 24, 1945, 6; March 31, 1949, 1; April 5,1949, 3; *Atlanta Constitution,* August 21, 1945, 15; Brown, "Interview with Polk Brockman, Recording Pioneer," 31; Lowry, "Atlanta

Black Sound"; Rijn, "Praying for the Pastor: The Life of Rev. Jim Gates"; Oliver, *Songsters and Saints,* 280.

4. *Atlanta Daily World,* August 24, 1945, 6.

5. Lillian Ashcraft Webb, *About My Father's Business: The Life of Elder Michaux* (Westport, Conn.: Greenwood Press, 1981); Nick Salvatore, *Singing in a Strange Land: C. L. Franklin, the Black Church, and the Transformation of America* (New York: Little, Brown, 2005); Best, *Passionately Human, No Less Divine.*

6. Walton, "Watch This!"

Abrams, Steven, and Tyrone Settlemier. "The Online Discographical Project," http://www.78discography.com.

Albertson, Chris. *Bessie*. New Haven: Yale University Press, 2003.

Archie Green Papers #20002, Folder 44. Polk Brockman, Southern Folklife Collection, Wilson Library, University of North Carolina at Chapel Hill.

Art Satherly, Taped Interview by Norm Cohen and G. Earle with Ken Griffis and Bill Ward, June 12, 1971. Audio Tapes FT1647- 1648 in the Southern Folklife Collection, The Wilson Library, University of North Carolina at Chapel Hill.

Atlanta Constitution

Atlanta Daily World

Auburn Avenue Research Library on African American Culture and History, Atlanta-Fulton Public Library System. Summerhill Community Oral History Interviews. Archives Division.

Auto Editors of Consumer Guide, *Encyclopedia of American Cars: A Comprehensive History of the Automakers and the Cars They Built*. Lincolnwood, Ill.: Publications International Ltd., 2002.

Baldwin, Davarian L. *Chicago's New Negroes: Modernity, the Great Migration, & Black Urban Life*. Chapel Hill: University of North Carolina Press, 2007.

Baltimore Afro-American

Bastin, Bruce. *Never Sell a Copyright: Joe Davis and His Role in the New York Music Scene, 1916–1978*. Chigwell, Essex: Storyville Publications, 1990.

———. with Kip Lornell, *The Melody Man: Joe Davis and the New York Music Scene, 1916–1978*. Jackson: University Press of Mississippi, 2012.

Bayor, Ronald H. *Race and the Shaping of Twentieth-Century Atlanta*. Chapel Hill: University of North Carolina Press, 1996.

Bean, Donald. "Books vs. Movies, Phonographs, and Radios." *Peabody Journal of Education* 17, no. 4 (1940): 253–260.

Berliner, Emile. "The Gramophone: Etching the Human Voice." *Journal of the Franklin Institute of the State of Pennsylvania for the Promotion of the Mechanic Arts* CXXV, no. 6 (June 1888).

Best, Wallace D. *Passionately Human, No Less Divine: Religion and Culture in Black Chicago, 191–1952*. Princeton: Princeton University Press, 2005.

Billingsley, Scott. *It's a New Day: Race and Gender in the Modern Charismatic Movement*. Tuscaloosa, Ala.: University of Alabama Press, 2008.

Bond, Horace M. "Negro Leadership since Washington." *South Atlantic Quarterly* XXIV, no. 2 (April 1925).

Bradford, Perry. *Born with the Blues*. New York: Oak Publications, 1964.

Brady, Erika. *A Spiral Way: How the Phonograph Changed Ethnography*. Jackson, Miss.: University Press of Mississippi, 1999.

Brawley, Edward M., ed. *The Negro Baptist Pulpit: A Collection of Sermons and Papers on Baptist Doctrine and Missionary and Educational Work by Colored Baptist Ministers*. Philadelphia: American Baptist Publication Society, 1890. Reprinted from a copy in the Fisk University Library Negro Collection, Freeport, New York: Books for Libraries Press, 1971.

Brooks, Tim. "'Might Take One Disc of This Trash as a Novelty': Early Recordings by the Fisk Jubilee Singers and the Popularization of 'Negro Folk Music.'" *American Music* 18, no. 3 (2000): 278–316.

———. "High Drama in the Record Industry: Columbia Records, 1901–1934." *ARSC Journal* 33, no. 1 (Spring 2002): 21–76.

———. *Lost Sounds: Blacks and the Birth of the Recording Industry, 1890–1919*. Urbana: University of Illinois Press, 2004.

Brown, Roger S. "Interview with Polk Brockman, Recording Pioneer." *Living Blues*, no. 23 (1975).

Buehler, E. C. *Chain Store Debate Manual: A Digest of Material on the Chain Store Question*. New York: National Chain Store Association, 1931.

Burkett, Randall K. "The Baptist Church in the Years of Crisis: J. C. Austin and Pilgrim Baptist Church, 1926–1950." In *African-American Christianity: Essays in History*. Edited by Paul E. Johnson, xi, 189 pp. Berkeley: University of California Press, 1994.

Bushell, Garvin, and Mark Tucker. *Jazz from the Beginning*. Edited by Richard Crawford. Ann Arbor: University of Michigan Press, 1988.

Butler, Anthea D. *Women in the Church of God in Christ: Making a Sanctified World*. Chapel Hill: University of North Carolina Press, 2007.

Calhoun, Charles W. *The Gilded Age: Perspectives on the Origins of Modern America*. 2nd ed. Lanham, Md.: Rowman & Littlefield, 2007.

Calt, Stephen. "The Anatomy of a 'Race' Label—Part 2." *78 Quarterly*, no. 1 (1989).

Calt, Stephen, and Gayle Dean Wardlow. "The Buying and Selling of Paramount—Part 3." *78 Quarterly* 1, no. 5 (1990).

———. "Paramount: The Advent of Arthur Laibly—Part 4." *78 Quarterly* 1, no. 6 (1991).

———. "Paramount's Decline and Fall—Part 5." *78 Quarterly* 1, no. 7 (1992).

Carpenter, Joel. "Fundamentalist Institutions and the Rise of Evangelical Protestantism, 1929–1942." *Church History* 49, no. 1 (1980): 62–75.

Carpenter, Joel A. *Revive Us Again: The Reawakening of American Fundamentalism*. New York: Oxford University Press, 1997.

"Chain Stores Organize to Build Good-Will, Fight Tax." *Business Week* (October 15, 1930): 10–11.

"Chains Will Now Court Public Opinion in Earnest." *Printers' Ink* (October 3, 1929).

Chapman, Erin D. *Prove It on Me: New Negroes, Sex, and Popular Culture in the 1920s.* New York: Oxford University Press, 2012.

Chernow, Ron. *The House of Morgan: An American Banking Dynasty and the Rise of Modern Finance.* New York: Atlantic Monthly Press, 1990.

Chicago Daily Tribune

Chicago Defender

Cohen, Harvey G. *Duke Ellington's America.* Chicago: University of Chicago Press, 2010.

Cohen, Lizabeth A. *Making a New Deal: Industrial Workers in Chicago, 1919–1939.* Cambridge [U.K.] ; New York: Cambridge University Press, 1990.

Cohen, Norm. "I'm a Record Man, Uncle Art Reminisces." *John Edwards Memorial Foundation Quarterly* 8, no. 25 (1972): 18–23.

Cohen, Norm, and David Cohen. *Long Steel Rail: The Railroad in American Folksong.* 2nd ed. Urbana: University of Illinois Press, 2000.

Cohn, David L., and Sinclair Lewis. *The Good Old Days: A History of American Morals and Manners as Seen through the Sears Roebuck Catalogs, 1905 to the Present.* [New York]: Simon amd Schuster, 1940.

Commerce, Bureau of Foreign and Domestic. *Consumer Use of Selected Goods and Services, by Income Classes,* 1935–1937. pt. Numbers 5–12.

Commerce, National Automobile Chamber of. *Facts and Figures of the Automobile Industry,* 1930.

Comprehensive Historic Preservation Plan, Prepared by Michael Sandler, New York City Community Planning Fellows. City of New York: Manhattan Community Board 10 Land Use and Landmarks Committee, April 2012.

Conot, Robert E. *A Streak of Luck: The Life and Legend of Thomas Alva Edison.* New York: Seaview Books, 1979.

Coolidge, President Calvin. "President Coolidge Pays Adverting Its Highest Tribute." *Printers' Ink* 137, no. 5 (November 4, 1926).

Craig, Steve. "How America Adopted Radio: Demographic Differences in Set Ownership Reported in the 1930–1950 U.S. Censuses." *Journal of Broadcasting & Electronic Media* 48, no. 2 (2004): 179–195.

Crichton, Kyle. "Thar's Gold in Them Hillbillies." *Collier's* (April 30, 1938).

Daniel, W. A. *The Education of Negro Ministers: Based Upon a Survey of Theological Schools for Negroes in the United States Made by Robert L. Kelly and W. A. Daniel Committee on Social and Religious Surveys, the Institute of Social and Religious Research.* Edited by Galen M. Fisher. New York: George H. Doran Company, 1925. Reprint, Negro University Press, 1969.

Daniels III, David Douglass, "The Cultural Renewal of Slave Religion: Charles Price Jones and the Emergence of the Holiness Movement in Mississippi, " Ph.D. Dissertation, Union Theological Seminary, New York City, 1992.

Daughters, Charles G. *Wells of Discontent: A Study of the Economic, Social, and Political Aspects of the Chain Store.* New York: C. G. Daughters, 1937.

Davis, Angela Y. *Blues Legacies and Black Feminism: Gertrude "Ma" Rainey, Bessie Smith, and Billie Holiday*. New York: Pantheon Books, 1998.

Davis, Benjamin J. *Communist Councilman from Harlem: Autobiographical Notes Written in a Federal Penitentiary*. New York: International Publishers, 1969.

Davis, Langston L. "Is the Church Fulfilling Its Primary Objective." *Half Century Magazine*, (September– October 1922).

"Dealers Expect Big Sale of Blues Records by Bessie Smith, Who Has Joined Columbia Artists." *Music Trades* (February 16, 1924).

Detweiler, Frederick German. *The Negro Press in the United States*. Chicago, Ill.: University of Chicago Press, 1922.

Dixon, Robert M. W., and John Godrich. *Recording the Blues*. The Blues Series, edited by Paul Oliver. New York: Stein and Day Publishers, 1970.

Dixon, Robert M. W., John Godrich, and Howard Rye. *Blues & Gospel Records, 1890–1943*. 4th ed. Oxford: Clarendon Press, 1997.

Donovan, William J. "How Anti-Trust Laws Affect Chain Stores: An Address Delivered before the National Chain Store Association in Chicago September 24, 1929." *Printers' Ink* (October 3, 1929): 133–134.

Dorsey, Allison. *To Build Our Lives Together: Community Formation in Black Atlanta, 1875–1906*. Athens, Ga.: University of Georgia Press, 2004.

Drake, St. Clair, and Horace R. Cayton. *Black Metropolis: A Study of Negro Life in a Northern City*. New York: Harcourt, Brace, 1945.

"Dramatic Action in Window Nets Big Sale in Record—-Jail House Blues Advertised by Live Boy in Striped Uniform in Window of Kaplan Furniture Co. Alexandria, La." *Music Trades* (January 26, 1924).

Driggs, Frank, and Chuck Haddix. *Kansas City Jazz: From Ragtime to Bebop—a History*. New York: Oxford University Press, 2005.

Du Bois, W. E. B. *The Philadelphia Negro: A Social Study*. Reprint of 1899: Publications of the University of Pennsylvania Series in Political Economy and Public Law, ed., *The Oxford W. E. B. Du Bois*. New York: Oxford University Press, 2007.

———. *The College-Bred Negro: Report of a Social Study Made under the Direction of Atlanta University; Together with the Proceedings of the Fifth Conference for the Study of the Negro Problems, Held at Atlanta University, May 29–30, 1900*. Second abridged edition. Atlanta University Publications. Edited by Corresponding Secretary of the Conference W. E. Burghardt DuBois. Atlanta, Ga.: Atlanta University Press, 1900. Reprint, 1902.

———. "The Religion of the American Negro." *New World: A Quarterly Review of Religion* 9, no. December (1900).

———. *The Souls of Black Folk*. Chicago: A. C. McClurg and Co., 1903. Reprint, Dover Thrift Editions Dover Publications; unabridged edition, 1994.

———. *The Negro American Family; Report of a Social Study Made Principally by the College Classes of 1909 and 1910 of Atlanta University, under the Patronage of the Trustees of the John F. Slater Fund; Together with the Proceedings of the 13th Annual Conference for the Study of the Negro Problems, Held at Atlanta University on*

Tuesday, May the 26th, 1908. Atlanta University Publications. Atlanta, Ga.: Atlanta University Press, 1908.

———. *The College-Bred Negro American: Report of a Social Study Made by Atlanta University under the Patronage of the Trustees of the John F. Slater Fund: With the Proceedings of the 15th Annual Conference for the Study of the Negro Problems, Held at Atlanta University, on Tuesday, May 24th, 1910*. Atlanta University Publications. Atlanta, Ga.: Atlanta University Press, 1910.

———. *Darkwater: Voices from within the Veil*. Edited by Julie Nord. New York: Harcourt, Brace and Company, 1920. Reprint, Dover, 1999.

———. "Phonograph Records." *Crisis* (February 1921).

———. "The Black Swan." *Crisis* (March 1921).

———. "The Problem of Amusement." In *W. E. B. Du Bois on Sociology and the Black Community*. Edited by Dan S. Green and Edwin D. Driver. Chicago: University of Chicago Press, 1980.

Duhamel, Georges. *In Defense of Letters* (New York: Greystone Press, 1939).

Dumenil, Lynn. *The Modern Temper: American Culture and Society in the 1920s*. New York: Hill and Wang, 1995.

Early, Gerald. "The New Negro Era and the Great African American Transformation." *American Studies* 491/2 (Spring/Summer 2008): 9–19.

Edison, Thomas A. "The Phonograph and Its Future." *North American Review* 126 (May–June 1878).

———. "Trial Books." Edited by Edison National Historic Site. West Orange, N.J. No date.

Edison, Thomas A., Inc. "A Special Request to a Selected List of Edison Owners: Thomas A. Edison Phonograph Surveys." In *Special Collections: Music Library, University of Michigan, Ann Arbor*. Ann Arbor: University of Michigan.

Edwards, Paul K. *The Southern Urban Negro as a Consumer*. New York: Prentice-Hall, 1932. Reprint, Negro Universities Press, 1969.

Ellington, Duke. *Music Is My Mistress*. Garden City, N.Y.: Doubleday, 1973.

Encyclopedia of Recorded Sound in the United States. New York: Garland, 1993.

Erickson, Hal. *Religious Radio and Television in the United States, 1921–1991: The Programs and Personalities*. Jefferson, N.C.: McFarland, 1992.

Evans, Curtis J. *The Burden of Black Religion*. Oxford: Oxford University Press, 2008.

Evans, David. "Interview with H. C. Speir." *John Edwards Memorial Foundation Quarterly* 8, no. 8 (1972).

Farrar, Hayward. *The Baltimore Afro-American, 1892–1950*. Westport, Conn.: Greenwood Press, 1998.

Ferguson, Karen. *Black Politics in New Deal Atlanta*. Chapel Hill: University of North Carolina Press, 2002.

Finney, Charles G. *Lectures on Revivals of Religion*. 6th ed. New York City: Leavitt, Lord & Co., 1835.

Fitzgerald, F. Scott. "Echoes of the Jazz Age." *Scribner's Magazine* XC, no. 5 (November 1931): 459–465.

———. "Early Success." *American Cavalcade* 1, no. 6 (October 1937): 74–79.

Foreman, Ronald C., Jr. "Jazz and Race Records, 1920–1932: Their Origins and Their Significance for the Record Industry and Society." Ph.D. dissertation, University of Illinois, 1968.

"Fortune Survey." *Fortune*, January 1938.

Frazier, E. Franklin. "Three Scourges of the Negro Family." *Opportunity* 4, no. 7 (July 1926).

Frazier, Edward Franklin. *Black Bourgeoisie*. Glencoe, Ill.: Free Press, 1957. Reprint, New York: Free Press, 1997.

Frederick, Marla Faye. *Between Sundays: Black Women and Everyday Struggles of Faith.* Berkeley: University of California Press, 2003.

Freeland, David. *Automats, Taxi Dances, and Vaudeville: Excavating Manhattan's Lost Places of Leisure.* New York: NYU Press, 2009.

Fry, C. Luther. *The U. S. Looks at Its Churches.* New York: Institute of Social and Religious Research, 1930.

Gaines, Kevin Kelly. *Uplifting the Race: Black Leadership, Politics, and Culture in the Twentieth Century.* Chapel Hill: University of North Carolina Press, 1996.

Gardner, Robert G. "Baptist Educational Institutions in Georgia." In *Georgia Baptist History Depository, Special Collections, Jack Tarver Library.* Macon, Georgia: Mercer University, September 12, 2007.

Garland, Phyl. *The Sound of Soul.* Chicago: H. Regnery Co., 1969.

Garrett, Charles Hiroshi. *Struggling to Define a Nation: American Music and the Twentieth Century.* Berkeley: University of California Press, 2008.

Gates, Reverend J. M. *Rev. J. M. Gates: Complete Recorded Works in Chronological Order.* Audio. Newton Stewart, U.K.: Document Records, 2005.

Gelatt, Roland. *The Fabulous Phonograph, from Tin Foil to High Fidelity.* Philadelphia: Lippincott, 1955.

"Georgia Department of Education, Fifty-Fourth and Fifty-Fifth Annual Reports of the Department of Education to the General Assembly of the State of Georgia." Edited by State Superintendent of Schools Fort E. Land. Atlanta, Ga.: Dept. of Education, 1927.

Giggie, John Michael. "'When Jesus Handed Me a Ticket': Images of Railroad Travel and Spiritual Transformation among African Americans, 1865–1917." In David Morgan and Sally M. Promey, eds., *The Visual Culture of American Religions.* Berkeley: University of California Press, 2001.

———. "Preachers and Peddlers of God: Ex-Slaves and the Selling of African American Religion in the American South." In *Commodifying Everything: Relationships of the Market.* Edited by Susan Strasser. New York: Routledge, 2003.

———. *After Redemption: Jim Crow and the Transformation of African American Religion in the Delta, 1875–1915.* Oxford: Oxford University Press, 2008.

Giggie, John Michael, and Diane H. Winston, eds. *Faith in the Market: Religion and the Rise of Urban Commercial Culture.* New Brunswick, N.J.: Rutgers University Press, 2002.

Gilroy, Paul. "Driving While Black." In *Car Cultures*. Edited by Daniel Miller. Oxford: Berg, 2001.

Goff, Philip. "'We Have Heard the Joyful Sound': Charles E. Fuller's Radio Broadcast and the Rise of Modern Evangelicalism." In *Embodying the Spirit: New Perspectives on North American Revivalism*. Edited by Michael James McClymond. Baltimore: Johns Hopkins University Press, 2004.

"The Golden Age of Blues-Recording." *Record Research* 2, no. 11, 1957.

Goldsmith, Peter David. *When I Rise Cryin' Holy: African-American Denominationalism on the Georgia Coast*. New York: AMS Press, 1989.

Griggs, Sutton E. *Life's Demands or According to Law*. Memphis, Tenn.: National Public Welfare League, 1916.

Grossman, James R. *Land of Hope: Chicago, Black Southerners, and the Great Migration*. Chicago: University of Chicago Press, 1989.

Hall, Stuart. "Encoding/Decoding." In *Culture, Media, Language*. Edited by Stuart Hall, Dorothy Hobson, Andrew Lowe, and Paul Willis. London: Hutchinson, 1980.

Hambrick-Stowe, Charles E. *Charles G. Finney and the Spirit of American Evangelicalism*. Grand Rapids, Mich.: W. B. Eerdmans, 1996.

Hammond, John. "Sights and Sounds." *New Masses* (May 25, 1937): 27.

Hammond, John, and Irving Townsend. *John Hammond on Record: An Autobiography*. New York: Ridge Press, 1977.

Handy, W. C., Arna Wendell Bontemps, and Abbe Niles. *Father of the Blues, an Autobiography*. New York: Macmillan, 1941.

Hangen, Tona J. *Redeeming the Dial: Radio, Religion, & Popular Culture in America*. Chapel Hill: University of North Carolina Press, 2002.

Hanson, Susan Atherton. "Home Sweet Home: Industrialization's Impact on Rural Households, 1865–1925." Ph. D. dissertation. University of Maryland, 1986.

Harris, Michael W. *The Rise of Gospel Blues: The Music of Thomas Andrew Dorsey in the Urban Church*. New York: Oxford University Press, 1992.

Hayden, Robert Earl. *Collected Prose*. Edited by Frederick Glaysher. Ann Arbor: University of Michigan Press, 1984.

Haynes, George E. "The Church and Negro Progress." *Annals of the American Academy of Political and Social Science* 140, The American Negro (November 1928).

Hemenway, Robert E. *Zora Neale Hurston: A Literary Biography*. Urbana: University of Illinois Press, 1977.

Hendershot, Heather. *Shaking the World for Jesus: Media and Conservative Evangelical Culture*. Chicago: University of Chicago Press, 2004.

Higginbotham, Evelyn Brooks. *Righteous Discontent: The Women's Movement in the Black Baptist Church, 1880–1920*. Cambridge, Mass.: Harvard University Press, 1993.

———. "Rethinking Vernacular Culture." In *African American Religious Thought: An Athology*. Edited by Cornel West and Eddie S. Glaude, Jr., 978–995. Louisville: Westminster John Knox Press, 2003.

Hoffman, Frank. *Encyclopedia of Recorded Sound*. Vol. 1. 2 vols. 2nd ed. New York: Routledge, 2005.

Holifield, E. Brooks. *God's Ambassadors: A History of the Christian Clergy in America.* Grand Rapids, Mich.: W. B. Eerdmans, 2007.

Horowitz, David A. *Beyond Left & Right: Insurgency and the Establishment.* Urbana: University of Illinois Press, 1997.

Hughes, Langston. "The Negro Artist and the Racial Mountain." *Nation* 122, no. 3181 (June 23, 1926).

Hulsether, Mark. *Religion, Culture, and Politics in the Twentieth-Century United States.* New York: Columbia University Press, 2007.

Humphrey, Mark A. "Holy Blues: The Gospel Tradition." In *Nothing but the Blues: The Music and the Musicians.* Edited by Lawrence Cohn. New York: Abbeville Press, 1993.

Hunter, Jane Edna. *A Nickel and a Prayer: The Autobiography of Jane Edna Hunter.* Nashville: Parthenon Press, Elli Kani Publishing Co., 1941. Reprint, edited by Rhondda Robinson Thomas, Morgantown: West Virginia University Press, 2011.

Hunter, Tera W. *To 'Joy My Freedom: Southern Black Women's Lives and Labors after the Civil War.* Cambridge, Mass.: Harvard University Press, 1997.

Hurston, Zora Neale. "The Hue and Cry about Howard University." *Messenger* 7 (September 1925).

———. *The Sanctified Church.* Berkeley: Turtle Island, 1981.

Hutchison, William R., ed. *Between the Times: The Travail of the Protestant Establishment in America, 1900–1960.* Cambridge, U.K.: Cambridge University Press, 1990.

Ingram, Paul, and Hayagreeva Rao. "Store Wars: The Enactment and Repeal of Anti Chain Store Legislation in America." *American Journal of Sociology* 110, no. 2 (2004).

Jackson, Mahalia, and Evan McLeod Wylie. *Movin' on Up.* 3rd ed. New York: Hawthorn Books, 1967.

Jhally, Sut. "Image-Based Culture: Advertising and Popular Culture." In *Gender, Race and Class in Media: A Text-Reader.* Edited by Gail Dines and Jean M. Humez, 249–257. Thousand Oaks, Calif.: Sage, 2003.

Johnson, Charles S. *Negro Housing: Report of the Committee on Negro Housing.* Vol. 6. The President's Conference on Home Buidling and Home Ownership Called by President Hoover. Edited by Chairman Nannie H. Burroughs, John M. Gries, and James Ford. Washington, D.C.: President's Conference on Home Building and Home Ownership, 1932.

Johnson, Guy B. "Newspaper Advertisements and Negro Culture." *Journal of Social Forces* 3, no. 4 (May 1925): 706–709.

Johnson, Henry. "Phonograph Music." *New Masses* (April 20, 1937): 35–38.

Jones, LeRoi. *Blues People.* New York: Morrow Quill Paperbacks, 1963.

Jones, William P. *The March on Washington: Jobs, Freedom, and the Forgotten History of Civil Rights.* New York: W. W. Norton, 2013.

Kazin, Michael. *A Godly Hero: The Life of William Jennings Bryan.* New York: Knopf, 2006.

Kelley, Robin D. G. "Notes on Deconstructing 'the Folk.'" *American Historical Review* 97, no. 5 (1992): 1400–1408.

Kenney, William Howland. *Recorded Music in American Life: The Phonograph and Popular Memory, 1890–1945.* New York: Oxford University Press, 1999.

Kent, Don. "An Interview with Reverend F. W. Mcgee." In *The American Folk Music Occasional: The Voice of Authentic American Folk Music.* Edited by Chris Strachwitz and Pete Welding. New York: Oak Publications, 1970.

Kimes, Beverly Rae, and Henry Austin Clark. *Standard Catalog of American Cars, 1805–1942.* Iola, Wis.: Krause Publications, 1985.

———. *Standard Catalog of American Cars, 1805–1942.* 2nd ed. Iola, Wis.: Krause Publications, 1989.

King, Martin Luther, and Clayton Riley. *Daddy King: An Autobiography.* New York: Morrow, 1980.

———. *Daddy King: An Autobiography.* Boston: G. K. Hall, 1981.

Kreiling, Albert. "The Rise of Black Consumer Magazines: The Case of the 'Half-Century.'" In *63rd Annual Meeting of the Association for Education in Journalism.* Boston, Mass., 1980.

Kuhn, Cllliford M., Harlon E. Joye, and E. Bernard Wes. *Living Atlanta: An Oral History of the City, 1914–1948.* Athens, Ga.: University of Georgia Press, 2005.

Kyvig, David E. *Daily Life in the United States, 1920–1940: How Americans Lived through the "Roaring Twenties" and the Great Depression.* Chicago: Ivan R. Dee, 2004.

Lacayo, Richard, et al. "Time Inc. Specials: Thomas Edison: His Electrifying Life." *Time* (2013).

Landman, Jacob Henry. "Phonograph Records as an Aid in the Teaching of American History." *School Review* 35, no. 9 (1927): 681–685.

Lears, T. J. Jackson. "From Salvation to Self-Realization: Advertising and the Therapeutic Roots of the Consumer Culture, 1880–1930." In *The Culture of Consumption in America: Critical Essays in American History, 1880–1980.* Edited by Richard Wightman Fox and T. J. Jackson Lears, xvii, 236 pp. New York: Pantheon Books, 1983.

Lebergott, Stanley. *Pursuing Happiness: American Consumers in the Twentieth Century.* Princeton: Princeton University Press, 1993.

Lee, Shayne. *T. D. Jakes: America's New Preacher.* New York: NYU Press, 2005.

Levine, Lawrence W. *Black Culture and Black Consciousness: Afro-American Folk Thought from Slavery to Freedom.* New York: Oxford University Press, 1977.

———. "The Folklore of Industrial Society: Popular Culture and Its Audiences." *American Historical Review* 97, no. 5 (1992): 1369–1430.

Levinson, Marc. *The Great A&P and the Struggle for Small Business in America.* New York: Hill and Wang, 2011.

Lewis, David L. *When Harlem Was in Vogue.* New York: Alfred K. Knopf, 1981. Reprint, Penguin Books, 1997.

Lewis, Earl. *In Their Own Interests: Race, Class, and Power in Twentieth-Century Norfolk, Virginia.* Berkeley: University of California Press, 1991.

Library of Congress Copyright Office. *Catalogue of Copyright Entries, Part 3: Musical Compositions for the Year 1926*. Vol. 21, nos. 1–12. Washington, D.C.: Government Printing Office, 1927.

Lienesch, Michael. *In the Beginning: Fundamentalism, the Scopes Trial, and the Making of the Antievolution Movement*. Chapel Hill: University of North Carolina Press, 2007.

Lincoln, C. Eric, and Lawrence H. Mamiya. *The Black Church in the African-American Experience*. Durham: Duke University Press, 1990.

Lowry, Pete. "Atlanta Black Sound: A Survey of Black Music from Atlanta during the 20th Century." *Atlanta Historical Bulletin* 21, no. 2 (1977).

Luhrssen, David. "Blues in Wisconsin: The Paramount Records Story." *Wisconsin Academy Review* (Winter 1998–1999).

"Lynch Young Negro Who Killed Farmer." *Janesville Daily Gazette* (May 13, 1913).

Lynd, Robert Staughton, and Helen Merrell Lynd. *Middletown; a Study in American Culture*. New York: Harcourt, Brace, Jovanovich, 1929. Reprint, 1956.

MacKenzie, John K., Collection. Manuscripts and Archives Department of the Indiana Historical Society.

Mahony, Dan. *The Columbia 13/14000-D Series: A Numerical Listing*. 2nd ed. Highland Park, N.J.: Walter C. Allen, 1973.

Marchand, Roland. *Advertising the American Dream: Making Way for Modernity, 1920–1940*. Berkeley: University of California Press, 1985.

Marmorstein, Gary. *The Label: The Story of Columbia Records*. New York: Thunder's Mouth Press, 2007.

Marsden, George M. *Understanding Fundamentalism and Evangelicalism*. Grand Rapids, Mich.: W. B. Eerdmans, 1991.

——. *Fundamentalism and American Culture*. 2nd ed. New York: Oxford University Press, 2006.

Martin, Albert T. "The Oral Interpreter and the Phonograph." *Quarterly Journal of Speech* 38, no. 2 (1952): 195–198.

Massey, James Earl. *African Americans and the Church of God: Anderson, Indiana—Aspects of a Social History*. Anderson, Ind.: Anderson University Press, 2005.

May, Mark Arthur. *The Education of American Ministers*. Translated by William Adams in colloboration with Frank K. Shuttleworth Brown, Jesse A. Jacobs, and Charlotte Feeney. Vol. 2: The Profession of the Ministry: Its Status and Problems. New York: Institute of Social and Religious Research, 1934.

Mays, Benjamin E. *Born to Rebel: An Autobiography*. New York: Scribner, 1971.

Mays, Benjamin E., and Joseph William Nicholson. *The Negro's Church*. New York: Institute of Social and Religious Research, 1933.

McLeod, Elizabeth. *The Original Amos 'N ' Andy: Freeman Gosden, Charles Correll, and the 1928–1943 Radio Serial*. Jefferson, N.C.: McFarland, 2005.

——. *Amos 'n' Andy—In Person: An Overview of a Radio Landmark*, http://www.midcoast.com/~lizmcl/aa.html. Retrieved November 11, 2010.

McLoughlin, William Gerald. *Modern Revivalism: Charles Grandison Finney to Billy Graham*. New York: Ronald Press Co., 1959.

———. *Revivals, Awakenings, and Reform: An Essay on Religion and Social Change in America, 1607–1977*. Chicago: University of Chicago Press, 1978.

Means Coleman, Robin R. *African American Viewers and the Black Situation Comedy: Situating Racial Humor*. New York: Garland, 1998.

Mencken, H. L., and George Jean Nathan. *The American Credo: A Contribution toward the Interpretation of the National Mind*. New York: A. A. Knopf, 1920.

Millard, Andre J. *America on Record: A History of Recorded Sound*. 2nd ed. Cambridge: Cambridge University Press, 2005.

Moloney, James H., and George H. Dammann. *Encyclopedia of American Cars, 1930–1942*. Sarasota, Fla.: Crestline Publishing Company, 1977.

Moore, R. Laurence. *Selling God: American Religion in the Marketplace of Culture*. New York: Oxford University Press, 1994.

Morgan, David, and Sally M. Promey, eds. *The Visual Culture of American Religions*. Berkeley: University of California Press, 2001.

Morse, H. N., Edmund de S. Brunner, and Institute of Social and Religious Research. *The Town and Country Church in the United States: As Illustrated by Data from One Hundred Seventy-Nine Counties and by Intensive Studies of Twenty-Five*. Institute of Social and Religious Research. Town and Country Studies, 11. New York: George H. Doran Company, 1923.

Mount Calvary Baptist Church Journal Committee. "100th Anniversary." Edited by Mount Calvary Baptist Church. Atlanta, 2000.

Murphy, Paul V. *The New Era: American Thought and Culture in the 1920s*. Lanham, Md.: Rowman & Littlefield, 2012.

Nevin, Reverend J. W. *The Anxious Bench*. Chambersburg, Pa.: Weekly Messenger, 1843.

New York Amsterdam News

New York Times

Nocera, Joseph. *A Piece of the Action: How the Middle Class Joined the Money Class*. New York: Simon & Schuster, 1994.

Norfolk Journal and Guide

Oliver, Paul. *Bessie Smith*. London: Cassel, 1959.

———. *Songsters and Saints: Vocal Traditions on Race Records*. Cambridge, U.K.: Cambridge University Press, 1984.

"The People's Forum." *Half Century Magazine* (November–December 1922).

"Persistent Advertising Necessary To-Day." *Talking Machine World* (March 15, 1922).

Philadelphia Tribune

Peters, Eric W. Rothenbuhler, and John Durham. "Defining Phonography: An Experiment in Theory." *Musical Quarterly* 81, no. 2 (Summer 1997).

Pierce, Joseph A., and Marion M. Hamilton. *The Atlanta Negro: A Collection of Data on the Negro Population of Atlanta Georgia*. American Youth Commission Negro Studies. Edited by Robert L. Sutherland. Washington, D.C.: American Youth Commission of the American Council on Education in Cooperation with the National Youth Administration of Georgia, 1940.

Pittsburgh Courier

Polk Brockman. Interview with Ed Kahn and Archie Green Atlanta, Georgia, August 11, 1961. Audio. Audiotapes FT-12660, 12661, and 12662 in the Ed Kahn Collection #20360, Southern Folklife Collection, Wilson Library, University of North Carolina at Chapel Hill.

Pope, Daniel. *The Making of Modern Advertising*. New York: Basic Books, 1983.

Powell, Adam Clayton. *Against the Tide: An Autobiography*. New York: R. R. Smith, 1938. Reprint, New York: Arno Press, 1980.

Raboteau, Albert J. *A Fire in the Bones: Reflections on African-American Religious History*. Boston: Beacon Press, 1995.

Raper, Arthur Franklin. *Preface to Peasantry: A Tale of Two Black Belt Counties*. Chapel Hill: University of North Carolina Press, 1936.

Recent Social Trends in the United States: Report of the President's Research Committee on Social Trends with a Foreword by President Herbert Hoover. Vol. 1. Edited by Wesley C. Mitchell-Chairman. New York: McGraw-Hill, 1933.

Reid, Ira De A. "Race Records." *Ira De A. Reid Papers, The Schomburg Center for Research in Black Culture*.

Rijn, Guido Van. "Praying for the Pastor: The Life of Rev. Jim Gates." *Living Blues*, no. 152 (2000): 48–51.

Roberts, Gene, and Hank Klibanoff. *The Race Beat: The Press, the Civil Rights Struggle, and the Awakening of a Nation*. New York: Alfred A.Knopf, 2006.

Roper Report, 77–3. February 1977. The Roper Center for Public Opinion Research, University of Connecticut in the iPOLL Databank http://www.ropercenter.uconn.edu.

"Rural Mail Service." *Half-Century Magazine* 18, no. 1 (January–February 1925): 14, 20.

Russell, Tony. "Recorded Sermons." Electronic personal communication with author, May 24, 2013.

Russell, Tony, Bob Pinson, and Country Music Hall of Fame & Museum (Nashville, Tenn.). *Country Music Records: A Discography, 1921–1942*. New York: Oxford University Press, 2004.

Sachs, William. "Land O' Melody: Melody Mart Notes." *Billboard* (September 18, 1926): 21.

Salvatore, Nick. *Singing in a Strange Land: C. L. Franklin, the Black Church, and the Transformation of America*. New York: Little, Brown, 2005.

Sanborn Map Company. "Digital Sanborn Maps, 1867–1970 Georgia." Ann Arbor, Michigan: ProQuest Information and Learning Company, 2001.

Sancton, Thomas. "The Negro Press." *New Republic* (April 26, 1943).

Sanders, Cheryl Jeanne. *Saints in Exile: The Holiness-Pentecostal Experience in African American Religion and Culture*. New York: Oxford University Press, 1996.

Savage, Barbara Dianne. *Broadcasting Freedom: Radio, War, and the Politics of Race, 1938–1948*. Chapel Hill: University of North Carolina Press, 1999.

Schlereth, Thomas J. "Country Stores, County Fairs, and Mail-Order Catalogues: Consumption in Rural America." In *Consuming Visions: Accumulation and Display of Goods in America, 1880–1920*. Edited by Simon J. Bronner. New York: Norton, 1989.

Schmidt, Leigh Eric. *Consumer Rites: The Buying & Selling of American Holidays.* Princeton, N.J.: Princeton University Press, 1995.

———. *Hearing Things: Religion, Illusion, and the American Enlightenment.* Cambridge, Mass.: Harvard University Press, 2000.

Schuyler, George S. "Traveling Jim Crow." *American Mercury* (1930): 423–432.

Scroop, Daniel. "Where Does the Local Have an End and the Nonlocal a Beginning? The Anti-Chain Store Movement, Localism, and National Identity." In *Consuming Visions: New Essays on the Politics of Consumption in Modern America.* Edited by Daniel Scroop. Newcastle: Cambridge Scholars, 2007.

Seeger, Mike. "'Who Chose These Records': Interview with Frank Walker on June 19,1962." In *Anthology of American Folk Music.* Edited by Josh Dunson et al., 8–17. New York: Oak Publications, 1973.

Sernett, Milton C. *Bound for the Promised Land: African American Religion and the Great Migration.* Durham: Duke University Press, 1997.

———. *African American Religious History: A Documentary Witness.* 2nd ed. Durham, N.C.: Duke University Press, 1999.

Shaw, Malcolm. "Arizona Dranes and Okeh." *Storyville* 27 (February 1970).

Sheer, Anita. "Blues Galore: The Story of Victoria Spivey." *Record Research* 2, no. 8 (May/June 1956).

Shilkret, Nathaniel. *Nathaniel Shilkret: Sixty Years in the Music Business.* Edited by Niel Shell and Barbara Shilkret. Lanham, Md.: Scarecrow Press, 2005.

Silver, Christopher. "The Racial Origins of Zoning in American Cities." In *Urban Planning and the African American Community: In the Shadows.* Edited by June Manning Thomas and Marsha Ritzdorf. Thousand Oaks, Calif.: Sage, 1997.

Simmons, Martha J., and Frank A. Thomas. *Preaching with Sacred Fire: An Anthology of African American Sermons, 1750 to the Present.* New York: W.W. Norton, 2010.

Somerville, John. *Chain Store Debate Manual: A Digest of Material for Debate on the Chain Store Question.* New York: National Chain Store Association, 1930.

Sooy, Harry O. *Memoir of My Career at Victor Talking Machine Company.* David Sarnoff Library, Princeton, New Jersey. http://www.davidsarnoff.org/soo-maintext.html.

Sooy, Raymond. *Memoirs of My Recording and Traveling Experiences for the Victor Talking Machine Company, 1898–1925.* David Sarnoff Library, Princeton, New Jersey. http://www.davidsarnoff.org/soo-maintext.html.

Spauling, Norman W. "History of Black Oriented Radio in Chicago, 1929–1963." Ph.D. dissertation, University of Illinois at Urbana-Champaign, 1981.

Spencer, Jon Michael. "The Black Church and the Harlem Renaissance." *African American Review* 30, no. 3 (Autumn 1996).

Starr-Gennett Foundation. "Gennett Records." http://www.starrgennett.org

Sterne, Jonathan, ed. *The Sound Studies Reader.* New York: Routledge, 2012.

Sterner, Richard Mauritz Edvard, Lenore A. Epstein, and Ellen Winston. *The Negro's Share: A Study of Income, Consumption, Housing and Public Assistance.* New York: Harper & Brothers, 1943.

Stout, Harry S. *The Divine Dramatist: George Whitefield and the Rise of Modern Evangelicalism*. Grand Rapids, Mich.: W. B. Eerdmans, 1991.

———. "Religion, Communications, and the Career of George Whitefield." In *Communication and Change in American Religious History*. Edited by Leonard I. Sweet. Grand Rapids, Mich.: W. B. Eerdmans, 1993.

Suggs, Henry Lewis. *The Black Press in the South, 1865–1979*. Westport, Conn.: Greenwood Press, 1983.

———. *P. B. Young, Newspaperman: Race, Politics, and Journalism in the New South, 1910–62*. Charlottesville: University Press of Virginia, 1988.

———. *The Black Press in the Middle West, 1865–1985*. Westport, Conn.: Greenwood Press, 1996.

Suisman, David. "Co-Workers in the Kingdom of Culture: Black Swan Records and the Political Economy of African American Music." *Journal of American History* 90, no. 4 (2004).

———. *Selling Sounds: The Commercial Revolution in American Music*. Cambridge, Mass.: Harvard University Press, 2009.

Sutton, Allan. *A Guide to Pseudonyms on American Records, 1892–1942*. Westport, Conn.: Greenwood Press, 1993.

———. *Recording the 'Twenties*. Denver, Colo.: Mainspring Press, 2008.

———. *A Phonograph in Every Home: The Evolution of the American Recording Industry, 1900–1919*. Denver, Colo.: Mainspring Press, 2010.

Sutton, Allan, and Kurt Nauck. *American Record Labels & Companies: An Encyclopedia, 1891–1943*. Denver, Colo.: Mainspring Press, 2000.

Sutton, Matthew Avery. *Aimee Semple Mcpherson and the Resurrection of Christian America*. Cambridge, Mass.: Harvard University Press, 2007.

Talking Machine World

"The Talking Phonograph." *Scientific American* XXXVII, no. 25 (December 1877): 384–385.

Thompson, Emily Ann. *The Soundscape of Modernity: Architectural Acoustics and the Culture of Listening in America, 1900–1933*. Cambridge, Mass.: MIT Press, 2002.

Tuuk, Alex van der. *Paramount's Rise and Fall: A History of the Wisconsin Chair Company and Its Recording Activities*. Denver. Colo.: Mainspring Press, 2003.

U.S. Bureau of the Census. *Fifteenth Census of the United States, 1930 Manhattan, New York, New York Roll 1577 Page 8a Enumeration District 1020 Image 342.0 Fhl Microfilm 2341312*. Washington, D.C.: U.S. Government Printing Office, 1930.

———. *Fifteenth Census of the United States, 1930 Philadelphia, Pennsylvania Roll 2094 Page 13b Enumeration District: 50 Image: 341.0 Fhl Microfilm: 2341828*.

———. *Negroes in the United States, 1920–32*. Washington, D.C.: U.S. Government Printing Office, 1935. Reprint of original 1935 ed. Edited by U.S. Department of Commerce. New York: Kraus Reprint Company, 1969.

———. *Negro Population in the United States, 1790–1915*. Reprint of 1918 ed. Edited by Department of Commerce. New York: Arno Press, 1968.

———. *Thirteenth Census of the United States, Population Schedule, Odessadale, Meri-wether, Georgia, Roll: T624_203, Page: 12a, Enumeration District: 0083, Image: 817, Fhl Microfilm: 1374216.* Washington, D.C.: U.S. Government Printing Office, 1910.

———. *Twelfth Census of the United States, Population Schedule, Mountville, Troup, Georgia Roll: 225, Page: 11a, Enumeration District: 66, Fhl Microfilm: 1240225.* Washington, D.C.: U.S. Government Printing Office, 1900.

———. *Sixteenth Census of the United States, 1940 New York, New York Roll: T627_2667 Page 5b Enumeration District: 31-1811.* Washington, D.C.: U.S. Government Printing Office, 1940.

———. *Sixteenth Census of the United States, 1940 Atlanta, Fulton, Georgia Roll T627_733 Page 13b Enumeration District 160–241.* Washington, D.C.: U.S. Government Printing Office, 1940.

———. *Sixteenth Census of the United States, 1940: Housing,* Vol. 2, pt. 2. Washington, D.C.: U.S. Government Printing Office, 1943.

U.S. Bureau of the Census and Enumerator 5778. *Fourteenth Census of the United States:192–Population Schedule of Atlanta, Georgia, Fulton County 3rd Ward Supervisor's District 5, Roll: T625_251 Page: 21a, Enumeration District 72, Image:1051.* Sheet No. 21. Washington, D.C.: U.S. Government Printing Office, 1920.

U.S. Bureau of the Census and Enumerator Mrs. Edward S. Wellons. *Fifteenth Census of the United States:1930-Population Schedule of Atlanta Ward 3 Roll: 361 Page: 31a, Enumeration District: 50, Supervisor's Distrct 4, Image: 138.0, Fhl Microfilm: 2340096.* Sheet No. 3A. Washington, D.C.: U.S. Government Printing Office, 1930.

U.S. Bureau of the Census and Enumerator Robert H. Hart. *Sixteenth Census of the United States: 1940 Population Schedule Atlanta, Fulton, Georgia Ward 1 Block Number 24 Sheet No. 4a.* Washington, D.C.: U.S. Government Printing Office, 1940.

U.S. Department of Commerce and the Bureau of Foreign and Domestic Commerce. *Statistical Abstract of the United States:1926.* Vol. no. 49. Edited by Department of Commerce: Bureau of Foreign and Domestic Commerce. Washington, D.C.: Government Printing Office, 1927.

U.S. Congress. *The Congressional Digest: Congress and the Chain Stores.* Vol. 9: August–September, nos. 8–9. Washington, D.C.: U.S. Government Printing Office, 1930.

U.S. Department of Labor. Bureau of Labor Statistics, http://www.bls.gov/data/inflation_calculator.htm

———. Bureau of Labor Statistics. *Family Income and Expenditure in the Southeastern Region, 193–36 Prepared by A. D. H. Kaplan, Faith M. Williams, Jessie S. Bernar,d Assisted by Lenore A. Epstein.* Study of Consumer Purchases: Urban Series, no.4. Edited by U.S. Bureau of Labor Statistics. Washington, D.C.: U.S. Goverment Printing Office, 1939.

———. Bureau of Labor Statistics. *National Occupational Employment and Wage Estimates.* May 2012.

———. Bureau of Labor Statistics. *100 Years of U.S. Consumer Spending: Data for the Nation, New York City, and Boston.* May 2006. Report 991.

——. Division of Negro Economics. *The Negro at Work during the World War and during Reconstruction; Statistics, Problems, and Policies Relating to the Greater Inclusion of Negro Wage Earners in American Industry and Agriculture*. Washington, D.C.: Governtment Printing Office, 1921.

U.S. Federal Trade Commission. *Chain Store Inquiry.* Vol. 1: Character and Extent of Chain and Cooperative Chain Store Business, 72nd Congress, First Session, Senate Government Document Number 31. Washington, D.C.: U.S. Government Printing Office, 1932.

——. *Chain Stores: Growth and Development of Chain Stores.* Vol. 1: Character and Extent of Chain and Cooperative Chain Store Business, 72nd Congress, First Session, Senate Government Document No. 100. Washington, D.C.: U.S. Government Printing Office, 1932.

——. *Chain Stores: The Chain Store in the Small Town.* Vol. 1: *Character and Extent of Chain and Cooperative Chain Store Business,* 72nd Congress, Second Session. Senate. Government Document No. 93. Washington, D.C.: U.S. Government Printing Office, 1934.

——. *Chain Stores: State Distribution of Chain Stores, 1913–1928,* 72nd Congress. Second Session, Senate Government Document No. 130. Washington, D.C.: U.S. Government Printing Office, 1934.

——. *Chain Stores: Final Report on the Chain-Store Investigation,* 74th Congress, First Session, Senate Document No.4. Washington, D.C.: U.S. Government Printing Office, 1935.

U.S. Work Projects Administration. Georgia. *A Statistical Study of Certain Aspects of the Social and Economic Pattern of the City of Atlanta, Georgia, Official Project 465-34-3-4. 1939.* [Atlanta], 1939.

University of Virginia, Geospatial and Statistical Data Center. *Historical Census Browser* http://mapserver.lib.virginia.edu, 2004.

Updegraff, Robert. "Tomorrow's Business and the Stream of Life." *Advertising and Selling* (April 20, 1927).

"The Victrola in Rural Schools." Camden, N.J.: Educational Department of the Victor Talking Machine Co., 1919.

Vreede, Max E. *Paramount 12/13000 Series.* London: Storyville Publications, 1971.

Walton, Jonathan L. *Watch This! The Ethics and Aesthetics of Black Televangelism.* New York: NYU Press, 2009.

——. "The Preachers' Blues: Religious Race Records and Claims of Authority on Wax." *Religion and American Culture: A Journal of Interpretation* 20, no. 2 (2010): 205–232.

Wardlow, Gayle D. Audio Field-Recorded Interviews, Center for Popular Music Archives Collection, Middle Tennessee State University, Murfreesboro, Tenn.

——. Interviews Alfred Schultz. August 2, 1968. Audio. Inventory Number: tta 0182i.

——. Interviews Harry Charles in Birmingham, Alabama. 1968. Audio. Inventory Number: tta 0182j and 0182K.

———. Interviews H. C. Speir in Jackson, Mississippi on May 18, 1968. Audio. Inventory Number: tta 0182w.

———. Interviews H. C. Speir in Jackson, Mississippi, N.D. 1969. Audio. Inventory Number: tta 0182hh.

———. Interviews H. C. Speir in Jackson, Mississippi. February 8, 1970. Audio. Inventory Number: tta 0182i.

———. Interviews P. C. "Polk" Brockman, March 20, 1970 in Atlanta, Georgia. Inventory Number: tta 0182j2.

———. "Rev. D. C. Rice: Gospel Singer." *Storyville*, no. 23 (1969).

Washington Post

Waters, Ethel, and Charles Samuels. *His Eye Is on the Sparrow: An Autobiography.* Garden City, N.Y.: Doubleday, 1951.

Waxman, Percy. "Are We as Mean as All That?" *Printers' Ink* (June 23, 1927): 41–44.

Webb, Lillian Ashcraft. *About My Father's Business: The Life of Elder Michaux.* Westport, Conn.: Greenwood Press, 1981.

Weisenfeld, Judith. *Hollywood Be Thy Name: African American Religion in American Film, 1929–1949.* Berkeley: University of California Press, 2007.

West, Cornel. "The New Cultural Politics of Difference." *October* 53. Humanities as Social Technology (Summer 1990).

White, Deborah G. *Too Heavy a Load: Black Women in Defense of Themselves, 1894–1994.* New York: W. W. Norton, 1999.

"Widening the Gap." *Half-Century Magazine* 18, no. 1 (January–February 1925).

Williams, Gilbert Anthony. *Legendary Pioneers of Black Radio.* Westport, Conn.: Praeger, 1998.

Williamson, Samuel H., and Lawrence H. Officer. "Seven Ways to Compute the Relative Value of a U.S. Dollar Amount, 1774 to Present." *Challenge: The Magazine of Economic Affairs* 49, no. 4 (2010): 86–110.

———. "Seven Ways to Compute the Relative Value of a U.S. Dollar Amount, 1774 to Present," MeasuringWorth 2013, http://www.measuringworth.com/uscompare/.

Wills, David. "An Enduring Distance: Black Americans and the Establishment." In William R. Hutchison, ed., *Between the Times: The Travail of the Protestant Establishment in America, 1900–1960.* Cambridge, U.K.: Cambridge University Press, 1990.

Wright, Richard R., Jr. "Social Work and Influence of the Negro Church." *Annals of the American Academy of Political and Social Science* 30, Social Work of the Church (1907).

Yellis, Kenneth A. "Prosperity's Child: Some Thoughts on the Flapper." *American Quarterly* 21, no. 1 (1969).

Yorke, Dane. "The Rise and Fall of the Phonograph." *American Mercury* XXVII, no. 105 (1932): 1–12.

INDEX

ABI. See Atlanta Baptist Institute

Advertising, 28, 40; for black newspapers, 77–78; in catalogs, 78–79; for phonograph religion, 63–64, 78–81; for phonographs, 15–16, 27, 76; predictions about, 88–89; for race records, 45–47, 58, 78–81; racism in, 46–48, 58; requirements for, 76; in stores, 78–79; symbolism in, 79–80; urban migration related to, 62. *See also specific clergy; specific companies*

Affordability, xvii, 25, 90, 166

AFL. See American Federation of Labor

African Americans: income increase of, 34–35; radios for, 30–31

Agriculture, 165

"Ain't Gonna Lay My Religion Down" (Gates, J. M.), 2

The American Credo (Mencken), 18

American Dream, 157–58, 160

American Farm Bureau Federation, 165

American Federation of Labor (AFL), 165

"Amos 'n' Andy," 25

"Antebellum Sermon" (Dunbar), 116

Anxious bench, 100

A&P (Great Atlantic and Pacific Tea Company), 150, 165

A&R. *See* Artist and repertoire

Armstrong, Louis, 2–3, 38; advertising for, *132*, 133; with Rainey, 67, 73

Artist and repertoire (A&R), 58, 64, 66, 81, 138

Artophone, 39–40, 86–87

Artophone Phonograph Corporation, 30, 86–87

Artophone Talking Machine Company, 18

"As an Eagle Stirreth Up Her Nest" (Dixon), 67–69, *68*

Atlanta, 86, 97, 120, 166–67; Ad Men's Club, 27–28; Auburn Avenue in, 144; churches in, 51–52, 96, 125

Atlanta Baptist Institute (ABI), 125

"Atlanta Compromise" (Washington, B. T.), 24

Authority, 4, 7–9, 33; of black clergy, 80, 125, 129–30, 171; of Gates, J. M., 130–31, 136; of New Negro clergyman, 130, 136–38, 140, 148

Automobiles. *See* Cars

Auxiliary of the National Baptist Convention. *See* Women's Convention

Baker, Josephine, 37

Baptist Ministers Union, 169

Baptist World Alliance, 50

"Baptist World Alliance in Atlanta" (Gates, J. M.), 120, 166–67

Berlin, Irving, 47

Berliner, Emile, 14, 29

Best, Wallace, 116

Black Baptists, 96, 111, 113, 125–26; musical instruments for, 108–9; rural culture of, 49; women, 43

Black Billy Sunday. *See* Dixon, Reverend Calvin "Black Billy Sunday"

Black celebrities, 141–42, 171

Black church, 54; mission of, 53; race records and, 33, 42–43, 50; racial uplift from, 50–51

Black church amusements, 49–50; competition for, 53–54, 58–59; Davis, L. L., against, 53; Du Bois against, 54; Hunter for, 51; Johnson, D., against, 54–55; Proctor for, 51–52; Wright, R. R., against, 54–55

Black clergy, 7, 138; authority of, 80, 125, 129–30, 171; education of, 129–30; new traditions for, 130–31;

ABOUT THE AUTHOR

Lerone A. Martin is Assistant Professor of Religion and Politics in the John C. Danforth Center on Religion and Politics at Washington University in Saint Louis.